THE LORDS OF THE ISLES

THE LORDS
OF THE ISLES
The Clan Donald
and the early Kingdom
of the Scots

RONALD WILLIAMS

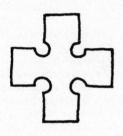

CHATTO & WINDUS

THE HOGARTH PRESS

LONDON

Published in 1984 by
Chatto & Windus · The Hogarth Press
40 William IV Street,
London WC2N 4DF

British Library Cataloguing in Publication Data
Williams, Ronald
The Lords of the Isles.
1. Donald *(Clan)* 2. Western Isles
(Scotland)—Genealogy
I. Title
929'.2'094114   CS479.D56. 1 9 8 4

ISBN 0–7011–2268–4

Maps by John Flower

Grateful acknowledgement is made to Penguin Books
for permission to reprint extracts from
a translation of the *Laxdaela Saga*;
and to J. M. Dent and Sons Ltd
for extracts from translations of
Njal's Saga and *Heimskringla*.

Phototypeset by Wyvern Typesetting Limited, Bristol
Printed in Great Britain by
Redwood Burn Ltd
Trowbridge, Wiltshire

Contents

Contents

Illustrations, maps
and genealogical tables

for LYNNE

Sagas come seeking me, tugging my heart strings;
Seafolk far-faring, call from the ghost-land:
Then sleep overwhelms me till birds cry at dawn.
                                    Lauchlan Maclean Watt

Preface

For almost a thousand years, the Western Highlands and the Hebrides were haunted by the memory of the great Lords of the Isles, chiefs of the Clan Donald who traced their ancestry back to the legendary Irish king, Conn of the Hundred Battles, and who embodied the poetry, the grandeur, and the ultimately doomed aspirations of the Celtic tradition in Scotland.

In early Celtic times the name 'Alba' applied to all the lands of northern Britain beyond the great estuaries of the Forth and the Clyde, which were inhabited by Pictish tribes called the *Cruithne*.

At the beginning of the sixth century three Gaelic clans of Irish *Scotti* – descendants of the warlike people who, in alliance with the Picts, had fought the Roman legions along Hadrian's Wall – landed in the western peninsula of Kintyre and established the Albain kingdom of Dalriada. Their leader was a chieftain called Fergus Mac Erc who was a descendant of the famous Irish king, Conn of the Hundred Battles, and the reputed ancestor of the Clan Donald. This Fergus Mac Erc settled his people along the West Highland coastline of Lorne and Argyll, and colonised the southern islands of the Inner Hebrides. Remote behind the great mountain ranges of *Druim Alban*, the Scotti consolidated their position, warring against their Pictish neighbours and the Celtic Britons of Strathclyde, and often threatened by Angle invaders who were spreading northwards from Northumbria into the Lowland plains of southern Alba.

In AD 843 the Dalriadic king, Kenneth MacAlpin, either by conquest or inheritance, assumed the crown of Alba and occupied the ancient Pictish capital at Scone. The Picts as a race thereafter disappeared from history, and the Scotti gave their name to the emerging realm of Scotland.

PART II THE VIKING PERIOD

The forefathers of the Clan Donald remained in the west as rulers of Argyll, but in the ninth century the Viking tide engulfed them, and during the confusion of the Norse period the thread of ancestry claimed by the clan genealogists became indistinct and incapable of substantive proof.

After colonising the northern isles of Orkney, the Norsemen settled in the two Atlantic archipelagos of the Inner and the Outer Hebrides, establishing Viking stations from which to conduct their summer raiding, and marrying into the local population. From this mixed race the later clans of the Western Isles evolved.

At the Battle of Clontarf, in 1014, a Viking army was defeated outside Dublin by the great Irish hero Brian Boru, and the independent power of the Hebridean Norse diminished. The Western Isles came within the orbit of the Kingdom of Man or the powerful Earldom of Orkney, which, during the eleventh century, also exercised an influence over events in northern Scotland. Towards the end of the eleventh century, however, the Norwegian king, Magnus Barelegs, formally annexed the Hebrides and the southern half of the Kintyre Peninsula, and they remained tributaries of Norway for 150 years.

PART III THE GAELIC REVIVAL

Despite the period of Viking occupation, in 1140 there was a Gaelic revival under the warrior Somerled, Thane of Argyll, who claimed descent from the ancient rulers of Dalriada, and recovered the southern Hebrides from the Norse kingdom of Man. Somerled was the great progenitor of the Clan Donald, to which his grandson Donald gave the name, and through whom the succession passed to the later Macdonald Lords of the Isles.

In Central Scotland meanwhile, the Celtic identity had been eroded by the influx of foreigners – Saxons, Normans, Flemings, and others – who had settled in the country, and Macbeth was the last Celtic ruler worthy of the name. The medieval kings of Scotland resented the Norwegian authority over their western seaboard, and the growing power of Somerled and his descendants excited the jealousy of the feudal baronage.

After the Battle of Largs in 1263, the Norwegian kings were forced to renounce their sovereignty over the Hebrides, and from this time the history of the western Gaels inevitably became more closely linked with events and developments in Scotland. Despite attempts by the Scottish crown to assert its authority, the descendants of Somerled continued to maintain their independence, and their support for Robert the Bruce during the Scottish War of Independence resulted in their being allowed to consolidate their hold over extensive territories in the western Highlands and the Isles.

PART IV THE LORDSHIP

When the Stewart dynasty succeeded to the throne of Scotland in 1371, the Chief of the Clan Donald, John of Islay, by inheritance, marriage, and other acquisition, had come to control a vast dominion in the west, far wider than the territories of early Dalriada, and began formally to style himself 'The Lord of the Isles'. During the period of the Lordship, from approximately 1350 to 1493, the entire Hebrides and the West Highland coastline formed a single Atlantic principality, and the Lords of the Isles conducted their affairs and governed this dominion as independent rulers in the west.

Their greed for territory led them to challenge the Scottish crown for possession of the Earldom of Ross which they eventually acquired for a time, thus adding to their domain a great tract of land in the north-west Highlands. In maintaining their claim to independence they exploited the political divisions within Scotland and the constant wars against England, frequently entering into conspiracy and alliance with the English kings – a policy which ultimately contributed to their downfall. For at the height of their greatness the symptoms of decline were already becoming apparent, as feudal impositions gradually undermined the early Celtic polity. In 1493, after an unsuccessful and ill-advised rebellion, John, fourth Lord of the Isles, proved incapable of controlling the clansmen, and upon such excuse the Lordship was formally forfeited to the Scottish crown.

This effectively removed the only focus of authority in the Western Isles, and the many clans of the Lordship embarked on a policy of individual aggrandisement which encouraged their constant feuding and rendered them vulnerable to the predations of the Campbells and other neighbours who long had envied the fabled wealth of the Isles.

After the grandson of the last Lord died without heirs, the several branches of the Clan Donald were never again united. But in decline, the memory of the ancient Lordship still sustained them, and the story of that former greatness remained their inspiration.

PART I
DALRIADA, AND THE CELTIC MEMORY

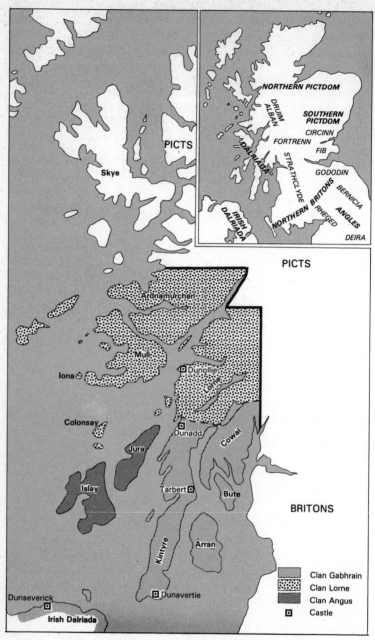

1 The Early Kingdoms of Dalriada and Northern Alba

CHAPTER I

The Lordship Remembered

The fort opposite the oak-wood –
Once it was Bruidge's, it was Cathal's,
It was Aed's, it was Ailill's,
And it was Maelduine's.
The fort remains after each in his turn;
And the Kings asleep in the ground.

In after centuries, when much of the old fierce blood was diluted or dispersed, the Seannachies would still remember. 'Without Clan Donald', ran the old saying, 'there was no strength. Without Clan Donald there was no joy.' And many still among the Highland men would recall the stories of the Clan Donald in might: when the tribal genealogy was a testament of greatness, and the names of their ancestors could inflame the swordsmen of the clan to battle.

They were a proud and factious people who called themselves the Seed of Somerled – steeped in the mythology of their race and counting their descent from Fergus Mac Erc who founded Albain Dalriada, and before that still from Conn of the Hundred Battles who had ruled in the halls of Tara. And although their pride fed on a tradition which with time became more mystic than substantial, and their contentiousness echoed old ambitions that had crumbled long ago, theirs to sustain was the memory of a time when their forefathers were Lords of the Isles, rulers of the Hebrides and the Western Sea, sib to heroes of the Viking sagas, descendants of kings, and the inheritors of a Celtic tradition unspoiled by Romans, Angles, Normans, and the rest, who made the lowlands mongrel and created the system which ultimately brought the old true Celts to ruin.

Gaelic, they were dreamers, and they had dreamed while others, greedier and more canny, scavenged among the Lordship for their share. Revenge had been theirs, brief and bloody, when under Montrose they cut the Clan Campbell to pieces along the shore at Inverlochy. But dreamers yet, they had not understood Montrose's

3

world; and dreamers still, they fought for the Pretender, and at Culloden found an end in blood and iron when Cumberland's artillery blew the clan to bits. An English government deported them. Gone the old valour, the nobility, wisdom, and defiance; and in their place an artificial and insipid preoccupation with the quaintness of the Highlands, which owed little to the fierce old legends from the western mists and much to the romantic fancy of a German-English king.

Culloden broke the fighting strength of the clans. The Clearances dispersed them. And with the recollection comes a sense of loss – at what was once, and was so callously destroyed. Romantic sentiment suffuses the stark tragedy. The chieftains in their eagle plumes depart. The Gaelic battle banners dip and fall, and ghostly captains lead their swordsmen back into the western mist. The coloured plaids melt slowly into the autumn heather; the music of the pipes dies on the wind; and they have returned to that older world of Celtic twilight to which they first belonged.

Departed, but not yet into oblivion: for the memory remains and the old feuds are not forgotten. The old pride lingers, and can conjure still the story of an ancient race of kings ruling over a fierce and independent people – whose many strongholds held inviolable their lands from Lorne to Kintyre, and who, ranging their galleys across the western sea to Ireland, Insigall, and Man, had the arrogance to style their scattered patrimony the 'Lordship of the Isles'.

And the lands of Lorne, and Argyll, and Kintyre bear witness to their passing. Their castles still rise stark and grim against the Hebridean sunset: Aros in Mull, and Ardtornish in Morvern; Sween the Mighty; Dunavertie of cruel memory; Dunyveg and Dunollie; Tioram that guards the narrows into Moydart; Eilean Mor Finlaggan, and Dunstaffnage of the king: these and many more whose stories are told in the runes of the Gael.

They are castles of the dead now. Their ruins crumble along the rim of the sea, watching over empty glens. No sentinel mans the tower to look for raiders on the tide, or listen to the Corrievrechan whirlpools. The sheilings are grass-grown and the peat fires are cold.

CHAPTER 2

Dunadd –
The Crowning Stone

I will tell you gentle boy;
With me the High Kings sleep.
I am the graceful, slender girl:
The Sovereignty of Scotland and Ireland.
                    DINDSHENCHAS

In Argyllshire, at Dunadd near Kilmichael Glassary, within the circle of a dark-age fortress, there is a footprint cut into the rock, which in Druidic times signified a crowning place of kings. The ruins of the ancient hill-fort crouch across the saddle of a low double-topped hill, rising out of the flat expanse of Crinan Moss – a natural bastion of earth and rock half-encircled by the River Add, and watching windswept over the Moss and seawards to Jura, Scarba, and the Isles.

This, according to tradition, was the stronghold of Dalriada's beginning, where, in about AD 500, a Celtic chieftain from Ireland called Fergus Mor, son of Erc, placed his foot upon the stone and facing north towards Cruachan, was invested of a kingdom along the western shore of the land which at that time was known as *Alba*.

There is no precise record as to the manner of Fergus's coming – whether he took the citadel by conquest, or through inheritance from some Pictish princess, or whether his crowning at Dunadd was the culmination of a gradual process of colonisation by Irish Dalriads who for generations had been plying across the Irish Sea. The ancient stronghold and other hill-forts within beacon-sight probably pre-date the founding of Albain Dalriada, and Dunadd may have been a traditional crowning place of kings for long before the Irish Fergus came. Excavation has revealed artifacts and other signs of occupation belonging to the dark-age Dalriadic time, but there was evidence too of an earlier iron-age settlement, built by a people whom time and history

5

forgot, but whose monuments are the duns and brochs and vitrified hill-forts beside which a traveller in the old Lordship may still stop, and pause to ponder something else again.

Sufficient now, that Dunadd occupied a special place in the memory of the early Gaels. Around it stretched their ancient patrimony – Lorne of the lonely sea-arms, Kintyre of their battles, Iona of their saints. Descent returned to Fergus Mor. Dalriada was his kingdom: Dunadd its stronghold; and the footprint on the crowning-stone conjured stories of a dim beginning – of the early Dalriads whose people brought the name of Scotland to all of Alba, and whose chieftains were the ancestors of Somerled, and Angus Og, and of the Macdonalds, Lords of the Isles.

According to the Clan Donald's genealogy (see List of Tables, p. vii), Fergus's ancestor, and the founder of the Dalriadic race, had been a third-century Irish chieftain called Cairbre Riada of the Liffey, who was a great-grandson of the famous Conn of the Hundred Battles, High King in Tara. This Riada had settled his followers first in Munster, but after famine caused him to abandon this land, he established a petty kingdom around Dunseverick in the north of Ireland between the Antrim mountains and the sea which came to be known as *Dal-Riada*, meaning 'Riada's share'. It was a small and narrow strip of coastland, but it lay poised along the northern channel looking east towards the long green finger of Kintyre and the mountains of Lorne against the far horizon. His heir, called Eochach Dubhlein, married a Pictish princess, daughter of the Albain King Ubdaire, and the three sons she bore him, known in legend as the 'three Collas', thus had blood kin and inheritance on both sides of the Irish Sea. The eldest, Colla Uais (Great Colla in the stories of the Gael) aspired to the High Kingship in Tara, but he was defeated by a cousin and forced with his brothers to take refuge among his mother's people in Alba (possibly in Colonsay where there are a number of stories associated with his name). In due time the three Collas returned to Ireland and won swordland among the old clans of the northern Ulaidh where they founded a small kingdom called Oriel (or Oirghialla).

Cairbre Riada's descendants also ruled their strip of Antrim coast for three more generations until Colla Uais's grandson, Erc of Dalriada, died, and his son Fergus Mor, land-hungry perhaps, or pressed by powerful neighbours, recalled a broader inheritance in Alba and led his people oversea to occupy the ancient citadel at Dunadd of the Kings.

The early Dalriads would have known by heart of Great Colla, Riada, and his descent from Conn – for genealogy was, above all, dear to the Gael. Stories of remoter ancestors became interwoven with the mythology of the tribe and the tales of heroes – Cuchulain and Maeve, the lament of Dierdre and the Sons of Uisneach – and all the legends of old Ireland. Recited by the harpers through successive generations, many of the old story cycles survived in the Highlands long after Dalriada itself was all but forgotten.

And within this heritage of genealogy and legend, they preserved also a myth of origin – the tribal memory of the first incoming of the Celtic peoples to Ireland. It was a story of how their ancestors had wandered from Scythia, through Thrace and Egypt, Gothland, Spain and Britain in search of an Island of Destiny in the west which had been promised them in the elder time – and how in Ireland that prophecy was fulfilled. It told that their leader had been the warrior, Goidel Glas, from whom they took the name Gaedheal or Gael, and how in Spain they followed his successor Miled who married the Egyptian princess Scota (and from whom were derived the names 'Milesians' and 'Scots'): how Scota had brought from Egypt a stone of black marble whereon strange runes were carved: how they landed in Ireland and fought the people there, and of Scota's death and later wars until a warrior of the Goidelic line called Tuathal founded a kingdom at Tara – and so at last to end, that they might begin again with Conn, and through his seed to Riada, each in his pride.

Prosaic history might differ.

The Celts as a race probably originated somewhere about the sources of the Danube. In the time of their greatness their influence stretched from the Baltic through middle Europe, and west as far as Gaul and Britain. From about 500 BC they conquered Spanish Carthaginia, settled in Cisalpine Gaul, and drove the Illyrians from Pannonia (Hungary). In 390 BC, they even captured Rome itself. However, from about 300 BC, time and conquest eroded their early ethnic unity, and the Celtic entity diminished as their confederacy lost cohesion. The tribes embarked on a series of individual wanderings – one to found the kingdom of Galatia, another to the sack of Delphi, others to defeat by the Roman legions or by the Teutonic tribes who were gradually spreading across central Europe. As early as the fourth century BC, small bands began to cross the Channel, and by the first century BC the Celtic tribes known as the *Belgae* were colonising southern Britain in large numbers, bringing with them a knowledge of the use of iron, both for weapons and heavy ploughshares, together with artifacts and ornaments of the bronze-age culture referred to as 'La Tène'. Gradually, as pressures on the European continent increased, they spread north and west to Ireland, and when Gaul and Britain passed under the Roman yoke, it was only in Ireland and northern Alba (Pictdom) that the old Celtic civilisation survived unconquered and unchanged.

The early Celtic colonisation of Ireland seems to have been undertaken by two principal tribes or groups, known to later scholarship as 'P' Celts and 'Q' Celts according to certain differences in their speech, and this has led historians to distinguish between two separate 'waves' of Celtic invaders. The earlier 'P' Celts, identified with the old clans of Ulaidh (Ulster) or the Erainn whose capital was Ermania and whose heroes of the 'Red Branch' feature in the Ultonian story cycles, were, by their Brythonic speech (close to Welsh, Cornish or Breton) akin to the people who inhabited the rest of Britain and to the *Cruithne* (Picts of the north). They were possibly Belgic in origin. The later 'Q' Celts, otherwise referred to as Goidels, Milesians, or *Scotti*, whose speech was closer to Gaelic Urse (and later Manx), came possibly from Galicia in Spain in about 100 BC. (The name of their legendary leader Milesius is probably a derivation of *Miles Hispaniae*.) Although perhaps they were in the minority initially, this second strain of Goidelic Celts became militarily powerful during the latter half of the first century AD, when after a period during which Ireland was torn with rebellion and internecine war, a Goidelic chieftain called Tuathal (the Legitimate) founded a principality in Meath with a stronghold on the sacred hill of Tara. Under his grandson, Conn of the Hundred Battles, this kingdom grew to challenge the rival states of Munster and Leinster, and encroach upon the old Ultonian clans of the north Ulaidh.

The legends of Tara are remembered in the stories of the heroes known as the *Fianna*. Of the kings, most famous perhaps was Cormac Mac Airt, grandson of Conn, and, according to tradition, father of Cairbre Riada. But the paramountcy of Tara more accurately dates from the reign of his descendant, Niall of the Nine Hostages, who ruled at the end of the fourth and the beginning of the fifth centuries. During his reign the traffic and movement across the Irish Sea increased, and in alliance with the Pictish tribes of Alba, he sent Irish warbands to raid the fat cattle lands of Strathclyde and carry havoc into northern Britain, as, with the weakening of the Roman legions, the old frontier began to crack and fail.

It was as the *Scotti* that the Romans knew them – a fierce and red-haired people who had joined the *Caledonii* to fight the legions on the Wall. Official Roman descriptions of the northern Celts were often secondhand, and treated in generalities as of an outland people. The ruins of the Roman camps remain to trace the northward progress of imperial ambition, but there is little to recall the barbarian tribes whom they marched to conquer. In earlier times, the Celts, before they came to these islands, had called the inhabitants *Pretani* – the 'people of the designs'. The Greeks also referred to the 'Pretanic Islands', but Julius Caesar in his *Memoirs* mis-spelled the name *Britanni*, and the Roman's ignorance endured. *Galli* was the Romans' name for the Gaels at large. The term *Caledonii* probably derived from the Celtic *Caile-Daoine* (spearman), and was applied generally to the warriors who descended from the central Highlands to harry the cohorts of the northern frontier, while the name Scotti was given specifically to their Irish allies. Ireland, which previously had been called *Hibernia*, became *Scotia* on the Roman tongue.

In the year AD 80 Agricola had invaded northern Britain, and Tacitus, writing of the expedition, recorded the first-known name of a northern Celtic chieftain – Galgacus, 'the Champion', who led a confederation of the tribes to defeat at Mons Graupius and defiantly told his conqueror: 'You have made a desert and called it peace'.[1] But although the Caledonian tribes were aided in their struggle by Irish allies, the Romans never penetrated into Ireland. Agricola had looked across the sea from Galloway and contemplated its conquest with a single legion, but he had been recalled in AD 85, and his successors were more preoccupied with consolidating their frontier than extending it. Roman armies marched north of the Wall, but they never seriously colonised beyond. In AD 400 it still marked the further limit of imperial civilisation, and the Darkness fell on all of Britain when the legions left.

Thus, although Fergus Mor may have been an incomer, the Dalriads were not strangers to Alba. Albain Picts and Irish Scots had been left to develop their various contacts undisturbed by imperial governors or occupying legions. For centuries coracles and curraghs plied the narrow sea between Antrim and Kintyre to link the two halves of a purely Celtic world. And in the wake of early commerce came more formal relationships – alliances, settlement, and dynastic marriage – from which grew the tradition to which the early Dalriads belonged.

CHAPTER 3

The Celtic Society
of Dalriada

A seventh-century manuscript called the *Senchus fer N'Alban* ('History of the men of Alba') provides a brief and later recollection of early Dalriada and the ordering of its society. From this and other early traditions it is clear that whatever process of settlement or gradual colonisation might have preceded Fergus Mor's landing, in about AD 500 there was a definite migration involving three tribes led by three brothers of whom, presumably, Fergus was the eldest.

The lands of Albain Dalriada were divided between them. Fergus, apart from establishing the king's seat at Dunadd in the Crinan isthmus, settled his people in Kintyre, Knapdale, Arran, and Bute, with principal strongholds at Tarbert and Dunavertie. It was the custom for each 'kindred' to adopt the name of its leader, but in recording the subsequent history, the old chronicles refer to the *Cinel* (Clan) Gabhran after Fergus Mor's grandson (from which one may infer that Fergus himself possibly died within a year or so of his crowning). Gabhran's elder brother Comgall also founded a small clan which occupied Cowal with a fortress at Dunoon.

The second brother, Lorne (or Loarne), established a stronghold at Dunollie, and settled his people in Colonsay, Lorne proper (to which they gave the name) and in the coastland north to Morvern where they encroached into the debatable lands beyond Ardnamurchan and the ill-defined boundary of northern Pictdom. Accompanying the Clan Lorne (but not part of it) were some men from Oriel who claimed descent from Colla Uais and made their settlement in Argyll.

Finally, the third brother, Angus, took his kindred and occupied the islands of Jura and Islay. Of the three clans, the Clan Oengus was least prominent in Dalriadic history. In early times the Kingship passed at irregular intervals between Clan Gabhran and Clan Comgall, and in the *Ulster Chronicle* the wars of Clan Gabhran received the greater attention. During the seventh century the Comgall dynasty appears to have died

out and from about AD 700 it was Clan Lorne who challenged Gabhran
for the Kingship.

The *Senchus* allows some calculation to be made concerning the
relative strengths of the clans and of early Dalriada as a whole. The size
of each clan was estimated in 'houses': Clan Gabhran having 560; Clan
Lorne 420; and Clan Oengus 430: relating presumably to the number of
families in client relationship to the chief. The numbering was important in relation to each clan's contribution to the war-muster when the
High King called the hosting, and at the time of Fergus's landing it is
possible that Dalriada could field a warband of 2000 fighting men out of
a population of between 7000–8000. In addition, every twenty houses
had to furnish twenty-eight oarsmen and two galleys or curraghs, which
would indicate that Dalriada was a maritime power to be reckoned with,
and this tradition was later inherited by Somerled and the Lords of the
Isles. Almost without exception, Dalriadic (and later, Macdonald)
strongholds commanded natural harbours or inlets where the galleys
could be beached beneath the fortress walls. In some places, the keel
marks, grooved into the rocks, are still visible today.

Dalriadic society, on the Celtic model, was determined by kinship.
The basic family unit was called the *derbfine* (certain kin) which
comprised four generations including the common ancestor. In earlier
pagan times, formal marriage had been unknown, with the group taking
a common responsibility for the rearing of children, and since paternity
was thus uncertain, succession was determined according to the
mother. The early Dalriads, who were at least nominally Christian, had
abandoned this custom in favour of patrilineal descent within the
derbfine of the father. Thus a man (or chief) was succeeded by a male
relative of 'certain kin' – son, grandson, brother, nephew, or first cousin.
The custom of matrilineal descent, however, persisted among the pagan
Picts, with whom the Dalriads were now in continuous contact. The
catalytic properties inherent in this situation would contribute eventually to the fusion of the two peoples as Dalriadic Scots took Pictish wives
and the inheritance that went with them. In later centuries, the
difference between Celtic custom and imported ideas of primogeniture
also prompted the struggles for succession which punctuated the early
history of Scotland.

Groups of interrelated families living in a particular area combined to
form a *Tuath* (people) under a *righ* (chieftain), who, with others of
similar rank, was in turn subordinate to an *Ur-righ* (over-king). These

petty kingdoms, roughly equivalent to independent clans, were then combined in a loose hegemony under the *Ard-Righ* (High King).

Even after the conversion of the Irish by St Patrick during the fifth century AD, the High Kingship retained a strongly sacral aspect inherited from Druidic times. The office of king had always been closely connected with the pagan tribal religion. In the elder days, when the succession passed through the female line, the Sovereignty resided in the person of the queen, who, as high priestess, was also the reincarnation of the Great Earth Mother and chose from among her warriors a man to mate with, lead her warband, and after the cycle of seven years, become the king-sacrifice and die to ensure fertility for the soil and prosperity for the tribe. By Dalriadic times, under a system of patrilineal succession, the High King had become rather the symbolic incarnation of the Tribal Ancestor. He was responsible for the tribe's *buada* (fortune), the preserver of its taboos and traditions, and the Sovereignty itself was conceived as a maiden to whom, as representative of the tribe, he was wedded in the ritual of investment at the crowning-stone.

It is possible, judging by later custom in the Isles, that at this ceremony there was no throne or formal crown-wearing as in later coronations, but that after the necessary preparations or mysteries of initiation according to the customs and totems of the tribe, the High King was brought to the stone 'to be made'. Robed in white with a golden torque about his neck and carrying a wand of white hazel, the king would set his foot upon the stone and swear to walk in the footsteps of his ancestors, and to do right between man and man. The oath was witnessed by the sub-kings, chieftains and clansmen ranged in the courts of the dun below who had come to the *feis* gathering to acclaim the king-choosing. Afterwards, there followed a nuptial feast in the great Mead Hall of the royal dun, its walls lined with the shields of warriors, when the king's champion was given the choicest of the meat, and the harper waited by the hearth to recite the Genealogy and sing the tales of tribal heroes.

The High King had to be a man without physical blemish – and it is told that the great Cormac Mac Airt himself was obliged to resign the kingship after he lost an eye in battle. Nor, as guardian of the tribe's customs and taboos, could there be any stain upon his *enech* (honour). A king who lost his *enech*, either through defeat in battle, or by some act of custom-breaking, or from whose brow the mark of sovereignty was thought to have passed, could be – and often was – deposed. For it was held that the power derived from the people, and their sanction had to be retained – and while rebellion against the High King, if unsuccessful, had unpleasant and usually mortal consequences, it never carried later connotations of treason.

In practice, the office of High King carried little actual power. The High King took hostages from sub-kings as security for tribute and obedience at a time of hosting. He secured his position by matrimonial alliance and by appointing his kinsmen to *Mormaerships* (Earldoms) or positions of authority, while he consolidated his military strength by employing mercenaries or forming a brotherhood of loyal warriors who lived with him at the royal dun. A High King had to be strong to survive.

Nevertheless, most descriptions of the kingship retain the Celtic concept of the responsibilities theoretically attached to the office. 'The King of the Hebudae', wrote Solinus in Cairbre Riada's time, 'was not allowed to possess anything of his own lest avarice should divert him from truth and justice.'[2] He was provided with such wealth, cattle, food, and service sufficient to support his state and maintain his 'face' and honour. He did not administer the Law – this being the exclusive function of the judges known as *brehons* (brieves) – but rather his duty was to uphold the Law to which he himself was also subject: 'The king must have patience, self-government without haughtiness, speak truth and keep promises; honour the nobles, respect the poets, adore God: keep the Law exactly without mercy. Boundless in charity, care for the sick and orphans; lift up good men and suppress evil ones; give freedom for the just, restriction for the guilty. At *Samhain* he must light the lamps and welcome the guests with clapping. He must appear splendid as the sun in the Mead Hall.'[3]

Samhain (The Feast of The Dead, November 1) was one of the festivals inherited from pagan time at which the High King, as guardian of the tribe's taboos, played a central role. On May Day he kindled the first of the *bealltuin* fires and took his place in the ancient Dance. He convened the tribal games, and once during his reign, he summoned his people to the great *feis* gathering for the king-choosing of his successor.

Succession to the High Kingship was hereditary within the royal *derbfine* in accordance with the general custom. The king chose and appointed his successor during his own lifetime, and his heir was called the *tanaire-righ* (second to the king) from which the later terms 'tanistear' and 'tanistry' evolved. The choice had to be acceptable to the tribe or clan, but in practice, both they and the king were influenced by the utterances of the Archdruid who claimed the ability to divine the names of future kings – a role which was readily assumed by St Columba on behalf of the early Christian Church. The 'tanist' system was intended to avoid the evils of interregnum or a disputed succession, and to ensure that the High Kingship passed only to a man whom the tribe accepted as fitted for the office. This custom would persist among the Gaels of the Hebrides but it was abandoned by the Scottish Kings after AD 1056, and the result was all too often the succession of a weak ruler. Nor was the old Celtic custom always successful in preventing a struggle for the office, particularly in cases where the High King died before appointing his heir. In such circumstances a feud could develop between rival claimants within the royal *derbfine,* for the kings were virile and their progeny ambitious.

Occasionally, under the old Irish Law, the extent of the *derbfine* itself might be in doubt, and there seems to have been a corresponding rule that if a king died without a tanist, any *derbfine* which had contributed a sovereign within the last three generations could again submit a candidate. The later history of Dalriada revolved mainly around the struggle between the Clan Gabhran and the Clan Lorne to possess and keep the kingship – with bitter consequences for the country. Another circumstance fraught with trouble was the accession of a minor – in which case the closest agnate (male heir) within the *derbfine* became regent – and remained as co-king for life after the tanist attained his majority. Sometimes this joint kingship prompted a murderous rivalry and tragic consequence, as was the case with Donald Bane during the eleventh century.

Finally, when an enemy threatened or ambition demanded that the tribe should take the war trail, it was the High King's most important duty to call the hosting at the Spear-stone. A king's war-luck was an essential part of his *enech*, and defeated kings, if not killed in battle, sometimes abdicated voluntarily. He was expected to lead his army to the fight, but if he was too old or otherwise incapacitated without reflection upon his honour, it was the custom to appoint a warleader or 'Captain' to lead the army in his place. But it was the warrior king who was best remembered. The Celts were reared to war and the blood-gold harpsongs of their ancient heroes, and they followed kings whose *enech* was bright in battle. And as Dalriada grew to encroach into the hunting runs of Pictdom and

Strathclyde it was the war-luck of their leaders that would ensure the survival of the little kingdom.

Below the king was a stratified society of nobles, commoners, and slaves. In theory, Celtic society was classless and each man had an equal right to arable and common pasture. By the nature of things, however, some men became richer than others. Wealth was reckoned in cattle (and a species of four-horned sheep), and a free man with twenty head was called a 'cow lord'. Such a person might rent out some of his cattle to poorer clansmen in return for certain obligations, and so a complex pattern of relationships developed which would persist in the Highlands until the eighteenth century. Slaves were usually captives or criminals – or native inhabitants overrun by conquest.

Three groups stood either temporarily or permanently without this class structure and free of tribal bonds.

A boy became free of parental control at the age of fourteen, but he did not receive any tribal privileges – house or land, or the right to marry – until he was full-bearded at the age of twenty. Young men usually spent this interval as warriors in the service of some other king who would give them an opportunity to blood their swords and reward their daring. Such unruly spirits would have disturbed the order of their own community or started blood-feuds, and so were sent to satisfy their hunger for adventure elsewhere. They formed or joined warrior brotherhoods under their own leaders, and went in search of war and glory in emulation of the heroes of the harp songs. In older times the most famous of brotherhoods in Ireland had been the 'Red Branch', but most of the later stories recall the deeds of the *Fianna* (the followers of the young hero Fionn MacCumhaill, who is better remembered as Fingal in the legends of the Gael).

The other two groups were known collectively as the *aes dana* (the men of skill), comprising the craftsmen and the complicated hierarchy of poets, judges, and priests referred to as the *filidhean*. The *aes dana* were held in high respect and permitted to travel at will across the tribal boundaries irrespective of their parent clan. This immunity often extended to times of inter-clan warfare.

The term 'craftsmen' covered a multiplicity of skills: technical, such as the working of bronze and iron, and the highly artistic, as in the fashioning of gold and enamel. This was an aspect of the Celtic culture which was neither so barbaric nor so crudely fierce as the stories of their warfare might otherwise suggest. Celtic art from earliest times had a rich and inspired individualism of its own, which showed an imagination, an originality, and in a sense, a refinement of mind which made them unique among the other dark-age warrior peoples.

In the hierarchy of the priesthood, the lowest rank was composed of bards and poets. To gain admission to the *aes dana* the aspirant had to study for seven years, to master the traditional metres and line schemes, learn the ancient lays by heart, and acquire the skill of song-making for himself. For the Gaels were given to the harp music and the speaking of ancient lore and riddles, and only when these arts were mastered could the young *filidh* take the bard's place at the chieftain's hearth or watch above the battle-wreck, and from the carnage and mêlée compose a tale of champions fighting hand to hand so that each might be remembered in his pride. The story would be told in the torchlight of the Mead Hall, put to a harp music that was set to draw the hearts of heroes, and when the warriors had drunk deeply of the *uisquebaugh* and boasted of the foemen's heads that hung beside their chariot wheels, they would call upon the bard again to sing the older fierce and sad songs of their past. And if the *filidh* was respected for his art, he was also feared, for among his magic he had the power of satire, and whereas praise exalted a warrior's honour, satire could so diminish it that a man's courage would wane, his respect be lost, and bad luck attend him as if he had been cursed.

Above the poets, among the *aes dana*, were the *brehons* (judges), admission to whose ranks required a further seven years of study. The Old Law had to be learned by rote and recitation since the Celts adhered to an oral tradition passed from master to pupil but never written down – thus preserving the mysteries of their caste. (The Old Irish Law was not formally codified until the *Senchus Mor* in AD 438.)

The *brehons* administered the Law and dispensed justice on the Judgement Mounds – in the open air where the proceedings could be seen and heard by all. (One such mound, Dundonald, is situated on the left-hand side of the road that runs into Crinan itself, while another overlooks Loch Indaal, a mile or so south of Bowmore in Islay. In fact there are many scattered across the Highlands.) Penalties imposed were usually in the form of fines, and compensation for injury was exacted according to the status of the offender and the consequences to the victim. Such fines were levied upon the offender's kinsmen as a group (which encouraged discipline within the *derbfine*) and the compensation was distributed likewise among the kindred of the plaintiff. A small portion also went to the *brehon* for his upkeep. In pagan times, extreme offences were punished by impalement and burning between two fires, but the Law became less harsh after St Patrick's conversion of the Irish.

Regarding the most revered sect of the *aes dana* – the ancient *druids* and high priests – much less is known since the Old Religion did not write down its secrets. Seven more years of study were necessary before a *brehon* might become a *druid,* but that knowledge or magery – whether of astronomy or divination – was locked in the mystery of druidic initiation. In pagan Ireland Celtic gods had mingled with a pantheon of local deities, while custom had also acquired native superstitions and taboos. But the names of those gods that can be quoted conjure only a fading invocation of forgotten faiths: Lugh of the Long Spear and the Many Arts, Lord of the Ravens; Epone the Horse Goddess; Tarvos Taranos, God of Bull and Thunder; Manannan MacLis who ferried the soul to *Tir nan Og* – the land of youth beyond the sunset, that *Emain Abhlaich*, the Vale of Apples where Arthur and his warriors sleep. There was magic in the streams and wells, and all places where earth spirits dwelt: magic and power in the rowan trees – proof against the evil eye and a charm for love and luck, and life's well-being. Blossom belonged to the Spring Maiden; summer's fruit to the Earth Mother; harvest to the Winter Hag who reigned in Autumn and was goddess also of red death and war. Even after the coming of Christianity, the Old Dance lingered – in the *bealltuin* fire, the *samhain* feast, in the curious imagery of Celtic design, and in the myriad of charms, taboos and faery legend that persisted in the Highlands. But the druidic order withered. Some of the old priests joined the new faith and brought knowledge with them; some disappeared and the knowledge was lost; a few kept secretly to the old gods and waited for their time to return.

For the people themselves, Irish sources seem to match Roman descriptions of the Gaullic Celts. They were large in stature, blue-eyed, their hair red or dark, moustachioed, and terrifying in the battle-rage. The majority charged into battle naked, their clan's identity elaborately tattooed across their bodies. Chieftains wore helmets and breast-plates, and were carried to war in two-horse chariots (though when the fight began they probably dismounted to seek an adversary on foot). In early times the weaponry of Picts and Scots may have differed. Apart from a short spear, the Picts carried oblong or circular shields and used a two-handed double-edged slashing sword. The early Scots seem to have preferred a short bronze sword, blade and hilt of one piece, but as they learned to fashion iron they also adopted the Pictish broadsword – the *claidheamth mor* – which was in use in the Highlands until the seventeenth century when it was replaced by the basket-hilted claymore. For close-quarter fighting the Gaels also carried dirks and small round shields or targes. Bows and arrows were used, but they were small and not particularly effective.

As the tattooing identified a man's clan, so his clothing identified his district and his rank. The Celts were noted for their production of fine linen and for their skill in dyeing cloth and yarn. The nobles and free men wore the Celtic tunic, belted at the waist and open at the front and sides to give ease of movement (the art of pleating came much later). Around the shoulders and fastened with a wooden pin or brooch, they threw a plaid or *sagum* which was usually striped in accordance with the pattern of their particular territory. The word 'tartan' derived from *tuar* (colour) and *tan* (district). The number of colours in the pattern indicated rank, and the *Senchus*, recording the Old Irish Law, ascribed seven colours for a king, six for a *druid*, and four for a noble. The poorer people wore cloaks of coarse wool or undressed sheepskin. Trews were sometimes worn, but more often men went about bare-legged or 'red-shanked', and they used untanned leather, fur side inwards, for shoes or *brogues*.

The hill-fort at Dunadd was a precarious beginning. The early Dalriads consolidated their hold upon the coastland and spread eastwards against the Picts to provoke resistance and retaliation until they had to fight for Dunadd itself – even as in later years they fought for it among themselves. Nor did they turn their backs upon the west. Their lands remained in Ireland also, where old ambitions lingered, old feuds persisted, and old enemies lived on. The galleys of Dalriada roamed widely among the islands, while the kings competed jealously with their kindred in northern Ireland, dreamed of an island hegemony for themselves, and coveted the Isle of Man.

More than thirty kings would rule in Dalriada before that Kenneth MacAlpin who, in AD 845, moved the High King's Seat east to Scone and claimed the sovereignty over all of early Scotland. Their names can be recalled still from the *Annals* – but they were kings of a dark age, feared and famous in their time but now without substance, flesh, or shadow. They are dimly perceived through the brief obituaries of the ancient regnal lists which in fragments record their life by the curt notice of their dying, while the names of long-forgotten battlefields provide only a faint echo of the 'dreadful clashings of their wars'.

Thus it was recorded that Fergus was succeeded briefly by Domangart his son, and then by his son Comgall, and then by Gabhran his brother, before the High Kingship returned to Conall, Comgall's son – who was by his obituary, unfortunate. In AD 574 the Dalriads fought a great battle in Kintyre, and in it 'Duncan son of Conal son of Comgall fell, and many others of the allies of the sons of Gabhran'.[4]

In this crisis, Dalriada found a warleader in a chieftain of Gabhran's line called Aedan the Fair-haired, who in the same year, AD 574, was brought to the stone to be crowned High King by a man no less fierce in spirit, though of a gentler calling, whose name is remembered as St Columba.

These were the two outstanding figures of Dalriadic history. But of the two – the warleader and the priest – it is Columba who is remembered now. Aedan in his lifetime carried his sword through all of northern Britain and the Islands, and his battles are recorded in the great Welsh epic of *Gododdin*. But the memory of the saint who worshipped on Iona has far outlasted the transient renown of a dark-age warrior king. In Columba, but for the pious imagination of an age which saw more to revere in a box of bones washed up on a Fifeshire beach, Scotland might have found her truer, native patron saint.

At Dunadd, the walls and ditches of an ancient fortress crumble still and the earth inexorably reclaims them. With the end of Dalriada the stronghold was abandoned and left derelict to wind and sky. The events, the kings, the killing grounds, seem unimportant now and the bards are gone to *Tir nan Og* from which there is no return. Within the citadel there is nothing left to see or touch – except the ancient rock with a hollow basin, some weathered lines of ogham writing that no-one living may decipher, and a footprint turned towards Cruachan – which some believe denotes the making of a king. Beside it a strange creature resembling a Pictish boar traced in the rock may signify some later rite or conquest – but that secret also sleeps with Dalriada.

On Iona nothing remains of the first mud and wattle chapel of Columba and the present ruins far postdate the early Dalriadic period. But the peace of Iona became part of the Gaelic mystery, and its sanctity did not diminish. Long after Dunadd was abandoned and the kings of Scotland rode in guilt or pride to wear the crown at Scone, they still were carried back in death to rest in the *Reilig Oran* on Iona.

CHAPTER 4

The Kingdoms of Alba

Alas for the Red Dragon, for its end is near. Its cavernous dens shall be occupied by the White Dragon, which stands for the Saxons, whom you have invited over. The Red Dragon represents the people of Britain, who will be overrun by the White One: for Britain's mountains and valleys shall be levelled, and the streams in its valleys shall run with blood.

Prophecies of Merlin Geoffrey of Monmouth

The better to understand the arena into which Aedan of Dalriada and St Columba now stepped, something must be said about the state of northern Britain and Alba during the early part of the sixth century AD. A truly accurate picture is impossible. A Darkness fell on Britain with the departure of the legions. It was a time of turmoil and dissolution, shifting alliances, disorder, massacre, invasion – and from this confusion few facts emerge that could be called incontrovertible. The little that is known derives mainly from the early Christian historians and hagiographers: Gildas, Nennius, Adomnan, and the Venerable Bede; from surviving copies of early manuscripts: the *Senchus Fer n'Alban*, the *Annals of Tigernach and Ulster*, the *Albain Duan, Leabhar Breac*; or from the poetry of British bards: Aneirin of Cumbria, and Taliesin of Wales. Accounts conflict, sources are confused, names are transposed and places have been long forgotten, interpolations have been added, and the veneer of later Christian bias has altered the emphasis of events.

At the time when Fergus Mor established Dalriada on the Crinan isthmus, three other peoples were occupying the more or less neighbouring regions of Alba and northern Britain (see map on p.2).

Closest and most threatening was the Albain Kingdom of the Picts, divided geographically into two parts, north and south of the Grampian mountains. Northern Pictdom had its capital near Inverness at the head of the Great Glen, but apart from Adomnan's account of St Columba's journey to the dun of King Brude, little is known about this region since it was too remote for English scholars such as Bede to attempt any accurate description. Southern Pictdom, however, was better known. It seems to have comprised four provinces around the valley of the Tay, bounded to the north by the Mounth, on the west by the mountain range then called *Druim Alban,* and stretching southwards as far as the crumbling Antonine Wall. The most central province was Circinn – the present area of Forfar, Angus, and the Mearns, with its capital at the Dun of Nechtan near Forfar. The second, Fotla, was centred around Dunkeld, encompassing the sacred mountain of Schiehallion and including the area of Atholl, the Upper Tay, and the Perthshire Highlands. The third, Fortriu, stretched south-west of the Tay and enclosed the present region of Strathearn and Menteith; while the fourth, Fib, was equivalent to the present county of Fife. By tradition there had originally been seven provinces – after the seven sons of Cruithne – and the other three, Catt, Cé, and Fidach, possibly comprised the northern kingdom. In St Columba's day, the High King Brude MacMaelchon ruled in the north, but later accounts seem to suggest that the King of Fortriu eventually became paramount, and had his dun at Scone.

It is the tragedy of the Picts that they are a forgotten people – their origins obscure, and their final disappearance unexplained. Little or nothing is known of their literature, religion, law, or written language – or even how they took their name *Pictae* (the 'painted people'). The name of their legendary ancestor, Cruithne, suggests that they too may have been of Irish origin, and one poetic tradition accords Cruithne a pedigree that goes back to the early Celts of Thrace. However, there is no memory of an invasion to prove them sudden incomers to Alba. Quite possibly the Picts were descended from early Irish immigrants who had settled and fused with the indigenous population whose customs they had adopted and to whom they brought a Brythonic variant of the Celtic speech.

By Aedan's time, they were a force to be reckoned with. Adomnan's account of St Columba's meeting with King Brude suggests a typical dark-age monarch ruling over a coherent people where once the Romans had encountered only disparate and divided tribes. Their history is thus a strange omission. Some hundred standing stones carved with strange designs, pieces of jewellery and silver artifacts, a fragmentary list of kings, are the only traces of a people whom, for their paganism, monkish chroniclers in their righteousness casually damned and wiped from off the historical record as deserving no posterity. The stones, the fragments, and the names of kings survive, together with some vague and often conflicting descriptions culled at second hand by Roman historians who briefly recorded the barbarian spearmen who fought the legions on the Wall.

A very little is known. Pictish society was matrilineal – and thus in contrast to that of neighbouring Dalriada. A king was succeeded by his mother's, sister's, or daughter's son. The women practised polyandry, a custom which the Romans prudishly called promiscuous but which the Picts preferred to the sly hypocrisy and secret fornication of Imperial Italian society. To the bravest warrior went the choice of a woman and the best of the meat: uncouth perhaps but heroic also. Exogamy was common, and as contacts between Picts and Dalriads developed across the *Druim Alban*, the eligibility of Pictish heiresses attracted Dalriadic adventurers, younger sons, and even princes, so that there developed also a complex pattern of intermarriage and mixed blood which, while producing a procession of disputed claims, rivalries, and dynastic wars, at the same time contributed during the following centuries to a gradual fusion of Picts and Scots, and so moulded the eventual destiny of Northern Alba.

But in Aedan and St Columba's time, the differences were more apparent. The Dalriads were incomers, the Picts long-settled. The first were Christians, the second were pagan followers of the Druidic religion. Two hundred years of intermittent warfare would pass before Kenneth MacAlpin of Aedan's line would wear the Albain crown at Scone.

The second people whose territory encroached into southern Alba were the Britons – descendants of the tribes known to the Romans as the *Dumnonii, Novantae, Selgovae,* and *Votadini.* There were three Celtic British kingdoms immediately to the south of Pictdom. The strongest was Strathclyde with its capital at Dumbarton Rock, stretching from the *Clach nam Braetann* (the Stone of the Britons) in Glen Falloch at the head of Loch Lomond, east towards Stirling. The second, called Manau of Gododin, extended between the two strongholds of Stirling and Dunedin (Edinburgh), while the third, Rheged, straddled the present border country around Carlisle.

These three kingdoms occupied the northern frontier region of post-Roman Britain, but they were closely connected with the other Romano-Celtic kingdoms that had emerged to the south – Gwynedd,

Dyfed, Powys, and Caerwent in present Wales, Dumnonia (Somerset, Devon, and Cornwall) in the south, and Elmet and Lindsey in middle Britain. In some cases the relationships were close. The Dumnonii of Strathclyde were the same tribe as the Dumnonii of Devon and Cornwall, while the Cunedda dynasty of Gwynedd probably originated in the Manau of Gododin before they were moved south and settled in north Wales by the Roman administration to defend the shores against Irish pirates.

During the last century of Roman rule, Britannia had come increasingly under barbarian attack. Saxon pirates were raiding along the coasts as early as the late second century AD, while in the same period, Irish warbands were landing in Wales to pillage, and in some places, to settle. The Romans attempted to counter these raids by building a series of coastal forts under the supervision of the Count of the Saxon Shore – a military commander responsible for organising this system of defensive garrisons and who patrolled threatened areas with a force of mobile cavalry. But the main threat came from the north. In AD 367 a confederation of Albain Picts with Irish *Scotti* and *Atacotti* burst across Hadrian's Wall. The frontier scouts defected, and the regular cohorts chose this moment to mutiny. The northern defences collapsed, and the Picts carried fire and sword throughout the northern provinces of Britannia – an awful foretaste of things to come. The situation was restored by Count Theodosius who offered an amnesty to the rebellious troops and drove the barbarians back into Alba. Hadrian's Wall was rebuilt, northern towns were fortified, and a system of watch-towers and signal stations constructed along the coast of Northumbria to give warning of seaborne raids.

Nevertheless, during the next fifty years, the defences of Britain were weakened further. In AD 383, the Roman general Maximus, who commanded the field army in Britain, made a bid for the Imperial purple, taking some of the precious legions with him. After his death in AD 388, these troops did not return. The Vandal general, Stilicho, withdrew still more troops to counter the growing threat on the continent. Finally, between AD 406 and 407, the army in Britain elevated Constantine III as Emperor in the West, and when he crossed to Europe to pursue his claim, he took with him the bulk of the field-army and much of the remaining frontier garrisons as well. From AD 410, Roman commitments in Europe precluded the sending of reinforcements to Britain, despite the desperate pleas of the Britons themselves.

In this pause, a confusion developed among the Britons. They had inherited Roman forms of administration, but the power behind that administrative system had now failed them, and this situation permitted the re-emergence of Celtic tribal groupings – sub-kings and petty warlords – and the consequent division of the country. A split began to develop between the Romano-British Party and a native pro-independence faction who saw that no help would be forthcoming from Rome and wished to dispense with the anachronistic and worthless trappings of the Empire. Whereas Christianity had been a unifying force among the Britons, the division now hardened between the Roman pro-Christian party and the native independent faction who inclined towards the Old Religion. The latter group (which included the Pelagian heretics) supported a king called Vortigern (by tradition a son-in-law of Maximus) who acquired the title of '*Superbus Tyrannus*' – approximating to the Celtic High King. Vortigern appointed a council of twelve Druids – and the pagan party thus achieved a temporary ascendancy.

Tradition also ascribes to Vortigern the fateful decision which brought the third and most powerful race of incomers to Britain and Alba – to the great bane of Britons, Dalriads, and Picts alike.

Cut off from Rome without hope of reinforcement and impoverished by famine, the Britons came under increasing attack from the southern Picts who now raided across the abandoned Wall deep into Northumbria. Having no means to counter this constant threat, Vortigern invited a warband of Germanic mercenaries to defend the north-eastern frontier against the invaders. A force of Angles landed in Northumbria (a region which had already acquired some Germanic customs through the settlement of retired German legionaries in the area) and swiftly drove the Picts back beyond the River Tweed. But this accomplished, the Angles did not remove themselves, and possibly on the excuse that the conditions of payment had not been fulfilled, they claimed the Deira Plain as swordland and large numbers settled in Northumbria.

Early chronicles record the *Adventus Saxorum* as if it were a single event. The Venerable Bede dates it as AD 446–447. Certainly the settlement of Saxons in large numbers marked a new era of early British history, but more likely the process extended over several decades as groups of Angles, Saxons, and Jutes landed and hacked out areas of settlement. Vortigern's invitation to the Angles was probably in about AD 428. By AD 450, the Saxon warleader Hengist was established in Kent. In those decades all Europe was convulsed. Rome, the centre of imperial administration, had fallen in AD 410. The Huns had swept out of Asia into Germany and Gaul, and the Saxon and Frisian peoples in their path were being driven west and overseas. Britannia had long been a raiding shore for Saxon pirates. Now it was a haven and a land for the taking.

By about AD 460, the Britons had been pushed westwards to a line running roughly north-south from Edinburgh to Southampton, while east of the Pennines the country was largely devastated or in Saxon hands. However, the last two decades of the fifth century saw a revival of Celtic resistance, and the barbarian advance was temporarily brought to a halt. Some sort of defensive coalition evolved among the British kingdoms along the frontier, with the Britons of Strathclyde as 'the men of the left' and south Wales as 'the right flank'. The title of *Superbus Tyrannus* seems to have lapsed as Vortigern's authority was rejected by the other Celtic kings, and military command was entrusted to a member of the old pro-Roman party called Ambrosius Aurelianus, whose role and position may have been modelled on the Roman military title of *Dux* or Duke of Britain. Ambrosius commanded a mobile field army, drawn possibly from conscripts or volunteers from the several British kingdoms, which campaigned along the ragged frontier to discourage Saxon raiding and engage any encroaching warband in force.

Onto this shifting battleground, in about AD 480, stepped that other shadowy Celtic Briton called Arthur, or Artos the Bear – who was to become by reputation the greatest warleader of the dark-age period. When the tales of Lancelot and Guinevere, Camelot and the Round Table, the Holy Grail and all the stuff of medieval romance are stripped away, there is evidence – in the terse entries of the *Easter Annals*, in the ninth-century *Historia Brittonum*, and surviving fragments of the old Welsh poems and battle lists – to indicate that this legendary figure did exist:

Then Arthur fought against them in those days with the kings of the Britons but he himself was leader of battles. The first battle was at the mouth of the river which is called *Glein*. The second and third and fourth and fifth upon another river which is called *Dubglas* and is in the district *Linnuis*. The sixth battle upon the river which is called *Bassas*. The seventh battle was in the Caledonian Wood, that is *Cat Coit Celidon*. The eighth battle was in *Fort Guinnion* in which Arthur carried the image of St Mary, ever virgin, on his shoulders and the pagans were turned to flight on that day and a great slaughter was upon them. The ninth battle was waged in the City of the Legion. The tenth battle he waged on the shore of the river which is called *Tribruit*. The eleventh battle took place on the mountain which is called *Agned*. The twelfth battle was on *Mount Badon* in which nine hundred and sixty men fell in one day from one charge by Arthur, and no-one overthrew them except himself alone. And in all the battles he stood forth as victor.[5]

Nevertheless, precise details are impossible. Arthur may have been a Dumnonian, since he appears to have been most active in their tribal areas – both in Strathclyde and in the south. The title of 'Warleader' seems to have been a formal one since other Welsh poems such as the *Elegy of Geraint* and *Llywarch Hen* also refer to him in this way, and may have been inherited from the ageing Ambrosius. And if there is any truth in a legend which fed also on oral traditions, he may have led a small, mobile army of professional warriors – after the fashion of the Celtic warrior brotherhoods perhaps – which might have been based on a revival of the Dumnonian cohort of Roman times called the *Britanniciani Juniores*. Nor is it clear precisely whom he fought on each occasion. The battle on Mount Badon was certainly against the Saxons, and the battles in *Linnuis* (Lyonesse of fable) may have been in defence of a river line merging with the Trent not far from Ilchester and Glastonbury in Somerset. A battle in the City of the Legion – either Chester or Caerleon – would also make sense in the context of a defensive campaign against a Saxon army thrusting west. The battle of Cat Coit Celidon, however, was almost certainly fought in the Caledonian Forest which lay to the north of Carlisle, and was probably against the Picts who had not ceased their attacks upon the northern kingdoms. One tradition also places the battle of Agned close to Edinburgh in the Manau of Gododin (near Arthur's Seat?), and the later battle of Camlann, at which Arthur was killed or mortally wounded, may have been at Birdoswald near the Wall. Another small piece of circumstantial evidence linking Arthur with the north (and indeed arguing for his historical authenticity) is that Aedan, who before becoming King of Dalriada, ruled a British appanage in Stirling of Gododin, named his eldest son after him – as did at least three other Celtic princes during the next century – a fact that is of some interest in so far as, prior to Arthur himself, the name had not before been known among the Celts.

The location of Arthur's twelve battlefields is a matter of dispute, and three of them – Bassas, Tribruit, and Fort Guinnion – cannot even be guessed at. Nevertheless, the spread of his supposed campaigns from

Gododin in the north as far south as Somerset is not impossible, given the length of the beleaguered frontier and the tribal connection between the two branches of the Dumnonii. There are other indications, not least in the battle history of Dalriada itself, that during the dark-age period, warbands and armies regularly raided and campaigned over considerable distances. A defensive strategy intended to counter the numerous and independent bands of Saxon raiders would have required a field army with a high degree of mobility.

That any references to the real Arthur have survived at all is due to their inclusion by monkish copyists – although his relations with the Church may have been at times ambivalent. The *Life of Cadog* and the *Life of Padam* (written in the eleventh and twelfth centuries) portray him as a perverse and avaricious tyrant – possibly because he exacted money from the Church to pay and feed his men. However, there are two clear references to him as the Christian champion fighting against the barbarian invaders – in the *Historia Brittonum* account of the eighth battle at Fort Guinnion where Arthur is said to have carried the image of the Virgin Mary upon his shoulders, and in an entry in the Welsh *Easter Annals* recording the decisive Battle of Mount Badon:

... Battle of Badon in which Arthur carried the Cross of Our Lord Jesus Christ on his shoulders for three days and three nights and the Britons were victors.[6]

In both cases, it has generally been taken to mean that Arthur either carried a holy relic into battle, or more probably, in the tradition of Constantine, displayed the Christian symbols of the Virgin or the Cross on his surcoat or shield. These two references, together with his title of *Dux Bellorum*, suggest that whatever his actual character or religious conviction, Arthur was regarded as the protagonist of the Christian Romano-British party – and his death was a serious political blow to that faction, and to the Church.

Camlann itself is not listed in the context of Arthur's battles against the barbarians, and if his victory at Mount Badon did secure the frontier and temporarily brought an end to Saxon incursions, then his last battle may have been fought between the Britons themselves – as later legend maintained. The *Easter Annals* record only:

... The strife of Camlann in which Arthur and Medraut perished. And there was plague in Britain and Ireland.[7]

It is unclear from this whether Arthur and Medraut fought on the same side or against each other, but one tradition, if there be truth in it, tells that after one of his northern campaigns, Arthur had entrusted the fortress of Dunpelder in Gododin to King Loth (from whom the Lothians take their name), who was described as *Rex semipaganus*. Subsequently, Loth's son, Medraut, headed an insurrection of the native Druidic party in alliance with the Picts. Arthur engaged them at Camlann, and in the battle both he and Medraut were killed.

A period of turmoil followed. Arthur appears to have had no successor as *Dux Bellorum* and the title vanished with him. Co-ordinated defence of the Saxon frontier ceased and the northern kingdoms were plunged into civil war. The Britons never again found a warleader of Arthur's calibre, and as the darkness closed around them, he passed into memory after the manner of the Celtic heroes. A hundred years after his death a brief reference in the great *Gododdin* epic whispers the beginning of his legend:

He (the hero Gwawrddin) glutted black ravens on the walls of the fort – but he was not Arthur.[8]

Owing to various discrepancies in the early references it has never been possible to quote precise dates for the battles of Badon and Camlann, but they are reckoned to have taken place in approximately AD 518 and AD 530 – which would make Arthur the contemporary of the early kings of Albain Dalriada. When Aedan became High King then, the memory of Arthur would have still been fresh, but Strathclyde had fallen to the Druidic party.

Of the English peoples who had secured swordland in Britain, it was the Angles of Northumbria who had the greatest impact on the northern kingdoms in Alba. In the *Historia Brittonum*, the short reference to Arthur's battles concludes on an ominous note:

And they, while they were laid low in all battles (against Arthur) sought help from Germany, and they increased many times without intermission, and they brought over Kings from Germany to rule over them in Britain up to the time when Ida reigned. . . . He was the first King in Bernicia.

In AD 547, Ida fortified a base at Bamburgh and proceeded to make himself master of Bernicia and the Deira Plain. From this date onwards, Strathclyde, Gododin, Rheged, and southern Pictdom all came under relentless attack by the Northumbrian armies, and within a short time the war engulfed Dalriada as well.

CHAPTER 5

St Columba and Aedan of Dalriada

Unto this place, small and mean though it be
Great homage shall yet be paid,
Not only by the Kings and peoples of the Scots,
But by rulers of foreign and barbarous nations
And their subjects.

St Columba

The precarious foothold which the early Dalriads had secured in western Alba was to be finally consolidated by two contrasting figures of early Scottish history: a saint and a warrior. St Columkil – the man who is better remembered as St Columba – was born at Garten in Ireland in AD 521. By birth he was descended from Niall of the Nine Hostages, and was thus a prince of the northern *Ui Neill*. His father, Phelim, was a chieftain of the Clan O'Donnell, and his great grandfather, a son of Niall of the Nine Hostages, was the warrior King Connall Gulban of Donegal from whom the province of Tyrconnell in north-west Ulster took its name. His mother was Ethne, eleventh in descent from Cathaire Mor, King of Leinster, and, to complete his genealogical credentials, he was through his father's mother, a great grandson of Lorne Mac Erc, the co-founder of Albain Dalriada.

According to the tradition which has grown up around St Columba, the first remarkable fact of his life was that despite the secular advantages which such a lineage undoubtedly afforded, he decided to enter the Church. It has even been claimed that he was eligible for the High Kingship of Erin itself but rejected the crown in favour of the cloister. Instead, he entered the ecclesiastical school at Moville, and was ordained deacon. After leaving Moville, he completed his Celtic education under Gemman, the christian Bard of Leinster, and then studied under St Finnian at the famous monastic school of Clonard where he became one of the 'twelve apostles of Erin'. When an outbreak of the

Yellow Plague caused the community of Clonard to disperse, Columba returned to Ulster, and the early part of his career, AD 545–62, was devoted to good works and the foundation of churches and monastic societies throughout Ireland – as at Derry, Kells, Swords, Tory Island, Raphoe, Boyle, and Drumcliff. These, and numerous other foundations attributed to Columba, were meticulously recorded by his eighth-century hagiographer Adomnan MacRonan, the ninth abbot of Iona.

Later tradition has also woven a story around Columba's coming to Iona, portraying him as a once proud and contentious man in defence of whose honour 3000 men died in battle – and who came to Iona as an exile in expiation of this sin. The tale is not redolent of simple piety. According to this version, Diarmait, the High King of Ireland, had dragged from sanctuary and murdered a kinsman of Columba's, and aside from this sacrilege and an impending blood-feud, he also imprisoned the priest himself at Tara after passing judgement against him in a suit concerning the ownership of a psalter which Columba had allegedly copied. Columba was rescued by members of his clan and the whole *Ui Neill* rose to avenge the insult. The armies met at Cooladrummon near Sligo, and Diarmait's host was slaughtered in this trial by battle. Diarmait thereafter arranged for a Synod at Meath to excommunicate Columba, but even in those early days the Church would not permit mere kings to meddle, and the sentence was annulled. However, for Columba, conscience-stricken and admonished, the consequence was a self-imposed penance of exile, never to look again upon his native Ireland until he had converted to Christ as many souls as he had caused to perish at Cooladrummon. And so he went to Iona, the Island of Hii, where Ireland was over the horizon, and founded a small sanctuary in the Bay of the Coracle in sight of Mull – at first a simple structure of mud and wattle, but which was to become the heart of the Celtic Church in Scotland.

Some parts of this tradition have their basis in known fact. Other parts, however, are inaccurate, or at the least, distorted. Moreover, the hagiographer's preoccupation with recording acts of saintliness and piety (however true many of these might be) has tended to obscure the central purpose behind Columba's mission and the circumstances which gave rise to it. The many stories that have grown up around the name of St Columba and Iona have distracted from a more practical appreciation of his impact upon Dalriada and the other Celtic kingdoms of Alba. Some reconstruction is therefore necessary.

Columba's parents probably intended him for the Church. His mother, Ethne, was a deeply religious woman who also devoted the later years of her life to the service of Christ in Dalriada, and she is (supposedly) buried on one of the islands of Lorne. As a child, instead of being put out to fosterage with another family of the clan as was Gaelic custom, Columba was sent to live with the family priest, Cruithnechan, who no doubt prepared him for entry to the ecclesiastical school of Moville.

After Moville, Columba's period of study under the christian Bard of Leinster was designed to complete his Celtic education – and the fact that this training was considered necessary, was an indication of the role for which he was being prepared. A decision to enter the priesthood did not automatically imply a withdrawal from the world. In pre-Christian times it would have been equivalent to a decision to join the ranks of the *filidhean*. Columba's high lineage, his priestly education, and his training under Gemman would qualify him as a christian *filidh* to play a prominent and influential part in the councils of the northern *Ui Neill*, while the intellectual background provided by the Church together with his accumulated knowledge of Celtic customs and political affairs also fitted him for the wider role which he was to play in Ireland and Alba. In a more personal sense, this period under Gemman also instilled in him a deep and abiding love of the old Celtic stories and traditions, and in later years it was under his supervision and instruction that many of the old tales were written down and so preserved. He himself continued to compose poetry, and such of it as has survived provides a fascinating insight into his character, since it reflects a deep emotion and a vibrant awareness, coupled with the power of description – of the scenery around him, the wind on the sea, and the 'thunder of the crowding waves' beating on the rocks around the small chapel on Iona.

His years at Clonard as the disciple of St Finnian, however, were certainly the most formative. For Clonard was in almost every sense a very special place.

The decay of the Roman Empire and the devastation of Europe by barbarian tribes following the fall of Rome itself, had also seriously weakened the fabric of the Christian Church. After Christianity had become widely accepted as a principal religion, the early Church began to acquire the characteristics of an 'established' institution, and in so doing, its organisation tended to parallel the secular administration of the Empire within which it developed. Its administrative centre was

Rome. It was hierarchical, diocesan in organisation, and, in general conformity with imperial institutions, largely urban in character. That amid the general disintegration, pockets of Roman order and civilisation continued to survive, was in some measure due to the Church, since although the Empire itself had become a barren thing, the prestige of the Church and the Christian ideology acted strongly in support of the beleaguered civic and provincial administration. But in another sense, the Church had become complacently dependent on the centralised order of the Empire, and although even after AD 410 Rome remained the spiritual centre of Christianity, the growing isolation of the individual Gallic and other European bishoprics made them increasingly provincial in outlook and endeavour, and thus a prey to local interest. The inefficiency and corruption latent in the local hierarchical system became more apparent, and the various centres of the Church fought a doubtful holding action to preserve their dwindling status and influence against the tide of paganism that was sweeping across Europe. But the Church seemed to have lost the dynamism that had inspired the first Apostles and the martyrs of the early persecutions, and was unable effectively to confront the barbarism which threatened to engulf the Western Empire.

Out of this disintegration and the growing disillusionment and despair, a religious revival took shape in the form of a new monastic ideal. The idea of retreat from the world in order to pursue a life of religious contemplation was itself by no means novel, and hermitic seclusion had long been practised by devout men in Egypt and the East. During the third century the example of St Anthony of Alexandria had attracted many followers, and a hundred years later, in AD 370 it inspired St Martin of Tours, an ex-soldier turned diocesan bishop, to form the *Magic Monasterium* in Gaul. Other foundations soon followed.

This new monasticism, however, while reflecting the growing disillusionment with the state of the Church and the spreading chaos within the Empire, was not merely concerned with providing sanctuary for those who sought religious refuge. The underlying purpose was to recover the purity of the early Christian teachings and recapture the zeal of the first Apostles so that a new Church might be generated from the ruins of the old. The movement did not have the formal support of the diocesan churches which at first regarded it with distrust and some alarm, but it attracted able and dedicated men from all levels of post-Roman society who came to these new schools of learning. A Christian intellectualism began to thrive. Old texts were studied, copied so that they might be preserved, and then disseminated to other monasteries so that others could read them. The early tenets of Christianity underwent a re-examination and revival. The example of poverty and discipline challenged the decaying order of corruption and chaos. Most important of all, out of this revival grew a missionary purpose – to carry the Christian message to the barbarian tribes who were settling in the lands which they had overrun.

The missionary activity had, of necessity, a political aspect. With the decline of the Empire and the central authority of Rome, old patterns of tribalism re-emerged. Pressure from the barbarian peoples who now rode unchecked through the broken frontiers forced Gauls and Goths, Franks and Burgundians to collide, as the various bands hacked out and strove to hold their share of country. Petty kings and warleaders fought each other and preyed upon the old civilisation of the cities. Warfare and pillage were endemic and the cohesion of Roman Europe disappeared. Against these warring divisions and the paganism which flourished among the barbarian tribes, the Church's one strength was that, in Christianity, it could offer an ideology around which kings and tribes might make common cause and from such alliances a chance of peace in which education might serve to restore a measure of order and civilisation. The conversion of the pagan tribes might check the process of disintegration when military conquest was clearly impossible.

In Europe, the movement at first met with only indifferent success prior to the rise of Charlemagne, but it had a strong appeal for the Celtic peoples of Wales and Ireland who developed the monastic ideal along their own Celtic lines.

The monastic school at Clonard was founded in about AD 540 by St Finnian, a *Cruithne* from Wales. This community quickly demonstrated the revolutionary aspects inherent in the new monastic movement. It broke the confines of tribalism and the barriers of caste. The monks shared a common discipline and a common purpose which claimed a higher loyalty than the demands of rank or clan. It attracted men of peculiar dedication, and the 'Apostles' of Clonard came from almost every possible background. Columba was the high-born prince of the Ui Neill. Cairan, who later founded the Abbey of Clonmacnois, was a carpenter's son. Brendan of Tralee was a sailor; Kenneth the son of a Pictish bard. They studied in the fashion of the old *filidh* – memorising the gospel texts and responding to the vigorous disciplines which St

Finnian made them undergo. The experience instilled in them a particular *esprit*, and a militancy which inspired them to action rather than contemplation. When the Yellow Plague in AD 548 forced the community to disperse, little 'Clonards' sprang up all over Ireland in the model of the original. Monasticism seems to have had a particular appeal for the Irish Celts, and although some of the original 'Apostles' were carried off by the plague, the movement begun at Clonard developed rapidly.

It might seem surprising that Columba, given his background, influence and reputation, did not become a bishop in the Church hierarchy. The reason almost certainly lies in the fact that the Irish Church viewed the activities of the Clonard militants with some alarm. Although Christianity in Ireland owed its origins to the missionary work of St Patrick, the Church that he founded was diocesan in character, and in the years since his death it had, like its counterpart in Britain, come to suffer a worldly infection which drew the criticism of religious purists. The British monk Gildas, a querulous historian, complained of the Bishops: 'Monsters of ambition who buy for cash the office which should be earned by a holy life'.[9] It was the weakness of an hierarchical system that candidates should vie for vacant office with consequent opportunities for bribery and corruption. The Church was failing to rise above tribal interests, its bishops often indolent, and caring only for their own. Clonard challenged this decline in religious morality and such differences which existed between the 'Apostles' and the established Church may have coloured the traditional account of Columba's feud with Diarmait and the incident of the psalter.

In AD 548, Ireland was not fully Christianised. Whereas the northern *Ui Neill* to whom Columba belonged had genuinely embraced the faith, the southern *Ui Neill* of which Diarmait was a member remained somewhat ambivalent. Diarmait himself was almost certainly a pagan. His election to the High Kingship had been contested by both Leinster and the northern *Ui Neill* (the two most Christian states in Ireland) and he did not actually become High King in Tara until AD 558. His first act was to appoint an archdruid as his chief advisor. The Church apparently was either unwilling or unable to challenge this – but quite possibly the struggle between the High King and Columba dates from this time.

Diarmait's intervention in the matter of the disputed psalter, however, is almost certainly a spurious fable, since, under the Canons laid down by St Patrick, no churchman could have submitted an

35

ecclesiastical dispute for judgement in a secular court. The psalter in question was possibly St Jerome's translation of the Vulgate which Columba is alleged to have copied while visiting the monastery of St Finbar at Dromin. It was undoubtedly an extremely precious manuscript and may originally have come from Tours, from whence it had been brought by St Ninian to Candida Casa – a monastery founded in Galloway to promote the conversion of the Picts. Bishop Finbar had been Ninian's pupil at Candida Casa, and when that monastery had to be abandoned in the face of pagan persecution, the psalter may have been entrusted to him for safekeeping. If this was the only copy in Ireland, Finbar might have wished to guard it, either to prevent the circulation of any spurious version of the sacred text, or as a treasure in his own monastery. Columba's view was more likely that it was a valuable evangelical tool to be copied and circulated for the benefit of other monastic schools. 'It is not right to extinguish a divine thing or prevent anyone copying, reading, or circulating it.' (This was the Clonard attitude again.) The two priests may have disagreed and the Church possibly saw an opportunity to discredit Columba by spreading the story of a quarrel. But the incident did not start a war.

The murder of one of Columba's 'kinsmen' also requires further examination. In AD 561, at the *Aenach* – a triennial fair held at Teltown, east of Tara, Prince Curnan, a son of King Aed of Connaught, struck and killed an opposing player during a game of hurley. Curnan fled to Columba who granted him the protection of sanctuary, a right of the Church which had already been accepted in Ireland. Notwithstanding this, Diarmait's soldiers dragged Curnan from the sanctuary and murdered him. By this action the High King had not only committed sacrilege, but, probably more important in Irish eyes, he had broken the Celtic *brehon* Law which entitled Curnan to trial and a pardon upon payment of the blood-fine. Whatever motive may have been behind this killing, the result was that Connaught declared war on Tara.

That the *Ui Neill* should then have risen in support of Connaught suggests there was more at issue than a mere blood feud. Besides any rivalry that existed between the northern and southern *Ui Neill*, the emphasis on religion which is apparent at the Battle of Cooladrummon indicates rather that this was a struggle for power between Christianity and a re-emergent Druidism. In such a context, Columba, as a prince of the northern *Ui Neill* and high in their councils, and also as the chief protagonist of an aggressive Christianity, may well have played an influential part in the decision. In the short campaign that followed, it was Diarmait who took the initiative by invading Connaught and trying to drive a wedge between the allies. But their combined army met him at Cooladrummon near Sligo. Before the battle, Diarmait carried out certain pagan rituals, marching his army sun-wise around a cairn while the Druids marked out an *airbhe* (a magic circle) around his position. By contrast, the Christian army carried as their standard the famous *Cathach* (the Battle Book) a psalter written in Columba's own hand, which in later centuries continued to be trooped before the Clan Conaill in battle, and is preserved as Ireland's most ancient book to this day.

The battle was a massacre. Diarmait's army lost 3000 killed, and the High King retreated to Tara. The *Ui Neill*, however, did not follow up the victory.

The next event in this rather tumultuous period of Columba's life was the Synod of Teltown at which certain members of the diocesan Church attempted to excommunicate him. That the Synod should have been convened close to Tara suggests that their action had Diarmait's approval, and that under secular pressure many of the hereditary clergy were ready to revert to local and clan loyalties. The intention was to excommunicate Columba *in absentia*, but he travelled through hostile territory to attend, and when he was supported by Brendan (his erstwhile colleague at Clonard) and by Bishop Finbar (with whom the alleged dispute concerning the psalter had been), the charges against him were dropped. The incident demonstrated the growing division between the monastic and episcopal Churches in Ireland.

Diarmait's time was almost come. In AD 563 he again broke the sanctuary in order to murder a man, the victim this time being under the protection of St Ruadhan of Lothra – another of the 'twelve Apostles of Clonard'. Ruadhan and his clergy surrounded the royal dun at Tara and began the ancient Celtic ritual of *Loscad* – a vigil of fasting during which they called down a curse that no king or queen would ever again dwell in Tara's halls. No one dared to break their siege. Supplies failed, and Diarmait abandoned the ancient dun. The thousand-year-old enclosure was never reoccupied.

Two years later, Diarmait's enemies trapped him in Banban's Inn at Rathbeg in Antrim and set fire to the building. When the king tried to break out, Black Aed MacSuibne of the *Cruithne* royal house drove a spear into his chest. Diarmait fell backwards into a huge vat and the burning roof collapsed on top of him.

Cooladrummon and the end of Diarmait swung the tide in favour of the Christian *Ui Neill* of the north who were soon to become the predominant power in Ireland – a fact which, because of ties of kindred, was of some importance to Dalriada. Columba, contrary to tradition, was not overcome with remorse, and he did not now embark for Iona as an act of penance or self-imposed exile. He had rather more positive reasons for going to Alba.

On the shore of Loch Caolisport, at Cove near Achahoish in Knapdale, there is a small cave which is associated with Columba. In front of it stands a chapel of a later date, but the cave itself was clearly an early Christian shrine. It is formed by a natural fissure and at some time it was walled across the mouth – as was the practice in many cave sanctuaries. Just inside the entrance a small hollow in the rock served as a stoup for holy water, while a natural platform supported an altar built with dry stones – above which there is a small cross carved onto the cave wall.

This, rather than Iona, may have been Columba's landfall. The cave is not far from the ancient hill fort of Torr which has been tentatively identified with the Cinelgon of Dalriadic times, where Conall son of Comgall son of Fergus Mor had his dun. Columba's journey to Alba was more likely in response to an urgent request from Conall, since Dalriada was in serious difficulty.

Arthur's death at Camlann was a disaster for the Romano-Christian party. The precarious alliance crumbled and the individual British kingdoms relapsed into civil war. The Roman party in Strathclyde rallied round the Christian king Rhydderch Hael, but within two years he was overthrown by the Druid faction led by the usurper Morken, and forced to flee to Ireland. In the north the Christian position had always been precarious and now a new tide of paganism engulfed the Church. During his brief reign, Rhydderch had invited St Kentigern (the Scottish St Mungo – by tradition the son of Tannoch, Christian daughter of King Loth) to become bishop of the small Ninian community at Cathures near Glasgow. When Rhydderch was defeated, Kentigern was also forced to flee. Christian monks were martyred in Gododin, and St Ninian's original monastic sanctuary at Candida Casa in Galloway also had to be abandoned. Another notable refugee was the monk Gildas who escaped to an island in the Bristol Channel where he composed his chronicle, *The Destruction of Britain* – less a history than an angry diatribe against the corruption of the Church and the wickedness of the pagan kings. Gildas, though a northman himself, directed his venom against the kings of Wales and Dumnonia, but nevertheless, as another historian put it: 'The christian religion in Strathclyde and Cumbria was almost entirely destroyed.'

Columba would have been fully informed of the deteriorating situation in Alba. He probably met and knew Rhydderch, and he formed an active association with Kentigern. Ireland had also witnessed a pagan revival under Diarmait, but there the situation had been retrieved by the victory of the Christian army at Cooladrummon. With the Church's position in Ireland thus secured, Columba and his colleagues turned their attention towards the re-establishment of Christianity in Alba.

The Kingdom of Dalriada was an essential part of such a plan since it was the only Christian beach-head available. Columba was not the first, nor the only saint of Lorne. Some twenty years previously St Brendan the sailor had founded a church at Tiree and established a number of small sanctuaries in the Garvelloch Islands – notably at Culbrandon and Aileach a Naoimh, the 'Rock of Saints' (Columba's Hinba where he and Brendan sometimes met and where Ethne is said to have been buried). St Moluog from Bangor in Erin had also founded a sanctuary on Lismore Island near Oban. There were small Christian communities in Skye, Raasay, Morvern, and Lewis. Having a similar background, and coming as they did from a very small Celtic world, these early saints were acquainted with each other, and despite a seemingly solitary existence there was probably a bond of association between them. Nevertheless, Columba was unique in that his actions displayed an acute political awareness and expertise. This political ability and his consequent preoccupation with the affairs of Dalriada were not altogether surprising, given his high birth and influence among the northern *Ui Neill* and his blood relationship to the royal *derbfine* of Lorne. Thus, a tradition which remembers him merely as a saintly hermit exiled on a remote Hebridean island does him less than justice. Columba was a highly political animal, and the pattern of events in both Dalriada and northern Ireland bear out this contention.

Cooladrummon was fought in AD 561. The same year, Columba embarked for Dalriada, probably at the request of King Conall, who had only recently become High King. The reason for such a request may be guessed at. Conall's predecessor Gabhran had been killed in battle the previous year, almost certainly by the Picts, and thus the indications are that Dalriada was under serious attack from the north. From Columba's point of view, if this Christian beach-head in Alba was to be preserved, security from Pictish attack was a first priority, but given Dalriada's size and vulnerability, this could only be achieved by treaty. His first task therefore, was to establish a Christian base and open negotiations with the Picts.

It is interesting to note that all Columba's monastic foundations were strategically located. Derry, for example, was within sight of Grianan in Aelach, the royal dun of the northern *Ui Neill*. Durrow was close to Uisneach, the capital of the southern *Ui Neill*, and Kells was only fifteen miles from Tara. Iona was no exception to the rule.

The island of Hii or Iova (the name Iona derives from a later mis-spelling) had been venerated by the Picts as a sacred place long before Columba arrived, and it may already have been a traditional burying ground of western Pictish kings. The earliest recorded Christian sanctuary was founded by St Oran, an Irish missionary from Tipperaray who had established churches in Colonsay and Mull before dying of plague at Iona in AD 549. Columba thus chose to establish himself on a spot which was already accepted as a holy place by both Picts and Scots. It was also a strategic location in that the disputed border between Dalriada and Pictdom bisected the island. This frontier, which ran across the island of Mull, through Iona and Colonsay, was marked by cairns. On Iona, the cairn was known as *Cul Ri Erin* (back to Ireland) while a matching cairn on the slope of Ben More in Mull was called the *Cul Ri Alba* (back to Alba), thus indicating the beginning of Pictish territory. The boundary may have been in dispute, and there are a number of contradictions in the early annals. *Tigernach* records that Iona was bequeathed to Columba by King Conall (the Irish contention) while the Venerable Bede maintained: 'The island belongs to the realm of Britain. The Picts who inhabit these districts donated it'.[10] In fact, the significance of Iona was possibly that its title had to be cleared with both the kingdoms and it thus provided Columba with a means of opening contact with the northern Picts. It also seems significant that he apparently landed on Iona in AD 563, after spending two years in Kintyre, and having presumably built the small chapel there. He set out almost immediately in that same year on a mission to the court of King Brude MacMaelchon who was High King in northern Pictdom.

Brude's dun was probably in the region of present Inverness and Columba's journey up the great glen was later recorded by Adomnan in the eighth century – an account, incidentally, which contains the first known reference to the Loch Ness monster with whom Columba had a short confrontation. The party had some difficulty in gaining access to Brude owing to the obstructive attitude of the Pictish Archdruid, but eventually Columba succeeded in meeting the king. Brude (a name commonly applied to Pictish kings) had, in accordance with Pictish custom, succeeded to the kingship by right of his mother, but his father is thought to have been the Welsh King Maelgwyn who had been a monk before seizing the throne of Gwynedd – in which case he may already have been familiar with the Christian teaching and thus not unfavourably disposed. Although Adomnan's account does not specifically state that Brude was converted (though a *Life of St. Comgall* reports his baptism two years later), the mission was undoubtedly successful. The monks were given freedom to preach, and land for their church-building. (The subsequent conversion of the northern Picts was undertaken by St Moluog of Lismore.) Columba himself became Brude's *anin chara* (soul friend) – a specifically Christian term which implies the king's conversion, and, most important for Dalriada, a peace seems to have been concluded since the Pictish attacks now ceased. Again, Adomnan's account does not record a specific agreement to this effect, but the Dalriads appear to have had confidence in it, since not only did they fight in alliance with the Picts against the Angles, but were also prepared to send their warbands south and their fleet overseas without apparently fearing for their flank. The truce was kept throughout Brude MacMaelchon's lifetime.

Having secured Dalriada's northern frontier, Columba could now turn his attention to the situation in Strathclyde. In Wales, the Christian party was rallying behind St David and St Cadoc, and the tide was beginning to turn their way. Kentigern persuaded the ex-monk, King Maelgwyn of Gwynedd, to allow a monastery to be built near his capital at Degannwy, and shortly afterwards, the king himself re-adopted Christianity. He died of plague in AD 563 and was succeeded as the 'Island Dragon' of Gwynedd by the more reliable Cadwallon, who was a devout Christian and a nephew of Kentigern's disciple St Asaph. During the next ten years, the Christian party built an alliance aimed at the re-establishment of the faith in Strathclyde. In AD 573, Rhydderch returned from his exile in Ireland and set up his standard of the Green Dragon. He was joined by Cadwallon and the Welsh, Urien the Golden of Cumbria, and a warband of Dalriads. The pagan army of Strathclyde was led by Gwendolew and his brother Elifer, and the Cumbrian Archdruid Merlin. The armies met at Ardderyd on the River Esk a few miles north of Carlisle and the pagan host was completely routed. The usurper Gwendolew was slain in the battle, while Merlin, according to tradition, fled to Ettrick Forest and eventually went mad. Rhydderch reclaimed his throne and summoned Kentigern to be his bishop. The Christian party claimed a complete victory, and for the first time since Arthur's death, the Celtic kingdoms of northern Britain achieved a frail alliance.

In AD 574, however, Conall died, and another serious crisis overtook Dalriada. Sometime that year (whether before or after the king's death is not known) there was a great battle in Kintyre at which 'Duncan son of Conall son of Comgall fell, and many others of the allies of the sons of Gabhran'. It clearly was a serious defeat.

The immediate question was the matter of the High Kingship itself. This was the first king-choosing since Columba's arrival in Dalriada, and he quickly arrogated to himself the old right of the archdruid to pronounce upon the succession – substituting for the customary trance utterance a vision of an angel who had shown him a great glass book in which were written the names of pre-appointed kings.

Columba may have had a political reason for intervening in the choice of High King. It seems likely that the succession might have been disputed. The inclusion of Duncan's death in the *Annals* suggests that he may have been the heir-apparent, and the next popular choice seems to have been Eoghan, a son of Gabhran. Instead, Columba named Gabhran's other son, Aedan, for the kingship – and a brief look at Aedan's ancestry may indicate the reason why. Both Aedan and Eoghan had the same father, Gabhran grandson of Fergus Mor, and thus may have had equal claims within the *derbfine*. Aedan's mother, however, was the daughter of an earlier Christian King of Strathclyde, and through her he was a nephew of the Christian King Urien of Cumbria. His wife was probably a granddaughter of King Brude MacMaelchon, High King of the Picts. In AD 574, by right of his mother, he was sub-king of Manau in Gododin, and had fought with distinction at the Battle of Ardderyd. His connections in Strathclyde and his support of the Romano-Christian party seem to be further demonstrated by the fact that he was the first of the Celtic princes to name his eldest son after the British hero, Arthur. Aedan thus had important blood ties with both of Dalriada's Albain neighbours – the Picts and the Britons. He had some experience of ruling a territory, and was already respected as a warrior.

He was invested of the Kingship by Columba, either at Dunadd or on Iona, and during the ceremony, Columba is supposed to have invoked both a prophecy and a warning: 'Believe certainly, O Aedan, that none of thine enemies will be able to resist thee until first thou work deceit against me or my successors . . . or against my relatives (the *Ui Neill*) in Ireland.'[11] As a prophecy it would come true during the time of Aedan's successors. In AD 574, however, Columba may have had something more immediate in mind. While the statement implies that Aedan had taken an oath to support the Christian cause, the reference to the *Ui Neill* suggests some other agreement – which may have been related to the situation in Dalriada following the defeat earlier in the year. That this battle should have taken place on the Kintyre peninsula indicates a seaborne landing by an invader (since Dalriada was at peace with the Britons and the Picts). The most likely candidate is King Baetan of Ulidia (Ulster) who, since his accession in AD 572, had embarked on an expansionist policy in the Isles. The lands of Irish Dalriada in Antrim were a tributary of Ulidia, and the Dalriadic kings had had to make the customary submission for them, yielding both the recognised tribute and hostages. The present dispute and Baetan's invasion concerned the status of Dalriada in Alba.

That Baetan apparently did not follow up his victory in Kintyre was probably due to the influence of the northern *Ui Neill* – no doubt advised by Columba – since their interests were also at stake. The tribute paid by a vassal to the overlord comprised a number of elements – *cain* (a yearly tax of seven shields, seven horses, seven hounds, and seven slaves), *cobach* (military service), *fecht* (participation in military expeditions), and *slogad* (hosting – a full-scale muster for war). These were generally recognised. The point at issue was the Dalriadic fleet.

Since the time of Fergus Mor MacErc, the Albain kingdom of Dalriada had been a sea power and, based in the *Senchus fer n'Alban* the fleet may have amounted to 150 galleys or more, even in Fergus's time. An armada of this size, if controlled by a hostile neighbour, would have posed a serious threat to the power of the northern *Ui Neill*, while from Columba's point of view, given that Baetan clearly wished to deploy that fleet in furtherance of his own predatory ends both in the Hebridean islands and along the coasts of Galloway and Wales, the participation of Dalriadic ships in such activities would almost certainly have fractured or disrupted the fragile alliances which he had built up with the other kingdoms in Alba and northern Britain.

It seems therefore, that Baetan was persuaded to cease his attacks on Kintyre (probably under threats from the *Ui Neill*) and submit his claim to a formal hearing in front of the *Olave Brieve* (the chief *brehon* judge in northern Ireland). The case was heard at the great Convention of Drum Ceatt in AD 575 – held on the ridge of Mullagh Hill near Limvady, east of Derry. Both Columba and Aedan attended, but Baetan himself was not present – no doubt because the result was a foregone conclusion, since the Convention was held on *Ui Neill* territory and in the presence of King Aed of Aelach who was cousin to both Columba and the then reigning High King of Erin. Instead, Baetan took the opportunity to invade and conquer the Isle of Man.

The judgement at Drum Ceatt was indeed in Dalriada's favour. Dalriadan *fecht* and *slogad* was 'with the men of Ireland forever' (which was not really practicable), while their *cain* and *cobach* was 'with the men of Alban and their sea service with Alban alone'. To all intents and purposes, Albain Dalriada thus became an independent kingdom. The judgement would no doubt have been guaranteed by the northern *Ui Neill* under whose auspices the Convention was held – and thus the significance of Columba's admonition to Aedan that he should keep faith with 'my relatives in Ireland'.

At the Convention, Columba also successfully represented Aed of Aelach in a case concerning the status of the *filidh*, and he took the opportunity to visit his old colleagues in Coleraine and Clonmacnois. But from now onwards, he began to withdraw from the centre of events. For the first time in its short history, Dalriada was relatively secure and its status recognised. There was peace with the Picts and the Britons, a strong king held the reins of power, and the priest could settle in Iona to concentrate upon the Christian work that was his greatest purpose. So the story passes to Aedan the warrior.

In southern Britain, the Saxons were on the march. In AD 577 their armies shattered the British forces at Dyrham above Bath. Cirencester and Gloucester fell, and the Saxon spear-thrust pressed east to the River Severn and the Bristol Channel. The Dumnonians of Cornwall, Somerset, and Devon were permanently cut off from the Britons of Wales.

In the north, the Christian victory at Ardderyd brought a few years of fitful peace. Here the threat was from the Angles in Northumbria whose warbands probed Gododin and Strathclyde. The Christian alliance of Dalriads and Britons combined to contain the raiders. Leadership in the field fell to Aedan, since Rhydderch and Urien of Cumbria were growing too old for the war trail, and the Dalriadic king seems to have had the Britons' trust. The alliance may have been further strengthened when Aedan took a princess of Strathclyde as his second wife.

However, his earliest campaigns do not seem to have been against the Angles, since Dalriada itself was still not without enemies. In AD 580 he led a seaborne expedition against the Orkney pirates who had taken to raiding in the Hebrides, and in AD 582 he drove his erstwhile overlord Baetan and his Ulidian Irish out of the Isle of Man. There was also sporadic fighting in Skye throughout Aedan's reign.

In AD 583, the Angles made an attempt upon Gododin, and Aedan defeated them at Manaan in Stirlingshire. The same year, Brude MacMaelchon died, and the centre of Pictish power shifted south to Abernethy on the Tay where the new High King Gartnaidh had his dun. The truce, it seems, still held, and Gartnaidh favoured Christianity since, during the early years of his reign, Columba and Kentigern founded a monastery at Dunkeld and began the work of converting the southern Picts. But Brude's power had weakened with age, and Gartnaidh's hold was less strong. Trouble came from the *Maeatea*, a Pictish tribe whose territory lay close to the old Wall. In AD 584 they invaded the hunting runs of the Gododin, whose ruler Mynyddog appealed to Dalriada and Strathclyde for help. Aedan gathered a mixed warband and caught the Picts near Catterick. According to the Gododdin epic, Aedan's host spent the night before the battle feasting in the Hall of Eydin (possibly Carredin, by the Wall) and in the morning, drunk on mead, they threw themselves recklessly upon a vastly superior enemy:

> The men went to Catraeth loquacious was their host;
> Fresh mead was their feast, and also their poison.
> Three hundred men were contending with weapons,
> And after the slaughter there was stillness.
> The men went to Catraeth with the dawn.
> They dealt peaceably with those who feared them.
> A hundred thousand and three hundred engaged in slaughter:
> Drenched in gore they were targets for the spears.

Their post they manfully defended
Before the retinue of Mynyddawg Mwynvawr.[12]

It was a slaughter after the old Gaelic manner, watched by the bards who composed the epic and told the death fights of the Celtic champions who fell. Tradition avers that Columba himself glimpsed the battle in his mind's eye, and like Moses before the Promised Land, raised his hands in supplication for Aedan's soldiers – prophesying victory, but a sad one. According to the epic, of the three hundred and three warriors who charged the Pictish battle line, only one survived. The figure doubtless derives from bardic licence, but certainly, although victorious, the Dalriads and their allies suffered fearful losses. Aedan himself left two sons, Eochaid and his chosen Arthur, on that killing ground.

The closing years of the sixth century brought the end of a small epoch in Albain history. Columba died in AD 597 and was buried on his beloved Iona. In AD 600 and 603 his old friends St Kenneth and St Kentigern followed him. Aed of the *Ui Neill*, latterly High King of Erin, had died in 598, and the year 603 saw also the death of Rhydderch of Strathclyde (he lies buried at the foot of the Cloridderck Stone by Loch Winnoch, West of Glasgow). A generation had blown away in a few short years, and Aedan the warrior was soon to follow.

In Northumbria, the Angle King Aethelfrith, having consolidated his hold over Deira and Bernicia, and being in Bede's phrase, 'very valiant, most avid for glory', set about the conquest and subjugation of the Britons. In AD 603, an Angle army under Aethelfrith's general, Hering, struck north across the Wall. The ageing Aedan mustered the warbands of the coalition – Britons from Strathclyde, Votadini from Manau, Dalriads, and friendly Picts, and barred the way at Degsastan (Dawstane in Liddesdale). The battle that followed was decisive. On the Angle side, Aethelfrith's brother Theobald was slain with all the royal body-guard; but the army of Dalriada and Strathclyde was virtually wiped out. The dead included Domangart, another of Aedan's sons.

'From that time to this [wrote Bede in AD 731] no King of the Scots in Britain has dared to come against the English in battle.'[13] Nothing could now stop the northward advance of the Angle armies. Dunedin (Edinburgh) fell in 638, Stirling in 642, and with them the old Gododin. Rheged succumbed to pressure and dynastic marriage. Dumbarton, the great fortress of Strathclyde, alone held out as an island of resistance in the west. On the east coast, the Angles drove northwards into the kingdoms of the Picts. Nor did their conversion to Christianity deter them from military expansion. Their advance was finally halted in AD 685 when the Pictish King Bridei, a great warleader after Aedan's mould, smashed their shield wall at Dunnichen near Forfar.

After Degsastan, Aedan himself retreated into Kintyre where he died (or abdicated) in about AD 605. He lies buried somewhere in Dalriada, but the place has been long forgotten.

CHAPTER 6

The Celtic Church on Iona

Isle of Sleep where dreams are holy,
Sails to thee a King who sleepeth.
With thy Saints we leave him sleeping.
IONA BOAT SONG

Aedan's body was not carried to Iona, but among the later kings it was
the custom – just as it had been perhaps in pre-Dalriadic times. During
the sixteenth century, the Dean of the Isles counted three tombs like
small chapels wherein forty-eight Scottish kings, four Irish kings, and
eight Norse kings lay buried. But beneath them there are probably
others whom time and historical obituary have ignored. They brought
them to the Martyrs' Bay, and laid their bodies on the mound called the
Eala – and then carried them along the Street of the Dead to the *Reilig
Oran* and the Place of Kings. Long after the centre of the kingdom had
been moved to Scone, the kings of Scotland returned to Iona to be
buried. Dalriads, Picts, and then Scots, ruled and fought, died, were
killed or murdered, and carried to Iona in seemingly endless procession.
It made a strange gathering even for the dead. Dark-age monarchs
remembered briefly for their valour or their violence, or the dreadful
manner of their dying, brought to peace. Here Duncan and Macbeth,
mortal enemies, lie together in the inevitable reconciliation of eternity.
And here too were buried the Lords of the Isles, and the chieftains of the
western clans. Macdonalds, Macleans, MacKinnons, Macquaries –
long after the Lordship was forfeit and the splendour gone. It was their
tradition – and their privilege.

Iona is now much visited – and much changed – though in quieter
moments it can be haunting still. As the ferry plies the short crossing
from Mull, to the left there is a small bay (later called the 'Martyrs' Bay')
which was the old landing-place where the bodies of the kings were first
brought to landfall and their biers placed upon the Mound of Lamen-
tation. From there, the Street of the Dead, a broad causeway paved with

48

rough red stones (which still lies beneath the present road) led through the ancient town of Sodora to the churchyard and the chapel of St Oran. The old causeway passed by the west wall of the ruined nunnery which stands close by the present jetty; founded in about 1200 by Ranald, son of Somerled, and ancestor of the Clan Donald. His sister Beatrice was the first prioress, and the early Benedictine nuns who lived there were drawn from the sisters and daughters of Highland chiefs. Parts of the ruin date from 1390, when the walls were partially rebuilt. The sisterhood later became Augustinian Canonesses, and the last prioresses were all Macleans. The nuns survived the forfeiture of the Lordship and the depredations of the Reformation, but in 1574, the nunnery and its lands were bestowed on MacLean of Duart who neglected them, and the convent buildings fell into ruins. When Dr Johnson and Boswell visited Iona in 1773, the church was a cow-shed, and the old sculptured tombs were buried under dung and mire. The stones had been taken for cottages and walls, and the vaulted chancel roof collapsed soon after. A tradition grew that the ruins were haunted. In 1899, the Duke of Argyll bequeathed the land to the Church of Scotland. The present garden and partial restoration date from 1923.

St Oran's Chapel, at the end of the Street of the Dead, is the oldest standing building on Iona. The present chapel marks the site of an ancient oratory raised over Oran's grave in pre-Columban times. It was rebuilt by Queen Margaret of Scotland in 1073, and the beautiful Norman arch added by the Benedictine community in about 1200. This is the most hallowed place of Iona. In 1098, Magnus Barelegs of Norway entered, intent perhaps on violence or plunder, and was seen to recoil, shaken, and order that none should enter – but it is not known what he saw or feared so much.

In the churchyard itself, there were once nine rows of tombs, and the earth around was literally paved with gravestones. Some were moved, some taken and destroyed during the Reformation, and today most of the surviving sculptured stones have been transferred to the Abbey Museum. Approaching through the first gate from the Street of the Dead, there is a railed-in space which is the traditional site of the *Ioman nan Righ* (the Ridge of the Kings), where three eastward-facing shrines contained the bodies of the kings of three realms. The centre shrine – *tumulus regium Scotiae* – was the tomb of forty-eight Scottish kings dating from AD 685. The southern shrine contained four Irish kings, two of whom had become monks and died the 'straw-death' on Iona, and the northern shrine housed the tombs of eight Norse kings of Man, the last of whom died in 1228. The three chapels still existed in 1549 and one survived still in 1695, but by Dr Johnson's time the violations of grave robbers had reduced the tombs to mere ridges of earth – formed by the broken arches of the vaults underground.

A second ridge marked the tombs of the MacLeans, Clan Gillean, and the grave of a single MacLeod (possibly MacLeod of Lewis who was killed at the Battle of Bloody Bay in 1480). This collection includes three of the most fascinating carved stones surviving in the Highlands. The first commemorates a Maclean of Duart – possibly Sallow Hector who was killed at Flodden, and it may mark the grave also of his father, Red Hector, slain at Harlaw – depicting a fighting man, tall and bearded, wearing ancient West Highland armour, a high conical helmet and a quilted leather war-coat reaching to his knees, and carrying a lance and shield. The second effigy is of a Maclean of Lochbuie – thought to be Ewen of the Little Head who was killed in rebellion against his father in 1538. The third is of a Maclean of Coll, a fifteenth-century warrior similarly armoured and clasping a claymore.

Inside St Oran's Chapel itself there were once other handsome tombs. South of the altar was a stone slab bearing the Macdonald Galley, and marking the graves of Angus Og of Bannockburn, and the first two Lords of the Isles – Good John of Islay and Donald of Harlaw. Facing the doorway is the *clach brath* (the doomsday stone), in reality the socket of a cross with a hollow worn in it that once supported 'three noble globes of white marble' – before they were thrown into the sea during the Reformation. For some centuries afterwards, other stones were kept in the cavity and every passer-by would turn them sun-wise – for it was prophesied that when the hollow was worn through, the world would come to an end.

Of Columba's sanctuary, there is little trace: a stone that may have been his pillow, a rock that might have been his table; the mill stream, and traces of an old earthwork. The rest is up to the imagination now.

The Celtic Church of St Columba established itself at a time when the movement of barbarian tribes in Europe largely prevented any consistent contact with Rome, and consequently it developed a number of independent characteristics of its own. It boasted no central authority, and its leaders were the individual 'saints' and abbots who founded monastic communities and sanctuaries after the pattern of Iona. Many of these 'clergy' retained a secular mode of life and fathered sons who succeeded them (the Clan MacNab are descended from one such), although this may not have been a general rule. The Celtic Church also had its fanatics – a sect called the Culdees, who referred to themselves as 'the Friends of God' and chose to live apart as anchorites. However, although many of its early leaders had been critical of the Patrician Diocesan Church in Ireland, there was no real divergence in terms of doctrine. There were minor differences concerning administration – the date of Easter and the shape of the tonsure, but the Celtic Church could not truly be described as schismatic.

Nevertheless, as the gradual settlement of Europe again permitted the advance of the Roman order in Britain, it was inevitable that the Roman and Celtic Churches should have found themselves in competition, and the independence of Iona was shortly challenged. This rivalry was most apparent in Northumbria where, since AD 634, the Celtic Church from its monastery at Lindisfarne had been working for the conversion of the heathen Angles. In 664, the Christian King Oswiu of Northumbria was prevailed upon by the Roman faction to convene a Synod at Whitby which would formally rule on the question of Iona's independence. Apart from such questions as the size of the tonsure and the date of Easter, the issue turned on the universal authority of Rome, and the acknowledgement of St Peter, the first Bishop of Rome, as the Keeper of the Keys of Heaven. The religious *realpolitik* of the Romans triumphed, for how could a small community on a remote island in the Hebrides claim to have a clearer revelation of the Truth than the powerful Universal Church of Rome – and if Oswiu, giving judgement, denied the right of St Peter, and was wrong, then who, on the Day of Judgement, would admit him into heaven? The Roman party also thus secured an alliance with the most powerful military kingdom in Alba.

And so the Celtic Church succumbed – in a sense – and withdrew into itself. Yet a part of it never died. Much of its art survived; monasteries still flourished, ruled by abbots of Celtic descent who still valued the old ways. Its saints were revered by the Highland men; the Celtic shrines retained their sanctity. It was the *Brechbennach* (reliquary) of Columba that the Scots carried to Battle at Bannockburn, and the old saint did not fail them.

On Iona, of the first eleven abbots, nine were blood kin to Columba. For a hundred years after his death, the community prospered. The fifth

abbot, Seghine (623–652), was responsible for the conversion of the
Bernician Prince Oswald and the founding of Lindisfarne in Northumbria. The ninth abbot was Adomnan (694–764), who is best remembered as the hagiographer of St Columba, but who was also responsible
for a number of social reforms in the Isles – not least the abolition of the
old Celtic custom that permitted women to fight in battle with their
menfolk. Constant to the political role of Iona, Adomnan was friend to
the kings of Dalriada, and also to the Pictish High King, the first to be
buried on Iona since Dalriada's founding, as well as, strangely, to the
Angle Egfrid of Northumbria who was killed at Dunnichen. He finally
brought the Ionan community into conformity with the Roman usage –
and his abbacy thus marked the formal end of the island's spiritual
independence.

But it was possibly the Vikings rather than the Synod of Whitby who
brought an end to the Celtic Church as Columba had known it. In 794,
Viking longships appeared off the coast of Mull and 'red martyrdom'
came to the islands. Monasteries and churches were an especial target
because of their accumulation of treasures, and many of the old
sanctuaries on the exposed coastline became untenable. Others built
watchtowers for warning and defence – or dispersed their precious
relics to places of greater safety inland.

During the next hundred years, Iona was sacked three times by Viking
raiders. In 806, sixty-eight of the community were dragged to the
Martyrs' Bay and murdered by the Norsemen. The abbot together with
the other survivors fled to Kells in Ireland taking the relics of St
Columba with him. But Iona was too important to be abandoned, and in
818 the next abbot rebuilt the monastery and replaced the relics. (The
little shrine behind the west door of the present Abbey – in a section of
an older wall and now called 'Columba's tomb' – may have been their
repository.) In 825 there was another massacre, but there was some
warning, and the abbot and many of the monks escaped in time. Among
those who remained was the son of an Irish king called Blathmac, who
looked for martyrdom, and whom the Norsemen, seeking the secret of
the Abbey's buried treasures, tore limb from limb when he would not
tell them. A further Norse raid took place in 986 when a band of Danes
from Dublin murdered the abbot and fifteen monks, but Norway by this
time had become Christian, and Sigurd, Earl of Orkney, caught up with
the raiders and put them to death. The red martyrdom passed with the
end of the Viking age, and in the years that followed, Iona recovered its

old atmosphere of seclusion and serenity – and the Gaelic chiefs, and even some from among the Norsemen, once more returned to the island to repent or die.

When the High King's seat was moved to Scone in Kenneth MacAlpin's time, the sacred relics of Iona were permanently dispersed, and the monastery was made subordinate to Kells. The final resting place of St Columba's bones is not known for certain, but an old poem places his grave at Downpatrick in Ireland beside St Bridget and St Patrick himself. His *brechbennach* was eventually housed in the monastery at Arbroath before being transferred finally to Monymusk – and it was perhaps significant that Arbroath should have been the scene of Scotland's Declaration of Independence, or that the Bruce should have found help and refuge with Angus Og of the Isles whose Islesmen held the right flank at Bannockburn.

However, Iona's particular association with the kings of Scotland came to an end in 1093 when Malcolm Canmore declined to be buried there. Instead, he and his wife Queen Margaret, were buried at her foundation of Dunfermline – probably as part of a deliberate break with the old Gaelic tradition, for which the queen may have been largely responsible. Her 'civilising' influence in Scotland was principally a matter of European innovation, and although she was responsible for rebuilding St Oran's Chapel, her saintliness was of the strictly Roman type, and she was contemptuous of the primitive Celtic mystery. Moreover, it was recalled perhaps that Macbeth's claim to the throne had been the better in accordance with Celtic custom, and with the claims of Donald Bane and the principal families of the Isles also pending, it was policy to seek a deliberate departure from the Celtic ways that now bedevilled the succession. Nevertheless the Norse kings of Man and the principal families of the Isles were still buried in accordance with tradition at Iona.

There is one other story concerning the influence of the early Church of Iona which is worth preserving as proof of Columba's early poetic prophecy. For while Margaret, a Scottish queen of Hungarian origin, rebuilt St Oran's chapel and yet despised the primitive Celtic tradition it enshrined, a small part of that mystery was even at that time being transplanted to her own European homeland.

In AD 617, during a struggle for the throne of Northumbria, the Angle Prince Oswald took refuge on Iona where he was converted to

Christianity. In due course, he succeeded to the Northumbrian king-dom where, in Bede's phrase, he reigned as '*rex christianissimus*' and was responsible for the founding of Lindisfarne on Holy Island from where the early missionaries from Iona began the work of converting the Angles. Oswald was killed in 642 in Shropshire by the great pagan warleader Penda of Mercia, and Lindisfarne, after the Synod of Whitby, became quite independent of Iona – but Oswald himself came to be revered as a martyr, and a cult grew around his name among the monks of Durham. (He is depicted in a stained-glass window of the cathedral.) Although technically before the time of formal heraldry, Oswald's blazon, taken from Iona, was a raven holding a ring in its beak, and he is usually depicted carrying this bird. During the tenth century, the evangelical movement in Europe began to turn back upon itself, and two monks from Durham undertook a missionary journey to southern Austria where they established the cult of St Oswald in the region of present Steiermark. Today, the village of St Oswald in that region still testifies to their mission, and the saint with his raven is painted on the reredos in a number of churches associated with his name. The cult became fashionable among the Steiermark nobility, and when the daughter of the ruler of Steiermark married the vizier of Hungary, it spread to the latter country also. In Hungary, the early part of the fifteenth century saw the rise of a Transylvanian family called Hunyadi, a descendant of whose house became the great King Matyas Corvinus of Hungarian history. When the Hunyadis were ennobled, they took the raven with its ring as their device, and so today, the traveller in Hungary may still see, among the sculptured monuments in Old Buda, the ancient blazon of King Oswald, worn by a famous Renaissance king who did not know, and may not have cared, that his shield recalled the piety of a dark-age Northumbrian monarch who once found sanctuary and Christian solace on a remote island of the Hebrides.

CHAPTER 7

The End of Dalriada

Little Dunadd of the Dalriad chiefs,
Sentinel rock of an ancient kingdom;
High place of Scots, far-famed for their valour;
Rulers of Lorne in a dim long ago.
T. Ratcliffe Barnett, 'A Rune of Lorne'

In AD 605, Aedan of Dalriada was succeeded by his son Eochaid Buidh, who ruled for sixteen years before he was overthrown and the kingdom plunged into civil war as rival claimants disputed the kingship. In 621, it passed to Eochaid's son, Domnall Breac – the 'Speckled' – whose reign appears to have been a disastrous one. In 634 and 638 there were new wars against the Picts, setting a pattern for the next hundred years, but, more serious than this, Domnall Breac also broke the old alliance with Columba's family, the *Ui Neill* of northern Ireland. In 637 he invaded Ulster in support of an exiled kinsman called Congal Claen against Domnall of the *Ui Neill*, the High King of Erin. The armies met at Mag Rath (Moyra) and Domnall Breac was soundly beaten. Three of his brothers, other sons of Eochaid MacAedan, were killed in the battle, and the Dalriadic king, according to the *Gododdin* battle-poem, was himself taken prisoner and held in Erin for a year.

On his return to Alba, Domnall Breac was defeated by a Pictish army at Glendmairison, and in 642, in a war against Dalriada's other allies of Columba's time, the Britons of Strathclyde, he was killed in battle at Strathcarron:

I saw the array from the headland of Adoyn,
Carrying the sacrifice to the conflagration:

I saw the men who made a great breach with the dawn at Adoynd;
And the head of Domnall Breac – the ravens ate it.[14]

Thereafter, Dalriada rarely existed as an organic whole. After Strathcarron the country itself passed under the overlordship of the Strathclyde Britons, but when they were defeated by Oswiu of Northumbria, power in the north lay with the Angles who kept it until the Picts finally broke their shield wall at Dunnichen forty years later. Within Dalriada, Domnall Breac's disastrous rule had seriously weakened the Clan Gabhran, and the Clan Lorne now challenged them for supremacy – so that the history of Dalriada over the next two hundred years was confused and bloody, and may be recorded briefly in so far as it relates to the traditional genealogy of Clan Donald and the Lords of the Isles.

Domnall Breac was succeeded by his son Domangart (d. 672) and then by his son Eochaid Roman Nose who was killed in battle against the Clan Lorne. This Eochaid married a sister of the Pictish King and the sons of that union, inheriting claims to two thrones (and thus representing the gradual process of fusion between Picts and Scots) would later contribute to the confusion and fratricidal warfare which became endemic throughout Alba.

In about 677, Ferchar the Tall of Lorne seized the throne of Dalriada and held it precariously against the Britons and Clan Gabhran for almost twenty years. On his death, his two sons – Ainfellach and Selbach – fought each other for the succession until Selbach eventually murdered his rival and was king until 723, when, weary or remorseful, he retired temporarily to a monastery. These were decades of obscurity – red and bloody years of ceaseless warfare, murder, truce, and treachery. The *Annals* speak of another Irish invasion, a sea fight (the first recorded in British history) in which Clan Gabhran were victorious, and the burning of Dunollie, Tarbert, and Dunavertie. There were frequent battles against the Strathclyde Britons, and in this warfare the earlier strength of Dalriada was spent, and no Aedan or Columba emerged from the chaos to restore unity or purpose. After Selbach, Eochaid III regained the Kingship for Clan Gabhran, but when he died (c.733) his son, Aed Find, was too young to rule and the dynastic struggle was renewed, with Clan Lorne again in the ascendant.

During this period, Dalriada was conquered by the Pictish king Oengus, who captured Dunadd, drowned the king, and drove the Dalriads almost into the sea. This was in about 741. The *Annals* briefly recorded 'the destruction of Dalriada', and for ten years it was a Pictish tributary. Oengus himself was eventually defeated by the Strathclyde Britons, and was otherwise dismissed by later chroniclers as 'a bloody murderer who persisted in the performance of bloody crime' – thus deserving no further details or valediction.

The *Annals* now falter – and then cease altogether. Aed Find of

Gabhran recovered his inheritance, though in what measure is not known, and he reigned for thirty years. He was remembered among the Gaels as a lawgiver. His son, Fergus II, reigned for three years, but was otherwise forgotten.

At this point the later genealogists of the Clan Donald, having traced the early ancestry of the Lords of the Isles from Conn of the Hundred Battles, Fergus MacErc, and those subsequent kings of the Clan Gabhran, claim that the line now passed through a younger son of Fergus II called Eacime, whose descendants were local chiefs in Argyll. Since their patrimony was restricted to the old Dalriadic territories along the western coastland, they gradually became detached from the dynastic struggles between the Picts and the Scots across the *Druim Alban*. In the ninth century the moving of the High King's Seat to Scone increased their isolation from the mainstream of early Scottish history.

In 843, Kenneth the Hardy, son of Alpin of the Gabhran line, became 'the first among the Gaels to assume the Kingdom of Scone'.[15] Yet precisely how this happened remains largely unexplained, since the old accounts, freakish and fragmentary at the best of times, are largely silent, and during the sixty years following the death of Aed Find, the history of Dalriada is conjectural and opaque. A battle between Picts and Scots in Fortriu in 768 suggests that the Dalriads were pursuing aggressive claims into Pictdom, and interim kings of Dalriada are sometimes recorded as ruling in Fortriu – which indicates that Dalriad armies penetrating across *Druim Alban* were not merely engaged in cattle raiding. It seems also that the Clan Gabhran finally asserted itself over the Clan Lorne, since many of the latter tribe appear to have spread North up the Great Glen into Moray. The claims of Clan Lorne would later emerge in the person of Macbeth.

Alpin is known to have fought against the Picts, and to have been defeated and beheaded by them. His son Kenneth, having a Pictish name and presumably a Pictish mother, may have had legitimate claim to both kingdoms, and various stories, legendary or contrived, have filled the vacuum of historical evidence. Aided perhaps by Irish allies, or by a marauding band of Danish pirates who were devastating the Mearns, he pursued his claim by battle and fought the Pictish army to extinction near Scone, following which he is said to have invited the seven Pictish Earls to a banquet, and, since they would have disputed his claim, murdered them in their mead. Thus the Picts, by chroniclers, are conveniently made to disappear, and Scone became the centre of a new kingdom, called Alba in the Gaelic, and Scotia in Latin.

According to legend, the transfer of the High King's seat involved also moving the 'fatal chair of marble' or 'throne of destiny' on which Scottish kings were crowned. Gaelic poetry recounted how Scota had brought it from Egypt, but another guess might be that the original stone of black marble may have been a travelling altar, associated perhaps with Columba and Iona. Certainly it was not the block of sandstone that Edward I later trundled south to England.

The move to Scone may also have been a matter of necessity – in the face of Viking raids which were making old Dalriada untenable. Dunadd was abandoned, and Kenneth's sovereignty barely extended west of *Druim Alban* after the throne was moved to Scone. To the north, he had little power beyond the Mounth where the *mormaers* of Moray were virtually independent, while in the south, the new kingdom was bounded by the line of the Forth and the Clyde.

Nevertheless, expansionism was the measure of a king's ambition and his war luck, and six times Kenneth invaded Angle Lothian before they carried his rotting body to Iona: to be followed by his brother and the two sons who followed him – in all, eight kings in a single century. For union did not bring peace – nor an end to Angle pressure from the south, much less the internal cycle of fratricidal warfare, ambition, death by assassination, poisoning, or other sinister occurrence. In these decades, the dragon's teeth were sown. The Scots gained Edinburgh by force, Strathclyde by marriage when the local dynasty died out, and Lothian by submission – submission that is, to the English, a new nation realised by great Alfred and passing to his grandson Athelstan who defeated Constantine II of the Scots at Brunanburgh in 938 and claimed overlordship of all Britain. Malcolm I, Constantine's successor, received from Edmund of England the lands of Strathclyde both sides of Solway, for which he did homage as an under-king, and Kenneth II, who poisoned and succeeded him, made submission likewise to the English Edgar for the grant of Lothian between the Forth and Tweed – to set a precedent for the bitter warfare that would last six centuries thereafter. Kenneth II was murdered also, and his successor and *his* successor in turn died either by the knife or by the sword in battle.

Next to be crowned on that fatal stone was Malcolm II who reigned for twenty-nine years and thus demonstrated a capacity for survival rare among early Scottish kings. Preoccupied initially with the problem of ending the constant feuds which were devastating the north, he embarked on a series of dynastic marriages to secure the loyalty of the more powerful warlords. He married one daughter to the secular abbot of Dunkeld, another to Sigurd Earl of Orkney, and a third to Finlech *Mormaer* of Moray – unions all of perilous consequence while the rule of succession still followed the Pictish custom – and having thus contrived to secure his rear, he marched south to fight the English. In 1018 he defeated the Angles at Carham, and in the same year, taking advantage of the vacuum caused by the death without heir of Owen the Bald, king óf Strathclyde, he installed his grandson Duncan, son of the abbot of Dunkeld, as king of Cumbria.

In retaliation, Canute, now King of England, marched north and occupied Lothian, but before he could take it, Malcolm was murdered by his nobles at Glamis, and the throne was seized by Duncan, who murdered one possible rival the day before his crowning and another immediately after it, but spared a third called Lulach because he was an imbecile. Lulach's mother, the widow Gruach, was promptly married by Macbeth, son of Malcolm's other daughter who had married Finlech of Moray. This Macbeth, reasserting the old claims of Lorne and the Pictish succession, and those of his wife for good measure, now aspired to the crown, and six years later, in alliance with the Viking Thorfinn of Orkney, defeated and killed Duncan in battle at Elgin. Contrary to popular legend, Macbeth seems to have been a creditable king. He reigned seventeen years thereafter, untroubled apparently by conscience, witches, or the neuroses of his wife (and even managed a pilgrimage to Rome) before Malcolm Canmore, Duncan's son, with help from Edward the Confessor and Seward of Northumbria, invaded Scotland in 1057 and defeated and killed him in Aberdeenshire. Macbeth's body was carried to Iona to rest next to that of Duncan, and to be followed shortly afterwards by the corpse of Lulach the Fool whom Malcolm dispiteously murdered in Strathbogie.

With Malcolm Canmore, Scotland emerged from a darker Celtic age into a newer epoch – and into the larger context of Britain and the European continent. The monarchy thus established was Celtic in origin, but it would change over the next two hundred years, turning against the old traditions and inspiration of its genesis, to accept a foreign feudal system, brought by another, fifth race of incomers, conquerors by invitation, from whom there developed gradually a new hierarchy, new customs, loyalties and ambitions, and a new impetus to the course of Scottish history. The Dalriads of elder days had given the land its name, and withal, its race of kings. But the kings in their turn now deserted them, and history itself began to pass them by.

Two factors in particular would contribute to the gradual isolation of the western Gaels. The first was the coming of the Normans – themselves a phenomenon of European history – who came to England with the Conqueror, and to Scotland by request. Strangely, it was Macbeth, the Celtic king, who first invited Norman mercenaries to the north, but they died for the most part at Dunsinnan Hill. Under Malcolm Canmore they came to stay, and for this, much credit – or responsibility – belongs to his second wife, St Margaret of Scotland.

Her story was an interesting one – and had its beginning in the earlier dynastic wars of England. On the death of Edmund Ironside in 1016, his two sons, to escape possible assassination by Canute, fled to Sweden and from thence to Hungary, where the elder, Edward, married Agota, a daughter of King Stephen – who granted the Saxon exile land in the south, at Mecsek-Nadasd, which was later to be known as the *Terra Britannorum.* Edward and Agota had three children – Edgar, Margaret, and Christina. Years later, when Canute was long dead, Edward the Confessor, torn perhaps between his Norman fosterage and his Saxon conscience, sent Ailred, Bishop of York, to fetch back the refugees from Hungary. It was an act of some significance, since Edward of Mecsek-Nadasd was by blood the true heir to the English throne. However, Edward died, perhaps suspiciously, immediately after making landfall, and his son Edgar, who was now the Atheling, though to all intents a foreigner, was too young to dispute the succession on The Confessor's death shortly afterwards. The bereaved family were a minor embarrassment to Harold of Wessex and The Conqueror in turn.

Edgar and his sisters passively survived the conquest, failed as pawns of further rebellions, and in 1068 escaped to Scotland where Margaret became the second wife of Malcolm Canmore. A deeply pious lady, she found Scottish society crude and uncivilised, and conceived a mission to convert the Scots from their northern barbarism and Celtic custom (which she held to be one and the same). Her piety being of the Roman sort, she regarded the Celtic Church as 'the defender of perverted custom', although, in addition to numerous ecclesiastical buildings and foundations of her own, she was also a benefactress to St Oran's Chapel on Iona. She appears to have dominated Malcolm Canmore. He forsook Gaelic for her language, substituted wine for mead, and welcomed to his court the strangers of her choice. These included a number of Hungarians who had accompanied the family to Britain and to whom Malcolm now gave lands in Scotland – Yorik de Marot, from whom are descended the Drummonds; Bertalan, from whom the Leslies, and possibly several more. After the conquest the influx of foreigners was further augmented by Norman adventurers, soldiers of fortune and landless knights – not least among them a hopeful Breton called Walter Fitzalan, a younger son of the Baron of Oswestry in Shropshire, who later became Steward of Scotland and ancestor of the Stewart Kings.

In 1093, Malcolm died at Alnwick with a spear-point through his eye, and the Celtic faction enjoyed a brief revival. Malcolm's brother Donald Bane came from the west to claim the kingship according to Pictish right, and drove the foreigners beyond the border. He was deposed by Malcolm's son Duncan, who had been brought up in exile in the south, more Norman than Scots, and was willing to barter his fealty for an English army. The Scots murdered him and Donald Bane again became king, until he was finally supplanted by his nephew Edgar (Malcolm's younger son) who put out his eyes (a Hungarian custom reserved for dynastic rivals and possibly another legacy of St Margaret) and left him to perish miserably in a dungeon.

Donald Bane was the last Celtic claimant worthy of the name. Those who followed, though by blood half-Celt, were by disposition Anglo-Norman, and the gradual Normanisation of Scotland proceeded through successive reigns. The now familiar names emerged – de Bruce, Soulis, de Morville, Cunningham, Hay, Mowbray, Sinclair, Menzies, Fraser, Grant – and others of Norman or Breton origin.

In the west beyond Druim Alban, the Gaels had become remote – excluded from the riches of the Lowlands and from the patronage of these Scottish kings. Even by the middle of the ninth century, the Hebrides and the coastlands of ancient Dalriada had been effectively lost to the emerging kingdom of central Scotland, for another, and more terrible race of incomers had reached the Isles and now dominated the Celtic Sea. The western Gaels were engulfed by the Viking tide from Scandinavia, and in the confusion of the Norse period, the Clan Donald's genealogy through the descendants of Eacime and the Celtic chiefs of Argyll was all but obliterated.

A GENEALOGY OF THE CLAN DONALD I

The Dalriadic Descent

1	CONN OF THE HUNDRED BATTLES	*High King of Tara*
2	AIRT	
3	CORMAC MACAIRT	
4	CAIRBRE RIADA	*founder of the Dalriadic race*
5	EOCHACH DUBHLEIN	*married Aelach, daughter of Ubdaire King in Alba*
6	COLLA UAIS	*d. c. AD 337; founder of Clann Cholla*
7	EOCHAIDH	
8	CRIOMTHAN	
9	ERC	*d. c. 502*
10	FERGUS MOR——LORNE——ANGUS	*founders of Albain Dalriada*
11	DOMANGART	*d. c. 511*
12	GABHRAN(d. c. 560)——COMGALL	
13	AEDAN (The Fair-haired)	*crowned by St Columba 574: d. 605*
14	EOCHAIDH BUIDH	*King of Dalriada: d. 621?*
15	DOMNALL BREAC	*King of Dalriada: d. 642?*
16	DOMANGART	*King of Dalriada: d. 672*
17	EOCHAIDH ROMAN NOSE	*King of Dalriada: d. 699*
18	EOCHAIDH III	*King of Dalriada: d. 733*
19	AED FIND	*King of Dalriada: d. 772*
20	FERGUS II	
	EOCHAIDH IV——21 EACIME	*Ruler of Argyll*
	ALPIN	
	KENNETH	
	Kings of Scotland	

A GENEALOGY OF CLAN DONALD II

The Ancestors of Somerled

22 GODFREY MAC FERGUS *Toiseach of the Isles: d. 853*
23 NIALLGHUSA
24 SUIBNE or SWYFFINE
25 ECHMARCACH or IMERGI *Possibly the Iehmare of the* Saxon Chronicle, *one of the Kings who submitted to Canute, the Danish King of England who invaded Scotland in 1031*
26 SOLMUND
27 GILLEDOMNAN
28 GILLEBRIDE *King of the South Isles: Gillebride of the Cave*
29 SOMERLED *Ancestor of Clan Donald: d. 1164*

PART II
THE VIKING PERIOD

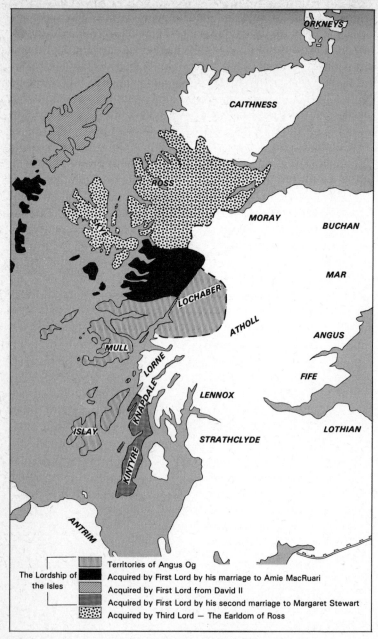

ORKNEYS

CAITHNESS

ROSS

SKYE

MORAY

BUCHAN

MAR

LOCHABER

ATHOLL

ANGUS

MULL

LORNE

FIFE

KNAPDALE

LENNOX

ISLAY

LOTHIAN

KINTYRE

STRATHCLYDE

ANTRIM

The Lordship of
the Isles

Territories of Angus Og
Acquired by First Lord by his marriage to Amie MacRuari
Acquired by First Lord from David II
Acquired by First Lord by his second marriage to Margaret Stewart
Acquired by Third Lord — The Earldom of Ross

2 The Lordship of the Isles

CHAPTER 8

Norsemen

Snapped roof-trees, towers fallen;
the work of Giants, the stonesmiths
mouldereth.

The *Anglo-Saxon Chronicle* contains the following entry for the year AD
787 – an ominous foretaste of things to come:

In this year, King Beorhtric took Eadburgh, King Offa's daughter to wife. And
in his days, came three ships of Northmen from Hordaland; and then the King's
Reeve rode to them and tried to make them go to the Royal Manor, for he did not
know who or what they were, and they slew him there. Those were the first ships
of the Danish men that sought the land of the English.

Since they came from Hordaland, the raiders were presumably Norwegians rather than Danes, but the early chroniclers, confronted by this
sudden and terrible phenomenon, were confused as to the identity and
origin of the first Vikings. However, they were not long ignorant of the
Norsemen's purpose. From 790 onwards, the sea-raiding continued in
terrifying earnest, and along the coastlands, churches and monasteries –
undefended and with their collections of treasure, ornaments and
wealth – quickly became principal targets. Monks in their cells prayed
for stormy weather, and came to dread the fair wind that brought the
longships with their dragon prows stooping towards the shore, to turn
their serenity into a red martyrdom of axe and arrow-flight. Settlements
clustering in the estuaries, by sheltered bays and sea lochs, fell easy prey
to the sudden Viking onslaughts: a longship sighted from the headland;
keels grinding on the shingle; screams and running feet, blood and
burning, slavery, and huddled corpses left to smoulder in the embers.
'Never before in Britain has such terror appeared as this we have now
suffered at the hands of the heathen', wrote Alcuin to his master
Charlemagne after the sack of Lindisfarne. 'Nor was it thought possible
that such an inroad from the sea could be made.'
    After Lindisfarne it was Jarrow, and in 794 the Vikings 'ravaged in

67

Northumbria'. In 795, Iona was attacked and the monastery destroyed, and in the same year Vikings landed in Lambey, an island north of Dublin. Another raid, into Glamorgan, was driven off by the Celtic Welsh. In 798, Norsemen attacked Innispatrick of Man and plundered throughout the Hebrides. In 802, 806, and 825 there were further raids on Iona and more slaughter on the little island.

The Britannic islands represented only one facet of the Vikings' bloody career into European history – which would take them east as far as the Black Sea, north to Iceland, south beyond Biscay, and west across the Atlantic itself. By the year 800 the peoples of Europe realised that a new force was upon them, and all the coastlands of Britain, Ireland, Frisia, Aquitaine and beyond witnessed and suffered the violence of the Viking breakout. A great harrying of Frankish Christendom began.

> Bitter is the wind tonight.
> It tosses the ocean's white hair.
> Tonight I fear not the fierce warriors of Norway
> Coursing on the Irish Sea.

Not unexpectedly, contemporary monastic chroniclers recording events of priest murder, sacrilege and rapine, lacked the facility for dispassion-ate comment, and their partial, often lurid, accounts made no inquiry into the lands or the civilisation from which the raiders had emerged. In general they were simply referred to as *Vikings* or *Nordmanni* (the 'Northmen'), with little or no distinction between Norwegians, Swedes and Danes. In Ireland, however, where the various Scandinavian groups conducted a protracted struggle for supremacy, the *Annals* refer more specifically to *Finngaills* and *Dubhgaills* – the White Foreigners and the Black Foreigners – corresponding to the two basic northern types and distinguishable as Norwegians and Danes. Some accounts also refer to them as *Lochlanns* (the people of the lakes or fjords) and *Danars*. Later centuries produced an abundance of unreliable written sources drawn principally from the traditions of the sagas and which, in the poetry of the skalds, embroidered an elaborate pattern of confusion over the precise chronology and events of the early Viking period.

In the beginning, the several peoples of the northern lands had little sense of nationality, but together they shared a common culture, language, and religion. Scandinavia was divided into a large number of petty kingdoms and independent lordships – indistinguishable in terms of boundaries, laws, administration or policy, but amounting rather to what a self-styled king could win and hold. This depended in turn upon the size of his following and the warriors whom he led. Such kings survived by force and their rule was directed towards self-aggrandisement and the accumulation of personal territory and wealth, but their authority over the remote and separatist communities in a wild and mountainous country was haphazard and slight. There were *Sea Kings* who commanded fleets of ships; *Host Kings* who led warrior bands; *Fylki Kings* who ruled on land; and *Scatt Kings* who paid tribute – when their overlord was strong enough to collect. Politically, it was an unstable society given to constant individual and local struggles for power, in which the strongest survived for a duration, and the vanquished sought their fortune elsewhere. This characteristic came to be perpetuated in the Viking settlements overseas.

The apparent suddenness of the Viking breakout may owe something to the hindsight of later chroniclers, but as a phenomenon it stemmed from a recognisable concentration of circumstance, and the flood once released took three hundred years to dry up. The root causes were overpopulation and land hunger, and from these a practical desire to make a better living and acquire wealth. The northern countries were wild; the small communities circumscribed by the land's topography, agriculture constrained by conditions of soil and climate, and the natural economy insufficient to support a population which grew out of a vigorous society in which large families were customary and polygamy was common practice. The pattern of small landholdings gave rise to a tradition of indivisible inheritance which resulted in numerous younger sons, whether of legitimate or hand-fast union, being turned adrift without maintenance or alternative but to settle new pasture or seek a means of acquiring movable wealth and thereby establish themselves, become famous warriors, or buy a steading of their own. As new land became scarcer, and wealth available only at the expense of neighbours, so there developed a reservoir of unruly spirits ready to join the Viking bands, take service abroad, or man the oars of longships and seek their fortune on the seaway.

It was under pressure of demand perhaps that by the middle of the eighth century, the Norse peoples had developed a technology of ship-building and design that far surpassed the European countries to the south, and by circumstance of history, the evolution of the longship coincided with the decline of the Picts as a sea power, and the destruction of the Frisian fleet by Charles Martel. The sea-ways were open – to trade and to piracy, and among the Norsemen, both were legitimate professions. To go 'viking' was a way of making a living – like agriculture, hunting, craftwork, trade – and fighting. In spring a man would plough his land and plant the corn. In early summer he might join a longship and go plundering west-over-sea, returning for the harvest, and when the crop was in, make a second raiding expedition till December. In this manner he obtained his sword-wealth, chattels, coin, jewels and slaves – and possibly a reputation for his sea-luck.

In the early days, these expeditions were generally small enterprises of one or two longships only. But as word filtered back of the countries oversea and the opportunities to be found there, larger expeditions were formed under recognised leaders which established summer bases from which to raid more widely, or penetrate inland. Settlement, and the annexation of territory, would follow.

From the first, a proportion among the Vikings were in search of fresh pasture and a place where the living was better. Such settlers would fix their steading in accordance with their own tradition – a right to water and wood, and to the land as far as a man could throw his knife around his house, provided it was fenced within one year. In many parts their landing was unopposed and they married local women and generally adapted to the customs of the country. The larger raiding expeditions established Viking stations on the islands and skerries off the coast where they could winter and regroup, while within the expanding Viking world, the *Kaupships* (merchantmen), developed a lucrative trade, and were, by Norse tradition, unmolested.

However, at the end of the ninth century, two strong kings in Denmark and Norway respectively, Godfred and Harald Thickhair, set out to impose a central authority over their kingdoms, and their warring caused an intensification of Viking activity as large numbers of Norsemen – fugitive, defeated, or rebellious – took to the sea-ways. Having found temporary refuge in the Viking stations west-over-sea, many returned to plunder the Scandinavian mainland, and the fleets of Harald Thickhair pursued them to burn their bases and levy *scatt*. Some, who had first settled in the Hebrides, migrated north again to the Faroes, and as far as Iceland, to evade the Norwegian authority established in the Isles.

Off the northern coast of Alba, the short voyage from Scandinavia to the Orkneys and Shetlands had been pioneered by northern trading ships, and the Vikings settled extensively in these islands from an early period. In the west, Lewis in the northern Hebrides became an important Viking station, under its own 'sea king', from where the Norsemen launched their early raids against the coasts of Ireland. In Lewis, the Uists, Benbecula, and Skye a high proportion of the present place-names are of Norse origin, while graves, coin hordes, loan words and other evidence of northern customs indicate fairly consistent settlement. In the southern Hebrides, among the western isles of Dalriada, settlement may have been less extensive, although Islay, Colonsay, Oronsay and Gigha were Viking stations, and there were Norsemen in Mull, and Knapdale in Kintyre, and along the shores of Loch Fyne. Throughout the Viking period the Hebrides were at least nominally under the control of Dublin, Man, or Orkney (often in dispute), and were administratively divided into the *Nordreyar* and *Sudreyar*, north and south of a line running west from the point of Ardnamurchan. To the inhabitants of mainland Alba, they came to be known as *Insigall* (the islands of the Foreigners).

By contrast, Viking penetration and settlement of the mainland was comparatively slight, apart from Caithness, which became part of the Orkney earldom; and although Norse armies raided into Dalriada and also into Fife, they never established themselves in the old Pictish kingdoms of Alba. No Viking graves have been discovered east of the Moray Firth, except for an isolated site at Errol in Perthshire. In later years Norse ambition was divided between the Viking kingdoms in Ireland (Dublin) and Northumberland (York).

In the Western Isles there are few tangible remains to recall the Viking settlement, since they were not, in general, builders in stone. A number of their customs did endure, however. In Mull, the local name *Pennyghael* derives from the Norse method of measuring land against a standard based on the weight of silver – a practice which was continued by the Scots. Thus twenty penny land amounted to an 'ounce land' and eight ounces then became 'one pound (one *merk*) land'. The old odal land law was occasionally preserved by Scottish courts in the Northern Isles, while the Highland due of *calp* (the payment of the best beast on the death of a tenant) was also of Norse origin.

A number of loan words passed into the language – the names of tools and fishing equipment, or features of topography – such as the suffix *nish* meaning 'bay'; *ey* or *aidh* for 'island'; *val* and *fell* and *dale*. In the Outer Hebrides a language akin to Norse and called *Norn* has existed until recent times. During the Viking period Norse and Celts intermarried widely, and most of the western clans have Norsemen among their forebears. Some names still reflect that connection: MacLachlan from *Lochlann*; MacLeod from *Liotr*; Lamont from *Lagman* (lawman), and others. There was much that was compatible between the two cultures, and the Norse when they settled, adapted easily to local custom – and were in turn assimilated.

However, no Viking panegyric survives to tell exclusively of the Norsemen in the Hebrides or of their dealings with the Dalriadic peoples there. The story has to be pieced together from references in the greater chronicles – such as the *Annals of Ulster*, the *Chronicle of the Isle of Man*, and the *Annals of the Four Masters*. But among the later sagas there are fragments also – of men, events and places, which may still evoke the Viking period in the Isles.

Shortly before 840, a Norwegian sea king called Turgeis (or Thorgills) set upon Ireland and established a pagan Viking kingdom in the north. Taking advantage of a civil war in Munster, he seized Armagh – a chief town in Ulster and the ecclesiastical centre of Ireland – and then embarked upon the subjugation of Meath and Connaught, entering the Shannon and taking his longships as far inland as Lough Ree.

The Vikings plundered the great monasteries of Clonmacnois and Clonfert, and desecrated the holy places of the Irish Christian church. Turgeis's wife, the priestess Ota, is said to have presided over pagan rites upon the high altar of ancient Clonmacnois.

Since the first raid on Lambey in 795, Ireland had suffered Viking depredations enough, but the appearance of Turgeis marked an end of sporadic raiding, and the beginning of a more permanent conquest. The Norwegians fortified the principal harbours along the coast – Dublin, Wexford, Wicklow, Limerick, Argassan and others, and Viking reinforcements came crowding from the sea to give these armed camps the aspect of established settlements. They were joined by numbers of disaffected Gaelic Irish, condemned in Christian annals as having reverted to paganism, who intermarried with the northern invaders to form a hybrid, mongrel race called the *Gall-Gaedhill*, and took to piracy in the Celtic sea and along the shores of Galloway and Man.

In about 839 Turgeis sent a great fleet of sixty-five longships to plunder into Leinster, and the Dalriads, with help from Fergus, King of

Oriel, fought against them in a battle somewhere on the shores of Western Alba:

The men of Dalriada fought with this fleet because it went northwards keeping Ireland on the left after destroying Leinster and Brega. In this battle, Eoganan, Angus' son, the King of Dalriada, was slain.[16]

The Clan Angus were driven out of Islay, and the Vikings took possession of the Dalriadic Hebrides:

The Scots, after being attacked by the Northmen for very many years were rendered tributary; and the Northmen took possession without resistance, of the islands that lie all around, and dwelt there.[17]

It was probably in the face of this growing Viking threat that Kenneth MacAlpin pursued his dynastic claims to Pictdom and moved the High King's seat to Scone in 843.

Turgeis's violent career in Ireland lasted seven years, until in 845 he was captured by the Irish King Mael Seachlainn of Meath and drowned in Lough Owel. After his death, the Norwegian Vikings in Ireland were challenged by a fresh wave of Danish invaders, and the Norsemen turned their axes on each other. In 851 the Danes seized Dublin. The following year they fought a great sea battle in Carlingford Lough, and the Norwegian Vikings were hacked to extinction in a three-day struggle at Argassan.

In 853 a second Norwegian host arrived led by Olaf (sometimes called the White), who was a son of the King of Lochlann (Norway). Olaf defeated the Danes, and established a mixed Norse kingdom in Dublin, ruling over white and black foreigners alike (see p.68), and securing his position by marrying (among others) a daughter of an Irish king, and also a daughter of Kenneth, King of Alba. This second marriage gave him claims in Pictdom, and with his brother Ivar Imhar, Viking lord of Limerick, he made a series of raids into Alba, laying waste the lands of the Picts and taking hostages. By 870 the Vikings controlled the Firth of Clyde, from where they launched attacks against Dumbarton and plundered into Cumbria. When Olaf was killed in 871, Ivar Imhar became *Rex Nordmannorum Totius Hiberniae et Britanniae*, and his descendants, until 1034, were kings of the *Gall-Gael* – styled *Rex plurimarum insularum* – Viking kings of the Isles.

Meanwhile, however, events in Scandinavia itself were to have a far-reaching effect upon the Viking impetus in the Hebrides. In about 870, an uplander called Harald Thickhair succeeded to the Kingdom of Vestfold, and set about the subjugation of all Norway. According to legend, Harald swore a great oath that he would never cut or comb his hair until he had 'subdued the whole of Norway with *scatt*, and duties, and domains; or if not, have died in the attempt'.[18] After putting down a succession of murderous relatives, he fought his way through Norway, subduing the disaffected petty kings and jarls (earls), which culminated in a great sea battle at Hafrsfjord, near Stavanger in 872. Following this victory, large numbers of dispossessed odallers and defeated war leaders fled to Orkney, Shetland and the Irish Sea, where they pursued a career of independent piracy, or launched retaliatory raids against the Norwegian coast, 'viking' in the summer months, and living in the islands on their plunder through the winter.

Among this fugitive migration, individual names persist – remembered usually for episodes of violence in the stories of the Norsemen's feuding through the Isles.

In the days of Harald Thickhair, King of Norway, certain pirates of the family of the most vigorous prince Ronald, set out with a great fleet and crossed the Solundic sea; and stripped these races of their ancient settlements, destroyed them wholly, and subdued these islands to themselves. And being there provided with safe winter seats, they went in summertime working tyranny upon the English and the Scots – and sometimes also upon the Irish, so that they took under their rule: from England, Northumbria; from Scotland, Caithness; from Ireland, Dublin, and other sea-side towns.[19]

One such was an uplander called Onund, who had a history of 'viking' in the Isles. In 869 he took five ships and plundered in the Hebrides and fought a great sea battle against a Celtic king called Karval off the island of Barra. 'For three summers they plundered in Ireland and Scotland; then they went to Norway.' In Hordaland, Onund joined Thori Longchin and King Kiotvi who were assembling a great force of longships to fight Harald Thickhair, 'and they made common cause because they were very eager to prove themselves, and declared they would be wherever the battle was most severe'.

Their encounter with King Harald took place in Rogaland in the fjord that is called *In Hafrsfiordr*. They had on each side a great force. This battle has been the greatest fought in Norway. And most sagas tell of it, because most is said of those things from which history chiefly springs.

Onund had his leg cut off during the battle and was known as Onund

74

Wooden-leg thereafter. Together with another fugitive Viking called Thrond, he returned to the Hebrides, 'going on warfare in the summers but staying in Barra in the winters'.

While there, Thrond and Onund Wooden-leg became enemies of two Hebridean Vikings called Vigbiod and Vestmar, who had eight ships and 'did many evil deeds'. Hearing that these Vikings 'had sailed to an island which is called Bute', Thrond and Onund pursued them with five longships:

And when the Vikings saw their ships and knew how many they were, they thought they had numbers enough, and they took their weapons and lay waiting. Then Onund bade lay his ships between two cliffs; there was a great channel there and deep, and ships could sail one way only, and not more than five at a time. Onund was a clever man; and he made his ships advance into the strait in such a way that they could let themselves drift with hanging oars, when they wished, because there was plenty of sea room behind them. There was also a certain island on one side of them. Onund bade one ship lie under it; and they carried many stones to the edge of the cliff where they could not be seen from the ships.

The Hebridean Vikings attacked, and Vigbiod taunted Onund on his mutilation – asking how he expected to fight when he could not even stand properly:

After that they laid their ships together. A great battle began and both sides fought fiercely. When the battle was fully joined, Onund let his ship drift under the cliff, and thinking that he was trying to escape, the Vikings closed on him. At this moment, those men who had been placed on the cliff-top cast upon the Vikings so great stones as nothing could resist. Many of the Vikings' crew fell and some were hurt so that they could not bear weapons. Then the Vikings tried to draw back, but they could not because their ships were caught in the narrowest part of the strait, and other ships and the current impeded them.

On the deck of Onund's longship, Vigbiod stood at bay. Onund's men wedged a log under his knee so that 'he stood quite firmly', and both sides paused to watch their leaders fight it out:

The Viking came forward until he reached Onund and hewed at him with his sword, and struck his shield and cut off what he touched. Then his sword struck into the log that Onund had under his knee, and lodged fast. As Vigbiod stooped to pull his sword free, Onund hacked him through the shoulder and cut off his arm.

The Vikings fled, and Onund mocked the dying man before him:

Look whether thy wounds are bleeding. Didst thou see me giving way? The one-legged warrior got from thee no scratch. To many a fighter is given more boastfulness than wisdom.[20]

Onund and Thrond despoiled the Vikings' ships and sailed back to Barra in the autumn.

Another Viking who settled in the Isles was Ketil Flatnose, a powerful odaller from Romsdale in Norway. According to the *Laxdaela Saga*:

In the latter years of Ketil's life, King Harald Thickhair rose to such power that neither provincial kings nor other men of stature could prosper in Norway or retain their rank and title without his sanction. When Ketil learned that King Harald intended to subject him to the same treatment as other chieftains, who had been forced to become the king's vassals and had been denied compensation for their fallen kinsmen, he summoned his own people to a meeting and addressed them thus:

You are aware of our past dealings with King Harald, and there is no need to recount them here: our more urgent task is to try to solve the problems that face us now. I have reliable reports of King Harald's hostility towards us, and I am sure we can look for no mercy from that quarter. It seems to me that there are only two courses open to us: either to flee the country or else be killed off each in his own place. I would much prefer to end my days as my forefathers have done, but I have no wish to commit you to such dangers on my decision alone, for I know the temper of my kinsmen and friends: I know that you would not wish to forsake me, whatever hazard there may be in standing by me.

Ketil's son Bjorn replied:

I can make my own intentions clear at once. I want to follow the example of other eminent men and leave this country. I cannot see how it would benefit me to sit at home waiting for King Harald's slaves to hound us off our lands or put us all to death.

This was considered bravely spoken, and there was loud approval. And so it was settled that they should leave the country, for Ketil's sons urged it strongly and no-one spoke against it. Bjorn and Helgi wanted to go to Iceland, for they claimed to have heard tempting reports of it; they said there was excellent land there to be had for the taking, with an abundance of stranded whales and plenty of salmon, and good fishing grounds all the year round.

But Ketil said:

That fishing place will never see me in my old age ...
Then he declared his own intentions: he preferred to go west across the sea to Scotland because, he said, he thought it was good living there. He knew the country well, since he had raided there extensively.[21]

Ketil Flatnose established himself first in Orkney and, in the event, appears to have reached an accommodation with King Harald who appointed him Norwegian Earl of the Northern Isles. However, Ketil neglected to pay the *scatt* which he had collected on the king's behalf, and was forced to escape to the west, where he remained for a time as Lord of the Hebrides. Despite his prediction, he eventually migrated to Iceland with others of his family.

During this early Viking period references to the Celtic descendants of Eacime (see the Genealogy of the Clan Donald I) are extremely rare, and the names given in the traditional Clan Donald genealogy are based on fragmentary or circumstantial evidence only. Not until the appearance of Somerled in the twelfth century as the undoubted ancestor of the Lords of the Isles can the true descent of the Macdonalds be traced with certainty. In 853 the death is recorded of Godfrey, *Toiseach* (or Thane) of the Isles, who was possibly the last Celtic incumbent of the Dalriadic line, since subsequent rulers or jarls (earls) in the Southern Hebrides have Norse names. King Harald seems to have appointed three Viking earls: Tryggvi, Asbjorn Skerryblaze, and Guthorm. Asbjorn Skerryblaze was possibly responsible for Ketil Flatnose's departure to Iceland, since he was subsequently murdered by Ketil's cousin, and his wife and children kidnapped into slavery. After Guthorm, the petty kingship of the Isles was held *de facto* by the grandsons of Ivar Imhar of Limerick. The Celtic chiefs were either forced into subjection or driven out. Alternatively they may have allied themselves with the conquerors through intermarriage so that their descendants were of mixed Norse and Gaelic blood.

Having subdued Norway, Harald Thickhair was eventually able to turn his attention to the bands of dispossessed Vikings who had escaped after the battle of Harsfjord, and were now using the Atlantic islands as bases from which to mount retaliatory raids against the Norwegian coasts. He sent a number of punitive expeditions to the Isles, but as these proved largely ineffective, he finally assembled a fleet with a view to imposing his authority upon the Viking settlements west-over-sea:

First he came to Scotland, and he slew all the Vikings who could not save themselves by flight. Then King Harald sailed southwards to the Orkney Islands, and cleared them all of Vikings (including Ketil Flatnose). Thereafter he proceeded to the Hebrides, plundered there, and slew many Vikings who formerly had men at arms under them. He then plundered far and wide in Scotland itself, and had battles there. When he was come westward as far as the Isle of Man, the report of his exploits had gone before him; all the inhabitants had fled over to Scotland, and the island was left entirely bare both of people and goods, so that Harald and his men got no booty when they landed.[22]

For as the panegyric ran:

> Bore the much-wise gold loader
> to the townships shields a many –
> The grove of Nith-wolves land-lance
> in the land prevailed in battle –
> Ere needs must flee the Scot-host
> before the fight proud waster
> of the path of the fish that plyeth
> around the war-sword's isthmus.[23]

Having successfully burned the Vikings out of their Atlantic skerries, Harald returned to Norway where he consented to have his hair cut, and was known as Harald Finehair thereafter.

Ketil Flatnose's daughter, called Aud the Deep-Minded, had for a short time been the third wife of Olaf the White, King of Dublin. Her son by this union, Thorstein the Red, now joined with Sigurd, whom Harald had appointed Earl of Orkney in place of Ketil Flatnose, to complete the Viking subjugation of Sutherland and Caithness. Crossing into Scotland, they raided south as far as Ross and Moray, but Sigurd came to an unfortunate end. In Moray, he killed a Scottish *Mormaer* (Earl) called Melbrig the Tooth, but having hung the victim's head to his saddle-bow, the 'tooth' (which was very prominent) scratched his leg – and the wound becoming inflamed, he died of blood poisoning. Sigurd was buried at the estuary of the River Oykel at the place which was known thereafter as Sigurd's Howe, by the present Cydenhall. Thorstein, however, made a treaty with the King of Scots whereby he retained 'Caithness and Sutherland, Ross and Moray, and more than half of Scotland', and his daughter married the *Mormaer* of Duncansby in Caithness. He was eventually murdered by the Scots in 875.

In the meanwhile, the Danes had established a Viking Kingdom at York. According to tradition, the legendary Norse pirate Ragnar Hairybreeks, having raided in Ireland during Turgeis's time, led an expedition into Northumbria, but was captured by the local King Ella and thrown into a pit of adders. In 865, three of his sons – Ubbi, Halfdan and Ivar the Boneless – led a Danish army into England, in revenge as was said for Ragnar's death – a matter which they accomplished by capturing King Ella and prising his ribs apart from the backbone to pull out his lungs in a ritual killing which the Vikings called the 'blood eagle'. In 866 they took York and in the following years fought their way south through Deira and East Anglia. By 874 Wessex and Mercia had fallen to them, and in the division of this swordland, Halfdan installed himself as king in York. From there, he cast covetous eyes over the Viking kingdom in Dublin and in 876 led a Danish invasion of Ireland. However, the Irish drowned him in Strangford Lough and the Danes were once more driven out of Erin. They crossed into Alba and defeated Constantine MacKenneth, King of Scots, in a battle near Dollar (in which the earth is said to have opened beneath the Scottish army). The marauders pillaged through Fife, and the following year killed Constantine in another fight at Inverdovet.

From this time onwards, Viking preoccupations were always divided between Dublin and York – and as Ragnar Hairybreeks had many descendants, there was no shortage of claimants to the two thrones. This dynastic rivalry, coupled with the Norsemen's predilection for incestuous and fratricidal warfare, withered the very roots of Viking power, and precluded any long-lasting stability among their settlements west-over-sea. Their history remained merely episodic – a kaleidoscope of shifting faction and alliance, ambition and revenge – as each and all pursued their claims, seized power for an interval, but never achieved a demonstrable unity.

In England, since the latter decades of the ninth century, the Saxons under Alfred and his line had moved onto the offensive. A ring of fortresses hemmed in the Danelaw, and in Mercia, East Anglia, and Wessex, Saxon armies were on the march. Although Norse infiltration continued, particularly in the Wirral and the north-west, Viking raiding obtained no lasting advantage, and as English ambition turned towards Northumbria itself, the Danish kings were forced to treat. In 910, Edward the Elder, Alfred's son, won a major victory at Tettenhall in

Staffordshire and pacified the southern Danelaw. Towards the end of his reign the Saxon advance was such that he was acknowledged overlord by 'the King of Scots and all the Scottish Nation, Rognvald King in York with all the Danes and Norwegians in Northumbria, and by the rulers of Strathclyde'.

But the power of the English kings, while imposing fitful peace, caused unease among their neighbours. Athelstan, Alfred's grandson and strongest of the line, having experimented with dynastic marriage and finding it a poor substitute for permanent conquest, expelled the Danish kings from Northumbria. In 938 he was confronted by a Celtic–Norse alliance – a confederacy of Scots, Strathclyde Britons, and Danes from Dublin – united only in their common emnity for the Saxons. The issue came to trial by battle at Brunanburgh, and the army of the confederacy was totally defeated:

Then the Norsemen departed in their nailed ships, bloodstained survivors of spears, on Dingesmere over the deep water to Dublin, Ireland once more, sorry of heart. The two brothers (Athelstan and Edmund) King and atheling both, sought their own country, the land of the west Saxons, exulting in war. They left behind them to joy in the carrion, the black and horn-beaked raven with his dusky plumage, and the dun-feathered eagle with his white tipped tail, greedy hawk of battle to take toll of the corpses, and the wolf, grey beast of the forest. Never until now, in this island, as books and scholars of old inform us, was there greater slaughter of an army with the sword's edge, since the Angles and the Saxons put ashore from the east, attacked the Britons over the wide seas, proud forgers of war conquered the Welsh, and fame-eager warriors won them a home-land.[24]

But Danish ambition survived the slaughter, and after Athelstan's death, the Danes of Dublin renewed their claims to York – the contenders often remaining only long enough to mint their coin and announce their pretensions before being driven out again. The Saxon King Edmund finally expelled them and ruled in Northumbria until his death in 946.

It is said that Harald Finehair had more than forty sons. His favourite and heir was Eric Bloodyaxe, who having permanently disposed of a large proportion of his nearest relatives, embarked on a career of such violence and rapacity that he was eventually expelled from Norway. For a while he plundered in the Isles 'to gather property', and then fixed his attention upon Northumbria where, since Halfdan's time, a succession of contenders from Dublin had briefly possessed and lost the throne of York.[25]

In this chaos, and the aftermath of Danish defeat, the Norwegian faction in York invited Eric Bloodyaxe to be their king – a choice displeasing to the Saxons. He took the throne twice – and was twice dispossessed in the short space of five years. Bloodyaxe embarked then on a great plundering, gathering the Vikings of the Orkneys and Western Isles to his longships – and raiding through Alba, the Hebrides, north-west England and Wales. This career came to abrupt end on a barren hillside called the Stainmore, where he was slain with five other Viking kings and sent at last to join the thousand ghosts that gibbered for him in Valhalla. But his brood would disturb Norway and the Northern Isles for a generation after.

In Orkney, following the deaths of Sigurd and Thorstein the Red, the Jarldom had reverted to Rognvald Earl of Moeri, who offered it to his son Hallad. Hallad visited the islands but found them so infested with Vikings that he decided to forego the privilege, and Orkney passed instead to Turf-Einar, an illegitimate son of Rognvald, who was altogether of a sterner constitution. He is described in the sagas as a mighty man, ugly, and blind of an eye – 'yet very sharp-sighted withal'. Orkney was attacked by Halfden Halega, another of Harald Finehair's sons, who having first burned Earl Rognvald in his hall at Moeri, seized the Northern Isles for himself. Turf-Einar caught up with him however, and having hacked the blood eagle in his back, paid the *Wergeld* to the Norwegian king, and made himself undisputed master of Orkney. Two of his sons were killed in England with Eric Bloodyaxe, but the third, Thorfinn Skullsplitter, married into the ruling family of Caithness, and thus reunited under the Norse line the lands first conquered by Thorstein the Red.

Thorfinn Skullsplitter begat five sons, of whom four married Ragnhild, the daughter of Eric Bloodyaxe. She was a lady of faithless and dangerous disposition who murdered each of them in turn or at least caused it to be done. The fifth son however, more circumspect or less susceptible, married an Irish princess, and his son in due time was Sigurd the Strong, the most renowned of the Jarls of Orkney.

Sigurd the Strong was a pagan (although many of the Norsemen were embracing Christianity), but shortly after his accession to the Orkney Earldom, he made an abrupt conversion. In Norway at this time, the

81

throne had passed to King Olaf Tryggvason – a notable Viking and latterly a saint. King Olaf

proceeded to England and plundered widely in the land. He sailed as far north as Northumberland and plundered there – thence he sailed to Scotland and plundered widely there – thence he sailed to the Hebrides and had some battles there.

He plundered also widely into Ireland. Then he went to Wales and plundered the land widely, and also the land which is called Cumberland. Then he sailed west to France and plundered there; then he sailed from the West and intended to sail to England. Then he came to the Isles that are called the Scillies in the sea to the west of England.[26]

Olaf spent the winter in the Scillies and was converted to Christianity by a local hermit. In the spring he departed peaceably and went no more 'a-Viking' – which was unusual, since among the Norsemen conversion to Christianity was not normally considered a deterrent to piracy.

Nevertheless, having adopted the Christian faith himself, Olaf Tryggvason felt that it was incumbent upon other Vikings to do the same – and took active steps to bring them to his persuasion. Landing in Orkney, he seized Sigurd's small son and vowed to put him to the sword, unless the earl and all his people were immediately baptised. Orkney then became Christian for a while.

Sigurd re-established his authority over Sutherland and Caithness in a series of battles against the Scottish *Mormaers*. He eventually made a treaty with Malcolm II King of Scots, and married one of Malcolm's three daughters. Sigurd's son, Thorfinn the Mighty, was thus first cousin to Macbeth (whose father Finlech of Moray had married another of Malcolm's daughters), and became his ally against their other cousin, Duncan.

Sigurd the Strong also revived the old Orkney interest in the Western Isles. Among the Hebrides, the descendants of Ivar Imhar had ruled as tributary kings of the *Gall-Gael*. Their names, but little more, survive: Arailt (Harold), grandson of Ivar; Magnus MacArailt, *Rex plurimarum insularum* (see p.73) – (who was one of the eight Norse princes who submitted to King Edgar of England and, according to tradition, rowed his barge along the Dee); Godfrey MacArailt (979–989) who was killed in battle against the men of Dalriada; Ragnal MacGodfrey, who died in 1004, and was succeeded by his nephew Svein MacKenneth. Norsemen all, but the Gaelic appellation may indicate a tradition of marriage or significant concessions to local Celtic custom. In about 1000 Sigurd, however, appointed his own Governor of the Hebrides, Earl Gilli, who was married to his daughter. Although Gilli was certainly part Norse, it is possible that he could claim Celtic descent from the Clan Cholla, and Clan Donald genealogies make him the possible grandfather of Somerled, and a descendant of the late kings of Dalriada.

Sigurd and Gilli did not have time, however, to pursue their ambitions in the Hebrides, before they were interrupted by a series of violent events, culminating in one of the greatest battles of the Viking Age. In Ireland a new hero had emerged. Among the Vikings of Dublin and the Isle of Man, fresh ambitions had been kindled by an unscrupulous woman and a disaffected king. In Orkney, Sigurd the Strong shook out his famous raven banner, and the *Valkyriur* were weaving the woof of war:

> The woof y-woven
> with entrails of men
> the warp hard-weighted
> with heads of the slain.[27]

CHAPTER 9

Clontarf (AD 1014)

I have been where champions battled;
High in Erin sang the sword.
Boss to boss clashed many shields,
Steel clanged sharp on warriors' helms.
I can tell of that fierce struggle;
Sigurd fell in storm of spears:
Brian fell but gained the kingdom
Ere the blood flowed from his wounds.
NJAL'S SAGA

In Ireland, the hero who emerged at the end of the tenth century was Brian Boriomhe – better remembered as the High King of Erin, Brian Boru. Born in 941, he was a younger son of Cenneide (Kennedy), chieftain of the *Dal Chais*, a tributary tribe of the southern kingdom of Munster.

The Celtic order had largely survived the Viking invasions and the old seven states of Erin continued to exist under their traditional kings, with the High Kingship itself generally alternating between the northern and southern branches of the *Ui Neill*. But the Norse presence was disruptive. In contrast to the English Danelaw, the Vikings in Ireland remained concentrated in their fortified harbour strongholds at Dublin, Waterford, and Limerick, and rarely attempted to settle widely in the hinterland. Rather, they continued to be raiders in the old Norse way, and preferred to exploit the Irish for the wealth and tribute they could take. Ever ready to intervene in local disputes or ally themselves with disaffected chieftains, they fostered conflict among the Irish kingdoms so that the tributary clans grew restive and ambitious for territory of their own, and the older, traditional loyalties gradually weakened.

Upon occasions the Irish had found champions strong enough to reverse the role and exact tribute from the foreigners, but such periods were transitory, and any peace untrusting and precarious. The last such leader had been Muirkertach, King of Aelach, who with his army of

84

'leather cloaks' had taken hostages from Danes and Irish alike and briefly subdued the country under the High King. But inevitably he was killed, in 941, and after his death the activities of the Norsemen again increased, while renewed rivalries between petty Celtic kings brought a return to the endemic warfare that was the common state in Ireland.

In 964, Mahon, chief of the tribe called the *Dal Chais*, seized the throne of Cashel (Munster) and started a war against the Danes of Limerick, who at that time were dominant in the south of Ireland. He was repulsed, driven from Cashel itself, and brought to truce. However, his brother, Brian Boru, refused to submit but retired instead into the wild fastness of Slieve Aughty on the borders of Connaught, and continued to hold out against the Danes. There, a legend grew around his name, as he fought a bitter guerrilla war – hiding in woods and caves, moving across trackless bogs, often hopeless and with fewer than fifteen men, but keeping rebellion alive in Munster. Yet in 968 the *Dal Chais* were again strong enough to move against the Norsemen, and in alliance with the neighbouring clans Thromond and Desmond, crossed the Shannon and sacked the Danish settlements in the south. The Viking King Ivar of Limerick, with his Irish allies Donovan and Molloy, was defeated at Sologhead near Tipperary and fled to Wales. Mahon ruled again in Cashel, and Limerick paid tribute.

However, in 976 Ivar returned with a great fleet, and having forced Mahon's abdication, instigated his murder by Donovan and Molloy. Brian Boru now assumed the leadership of the *Dal Chais*, and collecting the loyal clans of Munster, marched in vengeance for his brother's death. The Irish overran and burned the Danish settlements on the islands in the Shannon. They then fell upon the Viking army, and outside the earth walls of Limerick, Brian exterminated Ivar and his sons. Donovan and Molloy were hunted down, dispossessed, and killed, and having subdued also his erstwhile allies the Clan Desmond, Brian Boru installed himself as king in Cashel. By 979 he controlled all of Munster and his power was unchallenged in the south.

Meanwhile, in Meath, another Irish king, Mael Seachlainn Mor, was imposing his authority on the Vikings of Dublin. In 979 he routed an Irish warband outside Tara, and pursuing the survivors into Dublin itself, brought the Norse Kingdom under tribute. The Viking King, Olaf Kvaran, fled to Iona where he underwent conversion and eventually died a hermit. His son, Gluniarainn Iron Knee (whose mother had been a daughter of Muirkertach) submitted to the Irish, and in 980 Mael Seachlainn became High King of Erin.

Three years later Mael Seachlainn and Gluniarainn Iron Knee marched together against the Vikings of Waterford under their king, another Ivar, who was fomenting trouble in Leinster, but when Iron Knee himself rebelled in 989, the Irish again besieged Dublin. Thirst forced the Danes to surrender, and this time the tribute was crippling. When Gluniarainn died, the Dublin kingdom passed by default to Ivar of Waterford, who by this new concentration of Viking power felt strong enough to challenge Mael Seachlainn's authority. In 994 the Irish marched a third time on Dublin and took it by assault. The town was thoroughly looted, and in addition Mael Seachlainn seized the two great Viking treasures – the 'Sword of Charles', alleged to have belonged to Charlemagne himself and the symbol of royal power; and 'Thor's Torque', a pagan relic of religious value and significance. In place of Ivar, Mael Seachlainn installed another of Olaf Kvaran's sons, Sigtrygg Silk Beard, as king in Dublin. It was an unfortunate choice.

Inevitably perhaps, the two Irish kings eventually collided, and for some years Brian Boru and Mael Seachlainn fought each other to little purpose and no advantage. They finally became reconciled and divided Ireland between them, each to reign independent and supreme in his own country. Peace of a sort resulted, but the petty kings of Leinster, Aelach, and Cruachan saw little profit in it and awaited an opportunity to rebel. The kingdom of Leinster in particular had a tradition of conspiring with the Danes, and in 1000 its king, Maolmordha, formed an alliance with the Norsemen in Dublin and proclaimed his independence. Brian Boru promptly called Munster to the hosting and marched on Dublin. The armies met on the slopes of the Wicklow Mountains in the narrow pass called Glenmama near Dunlavin. The forces of Leinster were routed, and the Vikings of Dublin isolated in the pass and virtually wiped out. After the battle, Maolmordha, king of Leinster was found hiding in a yew tree (a fact of some significance later on). Brian occupied Dublin and received Sigtrygg's formal submission. Having brought Dublin and Leinster under the authority of Cashel it was a logical step to march next on Tara, where after a show of force, Mael Seachlainn was persuaded to abdicate. In 1002 Brian Boru became High King of Erin.

For a decade there was peace, as Brian proved an energetic and capable ruler. Monasteries and schools were reopened, ruined churches rebuilt, bridges and causeways repaired, and fortresses constructed at strategic points. There was a return to peaceful trade and a general revival of Irish art. Brian's palace at Kincora became the new centre of Ireland, and his power was accepted by the petty kings with more or less reluctance. Careful of his place in history, he had his name inscribed in the Book of Armagh with the title *Imperator scotorum.*

The unscrupulous woman was the Queen, Gormflaith: the disaffected king, Maolmordha, her brother.

Gormflaith was the widow of Olaf Kvaran, King of Dublin, and the mother of Sigtrygg Silk Beard. She was also the *divorced* wife of Mael Seachlainn, and the recent consort of Brian Boru. It seemed that possession of this dowager queen conferred a legitimacy upon claims of authority over the Dublin kingdom, and Brian Boru's marriage to her had been a part of his treaty with Sigtrygg. The flaw in this dynastic arrangement was that she conceived an implacable hatred for him, and at an early opportunity deserted Kincora for the *dun* of her brother, Maolmordha of Leinster, where she whispered sedition among the tributary kings.

These provincial Irish kings effectively separated the High King from the clans themselves, and although subject to Brian, they were jealous of the permanent authority of Kincora. The years of peace had not extinguished a nostalgia for the past, and idle warriors in the royal duns listened to the older stories sung in the hall at night, and hankered for the war trail. Brian himself was growing old. It merely wanted the occasion.

The opportunity presented itself when Maolmordha was visiting Kincora and interfered in a game of chess in which Brian's son Murchad was engaged. Murchad responded by taunting Maolmordha over his capture when hiding in a yew tree after the battle of Glenmama. The imputation of cowardice was excuse enough, and Maolmordha hurried back to Leinster and raised the banner of revolt.

Collecting to his army a number of malcontented chiefs from Connaught also, Maolmordha and his Leinstermen joined with Sigtrygg and the Danes of Dublin to attack Mael Seachlainn's kingdom of Meath. Brian Boru promptly summoned the loyal clans, repudiated Gormflaith, and marched to Meath's assistance, burning Leinster as he went. The rebels retreated into Dublin with Brian at their heels.

However, the approach of winter and the lack of provisions obliged him to raise the siege and await the spring.

The winter of 1013 was spent in preparations for what all now saw would be a decisive struggle. The Norse presence in Dublin had been seriously depleted since the massacre at Genmama, and the Queen Gormflaith now proposed that help should be sought from the Vikings in the Isles. Messages were sent to all the Viking stations of the west and the Atlantic islands – to the independent pirates and sea-wolves of the remote skerries, the *Gall-Gaedhill,* and the Norse raiders who still fought for plunder on the seaway. The pillaging of Ireland would be their portion, while for the leaders, the prize was to be the throne of Dublin and the hand in marriage of Gormflaith herself.

Sigtrygg Silk Beard carried the message to Orkney, where on Hrossey, Earl Sigurd the Strong was holding a Yuletide feast. Earl Gilli was there together with a number of other prominent Vikings, notably Thorstein Hallson, Hrafn the Red, and Erling of Stroma. They had gathered to hear an account of the burning of Njal – an event which had aroused some interest in the Viking world. In 1011, following a blood feud, Njal and his sons had been incinerated in their own mead hall, and one of the Vikings responsible for the deed was present at Sigurd's feast. His tale was so biased, however, that it incensed Njal's son-in-law, who, having landed at Hrossey with vengeance in mind, burst into the hall and beheaded him on the spot. This caused some confusion among the guests, but Sigurd had the tables scrubbed down and the body removed, and the story of Njal was told accurately to everyone's satisfaction. Sigtrygg was then allowed to broach the subject of his visit.

At first Sigurd was unenthusiastic, and the majority of his followers were not keen to join Maolmordha against Brian Boru. At length, however, he was persuaded by Sigtrygg's promises. Dublin was always a lodestone to a Viking, and the charms of the much-married Gormflaith were apparently irresistible. It was agreed that he should bring his longships to Dublin by Palm Sunday (18 April 1014).[28]

Sigtrygg sailed back to Ireland well pleased, and told Gormflaith that Sigurd had agreed to join the war against Brian. Considering possibly that the accident of battle might well resolve one promise of marriage more or less, she sent him next to the Isle of Man to strike a similar bargain with the Viking sea-king there.

The seaways of Man were at that time controlled by two Vikings,

Ospak and Brodir, who had a fleet of thirty longships between them. Sigtrygg spoke to Brodir, who also agreed to join him in return for the throne of Dublin and the hand of Gormflaith – but it was agreed that Sigurd should not be told of this. Ospak, however, refused absolutely to fight against the Irish High King, and when Brodir tried to kill him, he escaped with ten longships to warn Brian Boru what was afoot.

Brian called the hosting for the week before Palm Sunday.

Through the winter months the longships carried the word to the islands and skerries in the western sea, while in Dublin itself the anvils rang with the preparations for war. By March with the advent of calmer weather, the sea-Vikings were gathering at the mouth of the Liffey. Norsemen poured into Dublin, beaching their ships along the shore, to join the assembled warbands, and brawl and boast in Sigtrygg's hall.

In hindsight, men remembered portents and awful dreams of omen. The night rained boiling blood on Brodir's ships: a great clamour foretold the rupture of the world. Strange horsemen appeared against the skyline, and the black crows gathered by the gates in expectation of the heads which shortly would be hanging there.

In Orkney, Sigurd the Strong unfurled his famous battle banner, sewn to resemble a flying raven when taken by the wind. Woven with magic spells, it was the gift of the Seeress Audna at Skida Myre, who had prophesied that it would bring victory to those before whom it was borne, and death to him that bore it. In Orkney too, a man saw the ghastly vision of the twelve *valkyriur* weaving a terrible cloth of battle on the loom of slaughter. 'Men's heads were used in place of weights, and men's intestines for the weft and warp: a sword served as the beater, and the shuttle was an arrow.'[29] In the halls of Odin the old gods waited.

On St Patrick's Day, 17 March, the *Dal Chais* and the clans of Thromond mustered at Kincora, and Brian Boru was ready to march. Crossing Shannon, he gathered in the men of southern Connaught under their warleaders O'Heyne of Aidhne and O'Kelly of the Ui Maine, and advanced onto the great plain of Munster, where near Cashel he was joined by the Desmond clans and a band of Norsemen from Waterford who had decided to fight against the Dublin Vikings. Marching across the Osraidhe, he forded the River Barrow and moved into Leinster itself, but the fighting men of the province were with Maolmordha in Dublin, and his invasion was unopposed. Brian turned north, and keeping to the eastern edge of the Leinster plain, skirted the Wicklow Mountains and reached the high ground of Kilmainhan on the south bank of the Liffey, where he camped overlooking Dublin.

Dublin was at that time a small town on the south bank of the river, connected to the north by a single bridge. Earthworks and wooden fortifications guarded the landward approaches. The Viking fleet, assembling on Palm Sunday, was anchored or beached along the northern shore, across from the settlement, in the estuaries of the Liffey and the Tolka, and even beyond, towards the weir of Clontarf.

On about Palm Sunday, Mael Seachlainn joined Brian with the men of Meath, bringing the High King's force to almost 20,000. Apart from this detachment, however, Brian's army was drawn entirely from the southern clans, since the northern *Ui Neill* chose to ignore the hosting and waited upon events. The Irish now crossed the river and marched along the ridge of high ground which separated the valleys of the Liffey and the Tolka where they took up a position overlooking the shore between the estuaries, and threatening both the bridge into Dublin and the ships drawn up along the beach. The Vikings were thus forced to come out from their defensive positions in the town in order to protect their fleet.

The Battle of Clontarf was fought on Good Friday, 23 April 1014. Through the previous night there had been exchanges between the hostile camps – insults shouted, challenges given, and it seems possible that the Vikings made some attempt to ascertain whether Mael Seachlainn would really fight on the morrow. Towards dawn, the Irish prepared for battle. Brother said farewell to brother; men pledged faith with the companions who would fight on either hand, tested sword's edge or hefted battle-axe, and went to take their places in the lines.

At sunrise, the Viking army deployed in an extended battle-front with their backs to the shore. A cold wind was blowing off the sea, and rain squalls whipped off the water and carried across the fields into the faces of the advancing Irish. On the Viking left, Sigtrygg's brother Dubhgall led the Norse of Dublin, posted to guard the single bridge into the town where Sigtrygg himself stood to watch the battle from the tower above the gate.

In the centre, on rising ground, Maolmordha commanded the men of Leinster and the *Ui Cennselaigh*, Dungal of the Liffey and the provincial kings of Leinster with the chiefs and fighting-men of the rebellious Irish clans. On the right, defending the ships, were the sea-Vikings under their several leaders. Sigurd the Strong beneath the great Raven Banner led the men of Orkney, and in his shieldwall were Hrafn the Red, Asmund the White, Thorstein Hallson, Plait – called by the Irish the bravest of all the foreigners, and three other sons of the King of Norway. Close by, Brodir led the Danes of Man and the sea-wolves, the iron scales of their war-coats a dull rippling blue to the watchers in the Irish camp; their great sharp-honed Lochlann axes shaken aloft, conveying menace to the growing war-shout that swelled along the Danish line. The need to defend both the Dublin bridge and the ships now swinging on the high tide, caused the Vikings to extend their front over as much as a mile and a half, and in consequence the several divisions were separated by more than a bow shot from each other. The sea behind left no retreat.

Against this wide deployment, the Irish were also obliged to extend their front, and they advanced in a long, thin line, perhaps no more than twelve men deep, seventy battle banners carried before their chieftains marking the warbands of the clans of Erin. The old King Brian Boru declined himself to shed blood on the Holy Day, and waited behind his army in Tomar's Wood, where a skin was spread for him in a clearing so that he could spend the hours of battle in prayer for his soldiers. Command of the army was given to his son Murchad, called the Hector of Erin, and one of the famous ambidextrous warriors of Ireland who went into battle with a sword in each hand.

On the Irish right, facing the Dublin Vikings at the bridge, marched the men of Connaught under their chieftain O'Heyne, and next to them the Norse of Waterford with Ospak of Man and other Danish allies. In the centre, facing Maolmordha across the battle's anvil, were the clans of Munster under their leaders Mothla, King of the Desii, and Magnus of the *Ui Liathain*, while to their left and slightly in advance, Murchad led his own picked bodyguard – 'seven score sons of Kings', banded in a traditional warrior brotherhood around the High King's son. 'For there was not a king of any one tribe in Erin who had not his son or his brother in Murchad's household, for he was the Lord of the volunteers of Erin.' Supporting them were the Clan Desmond, while on Murchad's flank, the left wing under his son Tordelbach with the fighting strength of the *Dal Chais* advanced against the armoured Vikings of Sigurd the Strong and Brodir of Man. Finally, Mael Seachlainn and the army of Meath (whose loyalty Brian may have doubted) were stationed in reserve behind the Irish centre – their position partially concealed by a ditch which ran across the battlefield. In this order, the Irish moved off the ridge and approached the Viking divisions along the shore.

The battle began with a challenge and a single combat between Domnal, High Steward of Alban from Tordelbach's battalions, and the Viking Plait, who was son of the King of Lochlann.

Then Plait came forth from the battalion of the men in armour and shouted three times 'Faras Domhnall'; that is, 'Where is Domnal?' Domnal answered and said 'Here, thou reptile'. Then they fought, and each endeavoured to slaughter and mangle the other. And they fell, slain by each other, and were found in the morning with the hair of each in the fist of the other, and the sword of each in the other's heart.[30]

In the older times, such challenges would have been repeated as champions fought before the host to be remembered in the battle song. But the armies were closing fast under a hail of arrows, warriors lashing the turf with their swords as the battle-frenzy took them, and the two lines crashed together over the bodies. A terrible carnage began.

In the centre, Maolmordha and the Leinster clans hurled themselves down the short slope into the ranks of Munster. The Irish line buckled under the shock; bent, but did not break, as Murchad rallied the shieldwall round his banner; and a savage mêlée developed, with the Munstermen slowly giving ground before the ferocity of Maolmordha's spear charge.

On the Irish right, the clans of Connaught and Connemara with Ospak and the Norse allies, attacked the Danes of Dublin near the bridge, and a separate battle evolved, drifting away from the struggle in the centre as for a while neither side gained the advantage.

For some hours the lines fought chest to chest, until it seemed to the watchers in Dublin that they would hack each other to extinction, but gradually the Danish shieldwall began to waver, and isolated groups of Norsemen fought their way out of the press, and tried to reach the bridge. The surviving Irish chased them in a pack, dragged down Dungal of the Liffey and took his head, and completed the disintegration. Too few to fight their way into Dublin, they turned then across the battlefield to join Murchad whose men were taking a terrible mauling in the centre.

By the shore, meanwhile, Tordelbach and the *Dal Chais* were engaged in a desperate struggle against the more heavily armed Vikings.

Charging low under their shields, the Irish grappled with the Norsemen to drive sword through iron scales and muscle, or drag them down under the swinging axes and stumbling feet to stab and hamstring on the ground, in a savage confusion of knives and teeth. For a space the Norsemen were driven back, but then Sigurd rallied his shieldwall to form the 'swine-snout' fighting-wedge, and the Vikings started to cut their way into the press of Irish that boiled around them. The *Dal Chais* were in turn forced to give ground, bending around the inexorable Viking advance, as the great Lochlann axes rose and fell, bursting skulls and crunching bone, with the great Raven Banner of Sigurd towering over the battle and always where the fight was thickest. The *Dal Chais* retreated slowly, borne backwards by the weight of the attack, and their plight was watched with horror by the men of Meath in the Irish reserve.

Mael Seachlainn afterwards attested that: 'I never saw a battle like it, nor have I heard of its equal; and even if an angel of God attempted its description, I doubt if he could give it.' The wind was so strong that great gouts of blood were being blown across the field and into the faces of the Meath battalions. 'And it is doubtful to us,' he recalled, 'whether those who sustained that crushing assault were braver than we who had to endure the sight of it without going mad or distracted.'[31]

In Tomar's Wood, the old king paused from praying and sent his servant to report on how the battle went. He learned then of the confusion and the slaughter taking place: that the Munstermen were giving ground, but Murchad's banner was flying still and the Irish rallying where it passed their battle line. And he knew the battle was in the balance, and so returned to his prayers.

In the centre, the clans of Munster still retreated before the rebels, but Maolmordha himself was dead, killed early in the battle, and the Leinstermen were being carried forward by their own momentum behind their individual petty kings and chiefs. As the struggle moved across the field before him, Mael Seachlainn saw the opportunity, and prompt upon his moment, the old warrior led the Irish reserve in a wild charge into the enemy flank. The men of Meath poured across the ditch and smashed against the rebel centre. The Leinstermen began to panic, and when Murchad rallied the Irish for a counter charge, the battle suddenly swung against the Dublin army. Attacked from two sides, the men of Leinster were driven sideways, close to rout, until they were brought up against the Viking division of Sigurd and Brodir on the Irish left. Murchad and Tordelbach now combined to encircle the Norsemen who were in turn thrown into confusion by the fleeing rebels, and the final attrition began.

Brodir of Man formed his sea-wolves into a wedge and hacked his way out of the press. Cut off from the ships, he fought a way through the Irish who now swarmed around the isolated Norsemen, and with a few survivors, took refuge in a nearby wood. Other Vikings were also breaking out, and small groups were trying to reach the shore, or more remote, the Dublin bridge and the safety of the town.

Sigurd the Strong, however, chose to stand and fight, and the Orkney shieldwall still held solid around the Raven Banner. Twice, the banner-bearer had been struck down, and Sigurd called to Thorstein Hallson to take it up. But as Thorstein was about to lift it, Asmund the White shouted at him, 'Don't bear the banner, for they who bear it get their death.' Then Sigurd ordered Hrafn the Red to carry the banner. 'Bear thine own devil thyself,' replied Hrafn, and Sigurd tore the banner from its staff and stuffed it under his war-coat saying, 'It is fittest that the beggar should bear the bag.'[32] Plunging back into the fight, he charged through the press until eventually he came face to face with Murchad. Murchad hit him right-handed and broke the buckles of his helmet so that it toppled sideways off his head. The left hand stroke that followed clove his neck, and Sigurd the Strong fell beneath the trampling feet.

But Murchad's own death was near. Coming thereafter upon Eric, son of the King of Lochlann, the two fought alone against each other until Murchad was wounded in the hand:

And the sword of Murchad at that time was inlaid with ornament, and the inlaying that was in it melted with the excessive heat of the striking, and the burning sword cleft his hand, tearing the fork of his fist. He perceived that and cast the sword from him, and he laid hold of the top of the foreigner's head, and pulled his coat of mail over his head forward, and then they fought a wrestling combat. Then Murchad put the foreigner down under him by the force of wrestling, and then he caught the foreigner's own sword and thrust it into the ribs of the enemy's breast until it reached the ground through him, three times. The foreigner then drew his knife, and with it gave Murchad such a cut that the whole of his entrails were cut out and they fell to the ground before him. Then did shivering and fainting descend on Murchad, and he had not the power to move. So they fell by each other there.[33]

Murchad's eviscerated body was carried off the field, but according to the chronicle, he did not die until the morning.

In Tomar's Wood, Brian Boru again sent his servant to watch the fight, and so knew that the Irish were now close to victory but that Murchad's banner no longer flew above the battle-line. He understood then that Murchad had fallen, and having perhaps some premonition, named his younger son as heir to Erin before once more returning to his prayers. It was shortly after, that Brodir and his Vikings stumbled into the clearing, and recognising the old man kneeling on the ground, the Dane rushed forward and brained him with his battle-axe. Thus the High King Brian Boru was also slain at the moment of his greatest victory. But for this act Brodir of Man had a gruesome death, for the Irish found him by the body of their king with his axe still dripping brains and blood, screaming at an empty battlefield that he, alone of all the Vikings, had killed the mighty Brian Boru. And they tied his intestines to a tree, and made him walk around it clockwise until, still living, he was entirely disembowelled.

Elsewhere on the battlefield the Vikings were in flight, while the exultant Irish hounded after them, clubbing down the stragglers and taking heads. Among Sigurd's followers a few survived. Thorstein Hallson stopped running to tie his shoelace, and Tordelbach catching up with him, asked why he had not fled with the rest. 'Because', said Thorstein, 'my home is in Iceland and I cannot reach there tonight.' And Tordelbach spared him.

By the bridge, Ospak of Man, though badly wounded, had sealed off any escape into Dublin, and it was said later that out of all the Dublin Norse, only twenty reached the safety of the town. Nor on the beach could the Vikings find any hiding place. Sunset was now approaching and it was once more high tide, so that the fugitives could not reach their ships, and their iron war-coats dragged them under and drowned them in the current. Here also, the young Tordelbach rushed to his destruction. Leaping into the surf, he continued the killing in the water, but the tide took him, and exhausted as he was, swept him against the weir of Clontarf where he was impaled on a stake, and drowned without seeing the *Dal Chais* make an end.

Clontarf is a lost battlefield now, as over the centuries the city of Dublin encroached across the early site. Brian Boru has his place in Irish history. Gormflaith and Maolmordha, Murchad and Tordelbach, are remembered still and their deeds recorded in the chronicle. Sigurd's feast at Yuletide, his Raven Banner, and his final death in battle are written in the sagas. But only the story and their names remain. There is no grim landscape to conjure in the mind a scene of war and slaughter, no monolith to mark the dead, nor tumulus to indicate an ancient killing ground – upon the place which, in modern times, is known as Mountjoy Square.

CHAPTER 10

Thorfinn the Mighty;
Magnus Barelegs;
and the Kingdom of Man

Half a dozen homesteads burning
Half a dozen homesteads plundered
This was Swein's work of a morning.

The battle of Clontarf and Earl Sigurd's death put an end to any hopes that Gilli may have had of becoming Governor of the Hebrides, which now came under the control of the emerging Kingdom of Man and the Isles. The Earls of Orkney continued to claim overlordship in the Western Isles, however, and they also exercised a considerable influence over events in Scotland itself. Their activities in the west and the weakness of the Dublin Norse after Clontarf would arouse the predatory interest of the Norwegian kings.

Sigurd the Strong left three sons by his first wife – Sumarlidi, Brusi, and Einar – who divided the Orkney Islands between them. By his second marriage, to the daughter of Malcolm II King of Scots, he left also a five-year-old son, Thorfinn, who in time would become a mighty Viking earl, ruling Orkney, Shetland, the Hebrides, Caithness, Suther-land, Ross, and part of Moray.

Thorfinn was brought up at the court of his grandfather, Malcolm II, who bestowed on him the Earldom of Caithness. In Orkney, Sumarlidi shortly died, and his portion passed to Einar – who made himself so unpopular through acts of violence and extortion that he was killed by Thorkell Fosterer, so that Brusi eventually took possession of the whole earldom. When Thorfinn reached manhood, however, he challenged Brusi for a portion of the Orkney Islands, and the two half-brothers appealed to the King of Norway, Olaf the Stout, as their overlord. The king divided the Orkneys into three, reserving a part for himself, but promising Brusi that the extra third would revert to him in due course – an equivocal decision that led to bloodshed later.

The story of Thorfinn's turbulent career is told at length in the *Orkneying Saga*. In 1034, Malcolm II was murdered at Glamis, and the Scottish throne passed to his other grandson Duncan I, who attempted to exact tribute from Thorfinn for the lands of Caithness and Sutherland. When the earl with some justification refused, Duncan sent a creature of his own called Moddan to displace him. Thorfinn raised an army in Caithness where he was joined by Thorkell Fosterer and the men of Orkney, and in the face of superior numbers the Scots were forced to abandon their invasion of the north. Thorfinn then subdued Sutherland and Ross, and plundered deep into Scotland before returning to Caithness, where he disbanded his force – keeping only 'five warships and followers enough to man them'.

But Duncan meanwhile had despatched Moddan with a second army, and assembling a fleet of eleven warships under his own command, he trapped Thorfinn in the Pentland Firth as the Viking was about to sail for Orkney. Faced with the alternative of abandoning his ships and all the loot accumulated during the summer campaign, or fighting against a force twice the size of his own, Thorfinn promptly attacked the Scottish fleet:

> Once off Dryness to the eastward
> Came King (Duncan) in his mail coat
> Famous for its strength and brightness
> But the land was not defenceless,
> For with five ships, nothing daunted
> Scorning flight in warlike temper,
> Valiantly the Prince* went forward
> 'Gainst the King's eleven vessels.
>
> Then the ships were lashed together –
> Know ye how the men were falling?
> All their swords and boards were swimming
> In the life-blood of the Scotsmen;
> Hearts were sinking, bow strings screaming,
> Darts were flying – spear shafts bending;
> Swords were biting, blood flowed freely
> And the Prince's heart was merry.[34]

* Thorfinn

Despite their numerical advantage, Duncan's men began to lose heart, and cut their ships adrift from the battle to escape from the sea-Vikings who were leaping aboard in a determined attempt to seize the king. The skald completes his song:

> Never was a battle shorter
> Soon with spears it was decided –
> Though my Lord had fewer numbers,
> Yet he chased them all before him;
> Hoarsely croaked the battle-gull, when
> Thickly fell the wounded King's-men;
> South of Sandwick swords were reddened.[35]

Duncan fled to the Moray Firth to join his main army which had been summoned to assemble at Torfness (Tarbatness) on the Oykel estuary. Thorfinn recalled Thorkell Fosterer and the Orkneymen, and sailed in pursuit, plundering Scotland as he went. Hearing that Moddan was at Thurso awaiting reinforcement by Duncan's Irish allies, Thorkell landed in Caithness with a band of Vikings and surprised him in the night. The Vikings set the house on fire, and Moddan who 'was asleep in an upper storey, jumped out; but as he jumped down from the stair, Thorkell hewed at him with a sword, and it hit him on the neck, and took off his head. After this, his men surrendered, but some escaped by flight. Many were slain, but some received quarter.' Thorkell then rejoined Thorfinn, gathering up the fighting men of Caithness, Suther-land, and Ross.

Duncan had collected a large force drawn from all quarters of his Scottish kingdom, including a warband from Kintyre and a substantial number of allies from Ireland. The two armes met on the southern shore of the 'Broad Firth' – the Kyle of Sutherland – and in a fierce battle the Scots were routed:

> Reddened were the wolf's-bit's edges
> At a place – men called it Torfness; –
> It was by a youthful ruler
> This was done upon a Monday.
> Pliant swords were loudly ringing
> At this War-Thing south of Oykel,
> When the Prince had joined the battle
> Bravely with the King of Scotland.
>
> High his helm the Lord of Shetland
> Bore amid the clang of weapons;

In the battle ever foremost
Reddened he his gleaming spear-point
In the wounds he gave the Irish.
Thus my Lord, his mighty prowess
Showed beneath his Alban buckler
Taking many warriors captive;
Hlodver's kinsman burned the country.[36]

Thorfinn pursued the defeated Scots and pillaged the country as far south as Fife. The Vikings

went over hamlets and farms and burned everything, so that scarcely a hut was left standing. Those of the men whom they found, they killed; but the women and old people dragged themselves into woods and deserted places with wailings and lamentations. Some of them they drove before them and many were taken captives. After this, Thorfinn went through Scotland to the north, till he reached his ships, and subdued the country wherever he went, and did not stop till he came to Caithness where he spent the winter. But every season after this he went out on expeditions and plundered in the summertime with all his men.[37]

It is generally presumed that Duncan survived the battle at Torfness and escaped into Moray with the remnant of his army. He was defeated again and killed somewhere near Elgin by Macbeth, the Celtic *Mormaer* of Moray (the third of Malcolm II's grandsons), who now seized the throne of Scotland (1040).

Macbeth and Thorfinn appear to have been allies, and for the next sixteen years, during the period of Macbeth's reign in central Scotland, there was peace between them. Thorfinn was thus free to extend his influence in the Isles, and he is recorded as having established his rule in Galloway, 'making war' in the Hebrides, and raiding along the coasts of England.

When Brusi Sigurdson died, his son Rognvald received from King Magnus the Good of Norway confirmation both of his own odal rights and possession of the third part of Orkney which had belonged to Einar and been promised to Brusi by Olaf the Stout. Somewhat surprisingly, Thorfinn peaceably ceded two-thirds of Orkney to his kinsman provided that they became allies. For some years they went raiding together, sailing in the summer to the Hebrides and Ireland, so that for a while, the alliance seemed profitable to both. The Hebridean Norse were defeated in a sea engagement at Loch Vattin in Skye, and from their bases in the *Sudreyar*, Thorfinn and Rognvald sent warbands raiding along the coasts of north-west England.

This co-operation continued for eight years, and 'the kinsmen agreed very well whenever they met; but when bad men went between them dissensions often arose'. Eventually Thorfinn, who was finding it increasingly expensive to keep his Vikings in the winters, demanded Einar's share of Orkney for himself – and when Rognvald refused to give it up, gathered his followers from Caithness, Sutherland, and the Hebrides, and resolved to take it by force. Rognvald fled to Norway where he obtained men and longships from King Magnus, and thus reinforced, attacked Thorfinn's fleet off Dunnet Head in the Pentland Firth:

> Then I saw the two wealth-givers
> Hewing down each other's warriors.
> Fierce the fight was in the Pentland
> As the sea swelled and the red rain
> Crimsoned on the yielding timbers;
> While from the shield-rims sweat of hot blood
> Dripping, stained the warriors' garments.[38]

The Orkney ships were larger and higher than those of Rognvald, and Thorfinn's men were able to sweep the enemy decks with arrows and missiles, doing terrible execution among the Norwegian mercenaries. Rognvald's Vikings eventually broke off the fight, and standing out to sea, escaped under cover of the approaching darkness. Rognvald himself fled again to the court of Magnus, leaving Thorfinn in possession of all the Orkneys.

But despite this defeat, Rognvald would not rest content. Shortly afterwards, he obtained another ship from the Norwegian king, and sailing secretly to Hrossey where he knew Thorfinn was staying, he surrounded the hall during the night and set it on fire. Thorfinn got out by breaking down a wall at the rear of the building, and with his wife Ingeborg under his arm, escaped in the dark and rowed to Caithness. Believing that Thorfinn had been successfully cremated, Rognvald laid claim to all of Orkney together with Caithness and Thorfinn's territories in the Hebrides, and planned to spend the yuletide at Kirkwall entertaining his followers liberally.

Shortly before Christmas, Rognvald made a visit to the island of Papa Stronsay to obtain malt for brewing, and Thorfinn, getting to hear of it, repaid him in his own coin by burning down the house and killing everyone in it. Rognvald escaped and tried to hide among the rocks along the shore, but he was betrayed by his dog and slain by Thorkell Fosterer. Sailing next to Kirkwall, Thorfinn and Thorkell put the Norwegian garrison to death except for one man whom they sent to inform King Magnus of what they had done.

Thorfinn had always acknowledged the overlordship of the King of Norway, but since Magnus had been foster-brother to Rognvald a peaceful reconciliation seemed unlikely. Magnus was at that time at war with Swein of Denmark, and had anchored his fleet at Seley for the winter. One day, two longships rowed into the anchorage and moored alongside the King's vessel. A stranger in a white cloak stepped aboard and approached Magnus where he sat at meat. Saluting the King, the stranger took a loaf from the table, broke it, and ate. Magnus, handing him a cup to drink as was the custom, discovered to his considerable chagrin that it was none other than Thorfinn himself, who, having eaten his bread and drunk from his cup, was for the present safe from vengeance according to the Viking laws of hospitality. Thorfinn decided, however, that it was prudent to leave shortly after, without effecting a formal reconciliation, but following Magnus's death he made his peace with his successor Harald Hardradi who confirmed him in the Earldom of Orkney. 'And no-one spoke against it.'

In about 1050, Thorfinn went on a pilgrimage to Rome, possibly in company with Macbeth, and on his return he is said to have devoted more attention to the governing of his many territories and the welfare of his people. He also built Christ's Kirk at Birsay where he is buried, and established there the first Bishop's See in the Orkneys.

According to the saga, Thorfinn the Mighty was 'one of the largest men in point of stature, ugly of aspect, black-haired, sharp-featured, and somewhat tawny, and the most martial-looking man'. He 'retained all his dominions until his dying day, and it is truly said that he was most powerful of all the Orkney Earls. He obtained possession of eleven Earldoms in Scotland, all the *Sudreyar*, and a large territory in Ireland.' With pardonable exaggeration, the Orkney skald concluded his song;

> Unto Thorfinn, raven's feeder
> Armies had to yield obedience
> From Tuscar Rocks right on to Dublin;
> Truth I tell, as is recorded.[39]

On his death in 1064 'he was much lamented in his hereditary dominions; but in those parts which he had conquered by force of arms, many considered it very hard to be under his rule, and after his death many provinces which he had subdued turned away and sought help from the chiefs who were odal-born to the government of them'.

One of these territories which now regained its independence, was the Kingdom of Man and the Isles.

In the fateful year of 1066 the three greatest war-leaders of the age contended for the throne of England. On 6 January, Harold God-wineson was elected and crowned King in succession to Edward the Confessor – an inheritance which was claimed also by William the Bastard, Duke of Normandy, and coveted by the Norwegian King Harald Hardradi. In that autumn their claims were contested to the death in two great battles which effectively marked the end of the Viking era.

In 1066 Harald Hardradi was fifty-one years of age, and the most formidable warrior in northern Europe. Exiled from Norway in 1030, following the defeat and death of his half-brother, St Olaf, he had taken service for a time with King Yaroslav of Kiev as commander of his armies against the Poles on the western border of Russia. In 1034, with 500 followers, he sailed down the Dnieper and joined the Varangian Guard of the Byzantine Emperors, spending the next nine years fighting and plundering through the Mediterranean and the lands of Asia-Minor. He had fought the Muslims in Sicily, the Normans in southern Italy, the Bulgars at Thessalonika, and, according to the sagas, had participated in the uprising which overthrew the Emperor Michael Calaphetes. In 1043, events in Scandinavia drew him home, and he escaped from Constantinople, literally bouncing his longship over the great chains which barred the Bosporus, and gaining the Black Sea, returned to Kiev – where he gathered a Viking fleet and made war against King Magnus the Good. When Magnus died, Harald became undisputed master of Norway, and spent the next seventeen years trying, unsuccessfully, to conquer Denmark.

When Edward the Confessor died, Harald Hardradi revived a tenuous claim to the English throne as the nominated heir at one remove of Hardicanute – an argument which could only gain acceptance by the logic of conquest. Circumstances in England worked to encourage this ambition. Harold Godwineson was chiefly preoccupied with the threat from Normandy. The defection of his brother Tostig, Earl of Northumbria – first to the Danes, and subsequently to Harald Hardradi –

suggested that the country was already divided by internal rivalries and intrigue.

In 1066, Harald Hardradi assembled a large fleet of some 300 ships, and sailing first to Orkney and Shetland, gathered to his venture the island Vikings – Paul and Erlend, sons of Thorfinn, the Norse of Shetland, Lewis, the Uists, Skye, and the Isle of Man. He then cruised down the coast of north-east England, raiding after the old Norse manner among the coastal towns of the Danelaw – Cleveland, Scarborough, Holderness – before turning into Humbermouth and up the River Ouse to make a landing at Riccall. On 20 September, Hardradi and Tostig defeated the northern earls at Fulford outside York, and the Saxon garrison prepared to capitulate. After this victory the raiders were so confident that they left a third of their force to guard the ships at Riccall, together with most of their baggage and armour, and camped inland near Stamford Bridge, about eight miles from York itself. In this condition they were surprised by Harold Godwineson, who had marched north with the main English levy, and trapped against the east bank of the River Derwent.

Accounts of the battle vary. Harold is said to have offered to restore Tostig to the Earldom of Northumbria if he would make peace, but to Harald Hardradi he promised only 'seven feet of ground – or as much more as he is taller than other men'.[40] In the ensuing fight the Vikings were almost wiped out, and the English army suffered irrecoverable losses. Despite an epic defence by a giant Norwegian axeman who was said to have killed forty of the English before he was himself cut down, the Norsemen failed to hold the bridge at Stamford, and the English crossed the river and drove them in disorder to their ships. Harald and Tostig were both killed in the fighting, and the last great Viking raid of English history ended in slaughter and disaster. Harold of England was not permitted to savour his victory. Even as his battered army remustered after the battle, news came that William of Normandy had landed near Hastings, and he marched his weary house-carls south again – to defeat and death at Senlac nineteen days later.

Among the survivors of Harald Hardradi's army was Goddard, son of Sigtrygg, King of Man and the Isles. The greater part of the Hebridean contingent had perished in the battle and their ships been destroyed by the English in the aftermath, but the surviving remnant brought with them a number of refugees – among them Olaf, Harald Hardradi's son, and Godred Crovan, son of Harold the Black of Islay.

This Godred Crovan fixed his ambition on the Kingship of Man and the Isles, and in 1070 when Goddard of Man died and was succeeded by his son Fingal, he assembled a Norwegian fleet and seized the island at the third attempt. After this battle, Godred gave his Norse followers the option of either settling in Man or of despoiling the island, and when they chose the latter, he allowed them to depart with all the plunder they could carry. He then divided the land between the surviving Manxmen with the stipulation that 'none of them should at any time presume to claim any portion of the land by hereditary possession. Hence it came to pass [states the *Chronicle of Man*], that to this day the whole island is the exclusive property of the king and all its revenues belong to him alone.'[41]

Godred Crovan ruled the islands from Islay, and during the next sixteen years he 'subdued Dublin and the greater part of Leinster' in Ireland, and established such a hold over Galloway 'that no boatbuilder nor shipwright dared employ more than three iron bolts'. He died in 1087, leaving three sons – Lagman, Harold, and Olaf. Lagman seized the kingdom but was troubled for some years by the rebellion of his brother Harold, whom eventually he captured, castrated, blinded, and put to die in a dungeon. After reigning for seven years, he is said to have been overcome with remorse, and embarked on a pilgrimage to Jerusalem where he died in about 1095.

The third brother, Olaf, was still a minor, and the chieftains of the Isles persuaded the High King in Ireland to nominate a regent to rule *ad interim*. The King appointed one, Donald McTade, 'who conducted himself in the realm with great tyranny: and during three years he reigned wickedly and perpetrated many atrocious crimes. At length, all the chieftains of the islands conspired and rose against him and drove him out of their country. He vagabondised among the Irish, but did not return to Man.'[42]

These events were reported to King Magnus Olafsson of Norway, who had spent part of his youth in the *Sudreyar* since his father was that Olaf, son of Harald Hardradi, who had escaped to the Isle of Man after the battle of Stamford Bridge. Concerned at the new concentration of power established by Godred Crovan, and at Irish intervention in what he conceived to be an area of Norwegian interest, Magnus assembled a fleet and sailed to Brodick Bay in the Firth of Clyde.

The Scottish king at that time, Malcolm Canmore, was principally intent on invading the territories of the English William Rufus, and was therefore ready to buy off the Norwegian king if this would temporarily secure his western flank. He made a Treaty with Magnus 'to the effect that (the Norwegian king) should possess all the islands that lie to the west of Scotland, all between which and the mainland he could go, in a ship with the rudder in place'.

Magnus thereafter made good his claim to all the Hebrides: 'His men went into every firth and all the islands that lay in the firths; and they laid everything under King Magnus, in such a manner that they went with their ships between the mainland and the islands, whether they were inhabited or not.' Magnus also annexed the rich peninsula of Kintyre by having a skiff hauled on logs across the Tarbert isthmus while

the king himself sat on the after-deck and held the helm . . . And he took possession of the land that lay to the larboard. Kintyre is a great land, and better than the best in the Hebrides, excepting Man. A narrow isthmus is between it and the mainland of Scotland; there, longships are often drawn across.[43]

Having firmly established Norwegian sovereignty over the Kingdom of Man and the Isles, Magnus appointed two governors – Earl Ottar in Man itself, and Ingemund in Lewis – and then returned to Norway. During his expedition, he had adopted the dress of the Western Isles – going bare-legged, and wearing a short tunic and over-cloak – and so got the name Magnus 'Bareleg', or 'Bare-thigh'.

In Lewis, Ingemund proved to be a licentious and tyrannical governor who aspired to make the chiefs of the Isles appoint him king.

In the meanwhile he and his companions spent their time in rapine and revelling; they violated virgins and matrons, and gave themselves up to the pleasures and gratifications of the flesh. The chief men of the Isles . . . were exceedingly enraged; and during the night they burned down the house in which he was lodged, and either put to the sword or burnt himself and all his followers.[44]

Simultaneously, a revolt broke out in the Isle of Man which developed into a civil war between the north and south of the island, culminating in a fierce battle in which Earl Ottar also was killed.

These disturbances prompted Magnus Barelegs to undertake a second expedition to the west in 1098, and he now set about the complete pacification of the *Sudreyar*.

And when he came to the Hebrides he began at once to plunder and burn the inhabited lands, and he slew the menfolk. And they robbed everything wherever they went. But the people of the land fled far and wide; some to Scotland's firths, some south to Kintyre, or over to Ireland. Some received quarter and did homage. So says Bjorn Cripplehand:

The branch-scorcher played greedily up into the sky in Lewis; there was far and wide an eager going in flight. Flame spouted from the houses. The active King ravaged Uist with fire. The King made red the sword of battle. The farmers lost life and wealth.

The diminisher of the battle-gosling's hunger caused Skye to be plundered: the glad wolf reddened tooth in many a mortal wound upon Tiree. The Scots-expeller went mightily; the people of Mull ran to exhaustion. Greenland's King caused maids to weep, South in the islands.[45]

By some strange miracle, Iona was spared. Magnus gave quarter to the inhabitants of the island, and went alone into St Oran's chapel:

He closed the door again immediately, and immediately locked it, and said that none should be so daring thenceforward as to go into that church; and thenceforward it has been so.

But the general pacification continued:

Wide bore the active king his shields upon the level sand island; there was smoke from Islay when the King's men stirred up the burning. The sons of men South in Kintyre bowed beneath the swords' edges. The valiant battle-quickener then planned the Manxmen's fall.[46]

Arriving at Man, Magnus found the corpses of those who had fallen in battle against Ottar lying still unburied, and the survivors in such a miserable condition that, in contrast to his treatment of the other islands, he put the inhabitants to work on reconstruction, and set up his own headquarters on the island. From there he subdued Galloway and forced the Scots to supply him with the timber required to construct a series of fortresses on Man which was now brought firmly under his control. The Hebrides remained tributary to Norway for 150 years.

After he had reduced the Isles, Magnus also made a voyage to Anglesey and invaded Wales where he defeated the two Norman earls, Hugh the Stout (Earl of Chester) and Hugh the Bold (Earl of Shrewsbury) before returning north laden with plunder. In 1103 he made a final expedition – to Ireland, drawn by the old Viking ambition in that land, and died inconspicuously in an Irish ambush.

On his death, the chieftains of the Isles turned to Olaf, son of Godred Crovan, who in the interim had been a refugee at the court of Henry I of England. Olaf succeeded to the throne of Man and the Isles in 1104 and reigned for forty years. The *Chronicle* describes him as 'a man of peace

. . . who lived on such terms of union with all the kings of Ireland and Scotland, that no-one dared to disturb the Kingdom of the Isles so long as he was alive.'

The entry concludes by recording that Olaf 'took to wife a daughter of Fergus of Galloway named Alfreca, who bore him Godred. He also had several concubines by whom he became the father of three sons . . . and of many daughters; one of whom married Somerled, Prince of Argyll, who became the occasion of the ruin of the entire Kingdom of the Isles . . . and concerning whom we shall speak more fully in the sequel . . .'[47]

PART III

THE GAELIC REVIVAL

CHAPTER 11

Somerled

Strong as a horse's neck, shaggy as a stag's brisket,
Is the knee of the young torrent-leaper, the pride of the House of Crinan.
from *Hereward the Wake* by Charles Kingsley

Somerled, the warrior who led the Gaelic revival and restored the ancient Dalriadic claim to Argyll, is described by the Sleat historian: 'He was a well-tempered man, in body shapely, of a fair, piercing eye, of middle stature, and of quick discernment.' The name Somerled was Norse, meaning 'Summer Sailor', but after two hundred years of conquest, settlement, and inter-marriage, a Christian name alone was not a test of race, and all the leading families in the Isles and the coastland of Argyll were to a greater or lesser extent of mixed Norse blood.

Despite the long Viking occupation, Gaelic was again becoming the prevalent language in the Hebrides, but it borrowed extensively from the Norse. Many of the now familiar place-names on the coast or in the islands and the rough bounds north from Ardnamurchan are of Scandinavian origin – though often Gaelicised and not readily apparent on a modern map. In Islay, Loch Gruinart was 'The green fjord', and the suffix *-art* for *fjord* is constantly repeated – as in Sunart, Knoydart, Moidart, or Loch Snizort in Skye, while in Melfort (Melfjord), Broadfort, or Seaforth, a fuller form is still preserved. At Arran, Brodick is from Brathwik (The broad bay), while Oronsay was Orforisey (The island at the ebb tide). In Trotternish on Skye the *-nes* of Tradarnes has acquired the softer sibilant after the 'slender' vowel in accordance with Gaelic usage. Knapdale, Sunadale, and Saddell in Kintyre recall the names of Norse settlers in the peninsula, and the islands of Strathclyde have kept their Viking name of Kumbreyar (The Cumbraes). Among the emerging western clans Norse Christian names were Gaelicised in memory of a Viking ancestry and formed the now familiar patronymics – such as MacAulay from Olaf or Lamont from Lagman and many others – while by contrast the Gaelic name Gillemuire from whom the

MacLeans deduce, disguises a descent from Helga the Fair, grand-daughter of 'Old Ivar, King of Lochlann'.

The names of Somerled's father and grandfather were undeniably Gaelic, and in composing the Clan Donald genealogy most of the *seannachies* endeavoured to present him as a Gael in the male line, seventh in descent from Godfrey, *Toiseach* (Captain) of the Isles, who died in 853. It is possible to speculate that this Godfrey was not himself the direct descendant of the early Dalriadic kings but the son of Fergus, King of Oriel, who in 839 aided the Dalriads in battle against the Viking Turgeis when the sub-king of Dalriada was killed, and that Godfrey subsequently married the heiress. Certainly during the Viking period the old links with the descendants of Clan Colla in Ireland were revived – with whom the Dalriadic chieftains possibly took refuge. From Godfrey, most genealogies trace the pedigree through Niallghusa and Suibne to Echmarcach – who has sometimes been identified with the Iehmare of the *Saxon Chronicle* as one of the kings who submitted to Canute in 1031. Descent according to this tradition then passed through Solmund to Gilledomnan and Gillebride, '*Rig eilean shider*' (King of the South Isles), who was the father of Somerled. Some accounts have tried to equate Gilledomnan with the Earl Gilli who was Sigurd's governor in the Hebrides since he was not present at the Battle of Clontarf and continued to rule over Colonsay. But the dates do not fit such an hypothesis unless additional generations are interposed. It must suffice to say that Somerled's ancestry – particularly during the confused Viking period – remains clouded in obscurity, and the later seannachies had a tendency to opt for convenient solutions rather than established fact.

Be that as it may, not only did Somerled later claim a right both to Oirthirgael (the mainland of Argyll) and the South Isles by virtue of his 'predecessors', but the other chieftains who accepted his leadership clearly acknowledged his descent from the Clan Colla. Moreover, Norse accounts speak of him as being of the *Dalverja* family – that is, of the old royal house of Dalriada, whose name as *Dalir* had been preserved as the Norse word for Argyll.

What is beyond dispute, is that Somerled was the direct ancestor of the Clan Donald, and one of the greatest warrior kings born to the Gaels of Alba.

Somewhere in Morvern, on the shore of Loch Linnhe and looking

across the water towards Lismore, was a cave from which Somerled's
father took his name *Gillebride Na H'Uaimh* – Gillebride of the Cave.
Viking depredations, the conquests of Thorfinn the Mighty, the tyranny
of the kings of Man, and finally the terrible raids of Magnus Barelegs
which had scorched and depopulated the land, had brought about a
decline in the fortunes of the family, resulting eventually in their being
utterly dispossessed. According to the *Book of Clanranald*, Gillebride
took refuge in Ireland:

Giolla Bride, son of Gill Adamnan, son of Solamh, and from him the Thanes of
Argyll, having been among his kindred in Ireland, that is from the Clan Colla –
which are the tribes of Macguire and Macmahon, it happened that this tribe
held a meeting and conference at Fermanagh, on the estate of Macguire, and
among the matters to be transacted was that Giolla Bride should get some estate
of his own country, since he had been in banishment from his inheritance by the
power of the Danes and Norwegians. When Giolla Bride saw a large host of
robust young people in the assembly and that they were favourable to himself,
the favour he asked of his friends was that so many persons as the adjacent fort
in the place could hold should be allowed to go to Scotland with him in the
hope that he might obtain possession of his own inheritance and portion
of it.

Giolla Bride proceeded with that party to Scotland, where they landed. They
made frequent onsets and attacks on their enemies during this time of trouble,
for their enemies were powerful and numerous at that time. All the islands from
Man to the Orkneys were in the possession of the Danes, and such of the gael
whose lands as remained were protecting themselves in the woods and mountains. And at the end of that time Giolla Bride had a good son, who had come to
maturity and renown.[48]

The expedition must have failed since, in about 1130, Gillebride and
Somerled were reduced to living in 'a not very capacious cave' in
Morvern with neither followers nor apparent prospects.

At this time, the lands of Morvern and Ardgour were occupied by
people of the Clan MacInnes and their cousins the MacGilvrays who
had been suffering under continual attacks both by reivers from
Lochaber and bands of marauding Danes. In one such attack their chief
had been killed, and when another large force of Norsemen landed and
started to pillage the country, they gathered to elect a new warleader.
Internal rivalries and dissensions prevented them, however, from
choosing a member of their own kindred, and one of the elders proposed
that they should ask Somerled whom they knew to have taken refuge in

Morvern, and who, as the descendant of Clan Colla would be accepted by the warriors.

Accordingly they sent a deputation to Gillebride's cave, and subsequently found Somerled fishing in the Gear-Abhain – a little river that flows into Loch Aline – by tradition somewhere near to the present bridge at Claggan. Having convinced him that their intention was not hostile, they were eventually able to approach and speak their errand. According to the story, Somerled was preoccupied with a particularly fine salmon which was lying in the pool, and replied that if he caught this fish he would take it as a favourable omen and so agree. He duly hooked, played, and landed the salmon (which is now commemorated in the heraldic arms of Macdonald of Sleat), but said that he had to carry it back to Gillebride at the cave, and would join the muster on the following day. He ordered that an unusually large number of campfires should be lit during the night – presumably to indicate the presence of a big warband.

The next morning Somerled met the assembled warriors of Clan Innes at the spear-stone and agreed to lead them provided that they swore an oath of obedience to follow his command. When this oath was given, he marched his small force through the hills to where the raiders were camped in the vicinity of their ships. On scouting the enemy position, however, Somerled realised that his band was heavily outnumbered, and seeing a herd of cattle grazing nearby, he ordered that each warrior should kill a cow and skin it. He then had his men march several times around a small hill in view of the Norsemen – the first time wearing their own clothes and armour, then reappearing wearing the cow-skins with the hair side outwards, and a third time with the hair inwards – so as to convince the enemy that a large force had come against them.

The ruse succeeded, and as the Norsemen gathered round their ships and began to re-embark, Somerled led the Clan Innes onto the shore in a furious charge that threw the Danes into panic:

Withal he exhorted his warriors to be of good courage and to do as they would see him do, so they led on the charge. The first whom Somerled slew he ript up and took out his heart, desiring the rest to do the same, because the Danes were not christians ... So the Danes were put to flight and many of them were lost in the sea endeavouring to gain their ships.[49]

Others were pursued inland as the slaughter continued along the shore and northwards beyond the River Sheil. 'Two of the leaders, Boradill and Lundy, were slain in adjoining corries, which still bear their names, and another, Stangadill, was so closely pursued that to escape the sword he leapt into a boiling linn which is still known as *Eass Stangadill*.' And so the Norsemen were driven out of Morvern.

Possibly, the fight took place on the shore of Loch Sunart, but apart perhaps from Glen Borrowdale, a modern map contains no obvious recollection. Strangely, Somerled the warrior was never the subject of a panegyric bard song, and the principal accounts of his life are contained in the writings of the two Clan Donald seannachies: MacVurich's *Red and Black Books of Clanranald*, and the *History of the Macdonalds* composed by the Sleat historian Hugh Macdonald during the reign of Charles II. The story of this early battle is also drawn in part from a record of local traditions in Morvern 'handed down with great minuteness' and collected by the minister of the parish in 1846. In those days, when the oral tradition was still familiar, Morvern people might have identified the cave of Gillebride, or named the corries where Boradill and Lundy fell: but such things are forgotten now. The oral traditions have been slowly dying these hundred years. The old memory has faded, and the trail has grown cold.

After this successful beginning, Somerled embarked on the reconquest of his ancestral patrimony in old Dalriada, and by dint of allying himself with some clans and driving out others, he regained his mainland possessions and assumed the title of *Regulus* (Ruler or Thane) of Argyll. Thus established, he turned his attention to the southern isles which were under the dominion of King Olaf of Man, and began by setting his heart and ambition on marrying Olaf's daughter, Ragnhilda.

Olaf, who probably viewed this new concentration of power in Lorne and Argyll as an unwelcome development likely to threaten his own island hegemony, reacted unfavourably to Somerled's proposal, and the winning of Ragnhilda, as recorded by the Sleat historian, is another picturesque episode in Somerled's early career.

It chanced that Olaf of Man on his way north to raid in Skye, had anchored in Sanna Bay at the point of Ardnamurchan – probably to demand the galley service of the local chiefs. Approaching from the landward, Somerled hailed him at a distance and offered to assist the expedition on condition that Olaf agreed to grant him Ragnhilda's hand in marriage. Olaf refused and demanded Somerled's galley service as of right, whereupon the Thane of Argyll apparently submitted and joined the king with two galleys. However, during the night a shipwright called Maurice MacNeil, who was Olaf's foster-brother and also a close friend of Somerled, swam under the king's ship and bored a series of holes through the hull, sealing them with a mixture of tallow and butter. The next day, when the fleet entered open water, the pitching of the waves washed away the tallow, and Olaf's ship began to leak badly. When the galley seemed likely to sink, Olaf appealed to Somerled for help, but he refused to come to the rescue until the king agreed on oath to his marriage with Ragnhilda. Maurice MacNeil then boarded Olaf's vessel and plugged the holes with wooden pins which he had prepared for this purpose. 'From that time the posterity of Maurice are called MacIntyres (or "shipwrights' sons") to this day.'[50]

The matter of the marriage being agreed, the expedition proceeded to Skye and dealt violent justice to the chieftains of that island. 'Olaf and Somerled killed Maclier who possessed Strath within the Isles of Skye. They killed Godfrey Dhu or "the Black" by putting out his eyes, which was done by the hermit MacPoke, because Godfrey Dhu had killed his father formerly. Olaf, surnamed the Red, killed Macnicoll in North Uist likewise.'[51]

Somerled married Ragnhilda in 1140. But his policy in the Isles was not simply confined to a dynastic marriage. Since the early days of Dalriada, control over the Western Isles had depended on sea power, and throughout the Viking period for the defence of their extensive dominion, the kings of Man and the Isles had employed the war fleets which Norway required from all the tribute countries. In post-Dalriadic times the sea-muster of the Hebrides is not known, but the Isle of Man itself furnished crews for about sixteen large *skutas* of forty oars, or twenty-four galleys rowing twenty-six oars – the smallest ships accepted for war service. Norse power was based on the dragon-prowed long-ships which overmatched the traditional Celtic *birlinns* and ensured supremacy on the sea-ways. Somerled now began secretly to construct a new fleet of ships, smaller than the Viking *skutas*, but with two specific technical improvements which gave them a battle superiority over the conventional longships. Whereas the Viking *skutas* were steered by an oar called the 'steerboard' on the right-hand (or 'starboard') side of the vessel, attached to a tiller which passed across the stern, Somerled's new galleys had a hinged rudder to give greater manoeuvrability in a sea engagement, while a fighting-top at the mast-head for archers and slingers gave an advantage in fire power above the exposed decks and frail hulls of the longships.[52]

These new galleys were called *nyvaigs* ('little ships'), and as they proved effective Somerled rapidly expanded his fleet. In 1140 he had supplied only two galleys for Olaf's expedition. By 1158 he had fifty-three ships, and in his last campaign in 1164 he raised a fleet of one hundred and sixty galleys altogether. The *nyvaig* fleet was based at Lagavulin Bay on the southern coast of Islay where Somerled's grand-son Donald built the stronghold of Dunyveg (the Dun of the little ships). Somerled's own principal fortress was at Casteall Claidh (the Castle of the Trench) built in about 1154 on Fraoch Island overlooking the Sound of Islay (and recorded as the first castle in the Hebrides to follow the square design of the Norman keep).

This extension of sea power enabled Somerled to consolidate his hold over his island possessions, and eventually to intervene in the affairs of Man itself. In 1153 Olaf the Red was assassinated by two of his nephews at a time when Godred, the eldest son by his first wife, was absent in Norway. Godred returned to Man and promptly executed his father's murderers, thereafter establishing his authority and embarking on a series of raids against Ireland in the old pirate tradition. However, when Godred 'saw his kingdom established and that none could oppose him, he began to impose tyranny against his chiefs', disinheriting some and antagonising the rest to the extent that one of their number called Thorfinn son of Ottar went to Somerled and offered to make his son Dugall, king over the Isles: 'Hearing this, Somerled rejoiced greatly, and gave to him his son Dugall; and Thorfinn took him and conducted him through all the islands; and made them all subject to him, receiving hostages for each.'[53]

Word of this conspiracy soon reached Godred of Man who was 'dismayed in his mind' and promptly announced the sea muster. Somerled, with eighty galleys, intercepted the Manxmen off the west coast of Islay, and on Epiphany, 6 January 1156, there was a great sea battle – the fight continuing through the night, until dawn revealed the Norse fleet broken but the Gaelic force too badly mauled to follow up their victory. Godred and Somerled agreed terms of peace. According to the *Chronicle of Man*:

they divided the kingdom of the islands between them, and the kingdom became bipartite from that day to the present time. And this was the cause of the downfall of the kingdom of the islands, from the time when Somerled's sons took possession of it.

By this treaty, Godred retained the Isle of Man and all the Hebrides to the north of Ardnamurchan, but Somerled gained all the islands south of Ardnamurchan, including the rich peninsula of Kintyre.

The peace did not last, however, and two years later Somerled took fifty-three *nyvaigs* to the Isle of Man and displaced Godred, who fled to Norway. The Gaels devastated the island, massacring many of the inhabitants and even violating the religious sanctuaries. Norse, or Gael, warfare inflicted a similar desolation in a violent age of rapine and pillage – gilded always by stories of loyalty or heroism, but echoing to the clash of arms, the crackle of flames on burning thatch, and the sound of keening women. Somerled now held Man by conquest, and all the southern islands – Mull, Coll, Tiree, Colonsay, Islay, Gigha, and the lesser isles, as well as Kintyre, Knapdale, Lorne, and the old heartland of Argyll itself. He adopted the style of *Rex insularum*: it was a far cry from the small cave on the shore of Morvern.

While Somerled held the southern isles under the suzerainty of the king of Norway (to whom he and his successors paid tribute), the status of his mainland possessions was uncertain. Since the earliest days of Dalriada, the coastlands of the Gael had been protected from encroachment by the great barrier of the *Druim Alban* – a range of mountains and a debatable land of forest, moor and bog, that formed a natural defence along the ill-defined eastern frontier of Argyll. Although small bands slipped through Brander and raided down the old war-trails into Atholl, encumbered armies would not attempt that wilderness. Land access was by the established routes – north up the Great Glen to Moray and the ancient kingdom of the Picts, or south by the Firth of Clyde to Dumbarton and the land of the northern Britons. As in Dalriadic days, these were the vulnerable borders, with gateways to the east and the disputed grounds which had to be guarded by garrison or treaty: but with the difference that Somerled's neighbour was the growing, and increasingly coherent, Kingdom of Scotland.

Since the time of Malcolm Canmore, slayer of Macbeth, the remoteness of the western Gaels had become something more than the simple isolation of geography. Malcolm had been brought up in England and had grown attached to Saxon ways. After his accession, he encouraged the immigration of Saxon foreigners, and in the course of raiding into Durham and Northumberland he carried back prisoners whom he settled in various parts of the kingdom. As recorded earlier this policy was greatly accelerated after his marriage to St Margaret. The Norman conquest produced a steady influx of Saxon refugees – to be followed shortly by Normans themselves, riding north by invitation or in the hope of bettering their fortunes – landless knights and younger sons who had heard that the scavenging was good beyond the border. Malcolm forsook tradition by establishing a new capital at Dunfermline in the old Pictish province of Fife, and although the old moot hill and the crowning stone remained at Scone, the abbey which he built became the preferred burying place of successive Scottish Kings. Macbeth and Lulach were the last to be taken to Iona. Queen Margaret, in particular, was responsible for much of the social and religious reform which was inflicted on the Celtic population. The ancient language of the court was abandoned; manners and institutions brought into conformity with English or continental models. Foreigners were given land, or, more confusing to the Gaels, rights over land, and places of influence in the new Baron Court. Preference was given to Saxons, Hungarians, and Norman adventurers – to the gradual alienation of the Gaels.

These changes caused offence – particularly in a race wedded to tradition and claims of ancestry. The Gaels resented the pious contempt directed at their Church, the abandoning of custom, the dismissal of their culture. But the changes were backed by an increasingly efficient feudal organisation led by heavily armoured horse-knights (that other foreign innovation) and Celtic resistance was savagely put down and crushed.

Macbeth was the last of the Celtic kings of Scotland – in the proper sense of the word – but since he had an ancient claim to Lorne, he was probably no friend to the House of Argyll. As previously recorded, when Malcolm Canmore died, his brother Donald Bane seized the throne by Celtic right and issued a sentence of banishment against all foreigners, so that the Saxon importation temporarily ceased. But Donald Bane was driven off the throne by another English army, and the sons of Malcolm Canmore were southern-schooled and continued to develop the feudal order.

There is some evidence to suggest that Gillebride of the cave had supported Donald Bane, and some of his misfortune may have stemmed from this Celtic defeat. Somerled himself appears to have pursued a deliberate Celtic policy – which inevitably brought him into conflict with the Scottish king. During the early period of Somerled's rule over the Isles, this was David I (1124–1153, see p.145), a strong king whose succession to his brother Alexander I (1107–1124) satisfied both feudal law and Celtic custom, but whose reign was disturbed by two rebellions, in one of which Somerled took an active part.

The first revolt was led by the adventurer monk Wimund, an unusually large man who was born in Skye, and after a doubtfully religious career became the Bishop of Man. Not satisfied with the rank of episcopal office, he advanced a spurious claim to be the dispossessed son of the rightful Earl of Moray and deceived a number of discontented Celts into supporting his cause:

He made incursions into the provinces of Scotland, harrying everything with rapine and slaughter. And when the royal army was sent against him he retired into remoter passes, or fled back to the ocean, and escaped all the preparations of war; and when the army had returned broke out again from his hiding places to molest the provinces.

Wimund eventually took possession of the region around the monastery of Furness – which satisfied his greed for a time, but also brought about his downfall:

But while Wimund was borne in glory like a king surrounded by an army through the province which had been made subject to him, and was severe beyond measure with the very monastery where he had been a monk, certain provincials who were galled by his power or by his insolence laid a trap for him with the consent of the nobles. And finding a favourable opportunity when Wimund had sent the host on to their quarters, and was following them at an easy pace with only a small escort, they seized and bound him and put out each of his eyes (since each was wicked) – and with mutilation emasculated him, for the peace of the Kingdom of Scots, not for the sake of the Kingdom of Heaven.[54]

More serious was the rebellion, at the same time, of Malcolm MacEth – since his claim was a legitimate one, and Somerled was deeply implicated.

In the time of early Dalriada, following the wars between Gabhran and Lorne, the descendants of Ferchar the Tall had emigrated up the Great Glen into Moray ('the sea settlement'), where as *Mormaers* they kept alive the old aspirations of Lorne – which were later represented, not least, in the person of Macbeth. To strengthen his claim, Macbeth married the Princess Gruach who was the heiress of the royal line of

King Duff (died 962) and through whom he also had pretension to the Duff lands in Fife. By a previous marriage, Gruach had a son called Lulach the Fool, later murdered by Malcolm Canmore, who also left two children: a son, Maelsnechtan, who was the last 'King of Moray' and died in 1058, and a daughter who married Aedh, the Bishop of Dunkeld and brother to Alexander I and David I. In 1130 Aedh's sons, Angus of Moray and Malcolm MacAedh (MacEth) rebelled against the king their uncle, but were defeated by Norman mercenaries brought from England, and in the battle Angus was killed.

Malcolm MacEth continued the struggle alone, receiving substantial support from the western Gaels, among them Somerled, with whom he made a formal alliance by marrying his sister. The rebellion collapsed in 1134 when Malcolm was captured in Galloway and imprisoned by David I at Roxburgh Castle. Somerled, however, maintained his support for Malcolm's sons until the eldest, Donald MacEth was also captured in 1156, and a settlement was agreed whereby Malcolm MacEth became reconciled to the new king Malcolm IV and was granted the title of Earl of Ross (the lands of northern Moray). In 1163 Malcolm IV attempted to dispossess him in favour of the Count of Holland (the king's brother-in-law) since many Flemings were settling in that region. Large numbers of the inhabitants of Moray were forcibly evicted and transported 'beyond the mountains of Scotland' – that is, into Strathnaver, where their descendants, the Clan Mackay, established themselves during the thirteenth century. Malcolm MacEth died in 1168. His grandson Kenneth made a further attempt to gain the crown following the succession of Alexander II in 1214, but was beheaded by his neighbour Ferchar Macantagart, who afterwards himself became Earl of Ross.

Another family of claimants to the throne whose rebellions, with Gaelic support, disturbed this period of Scottish history, were the MacWilliam who were descended from King Duncan II (killed in 1094). The MacWilliam claimants were princes appanaged in Lochaber and Badenoch (then provinces of Moray), and were supported by the MacMartins from Loch Lochy (from whom the Clan Cameron have partial descent). Their revolt was unsuccessful. At the close of the twelfth century, Donald Bane MacWilliam was slain by William the Lion in a battle outside Inverness. In 1230 his successor Gillescop MacWilliam was also defeated and killed by Alexander II, and the whole family were hunted down and murdered – including the last MacWilliam's infant daughter who was barbarously executed and her brains dashed out against the Market Cross in Forfar.

In 1153, David I died, to be succeeded by his grandson Malcolm IV – called 'the Maiden' – who was still a child. Somerled's intervention in the MacEth rebellion, and his growing power in Argyll and Lorne, had excited the envy of the lowland nobility. Malcolm was much under the influence of his Norman councillors whose greedy eyes saw profitable opportunity in the dismemberment of Somerled's dominion and a new sheriffdom in Lorne. They therefore persuaded the young king that the Gaelic power had to be crushed if Malcolm was to gain control over the mainland territories of Argyll, and an army under Gilchrist, Thane of Angus, was sent into the west to bring the Gaelic coastland under the crown. Gilchrist began to lay waste the country:

> ... but Somerled, making all speed in raising his vassals and followers went after them; and joining battle, they fought fiercely on both sides with great slaughter until night parted them. Two thousand on Somerled's side and seven thousand on Gilchrist's side were slain in the field. Being wearied, they parted and marched off at the dawn of day, turning their backs to one another.[55]

After the failure of this invasion, Somerled and Malcolm reached an agreement which restored the peace between them. The terms included the release of Malcolm and Donald MacEth from Roxburgh Castle, and the restitution of their lands in northern Moray. This treaty was considered to be of such consequence that certain of Malcolm's charters were dated by it, as ' . . . on the next Xmas day after the treaty between the King and Somerled'.

But the peace lasted only five years. Even after Malcolm attained his majority, 'the nobles were still in his ears, desiring him to suppress the power of Somerled, hoping if he should be crushed, they might get his estate to be divided among themselves, and at least get him expelled from the country'. In 1164, on learning that another invasion of Argyll was planned, Somerled 'resolved to lose all or possess all he had in the Highlands', and with a great fleet of a hundred and sixty galleys, sailed up the Clyde to Greenock where he landed and advanced up the Southern shore towards the Scottish army which had leaguered at Renfrew.

Although it was put about that Somerled's intention was to invade southern Scotland, Malcolm was reluctant to offer battle, and sent

Walter Fitz-Alan, Baron of Renfrew and Steward of Scotland, to negotiate terms. At the time of this meeting with Somerled, this ancestor of the Stewarts was developing an acquisitive interest in Arran and Bute.

Malcolm declared that he would not molest Somerled for the Isles since they were properly his wife's right, but he demanded the immediate 'restoration' of all the lands of Argyll and Kintyre. Somerled's response as recorded (and no doubt embellished) by the Sleat historian, encompassed the claim which would be echoed by his descendants and the Lords of the Isles for as long as their power and independence lasted, or the memory remained – asserting that he was more than a mere subject or feudal liegeman of the Scottish king:

Somerled replied that he had as good a right to the lands upon the mainland as he had to the Isles. As to the Isles, he had an undoubted right to them, his predecessors being possessed of them by the goodwill and consent of Eugenius the First, for obligations conferred on him: That, when his forefathers were dispossessed of them by the invasion of the Danes, they had no assistance to defend or recover them from the Scottish king, and that he had his right of them from the Danes: but, however, he would render assistance to the king in any other affairs, and would prove as loyal as any of his nearest friends, but as long as he breathed, he would not condescend to resign any of his rights which he possessed to any; and that he was resolved to lose or keep all, and that he thought himself as worthy of his own as any about the king's court.[56]

This message was conveyed to Malcolm, who still hesitated to give battle, having, it is said, no animosity towards Somerled – 'but as the most kings are commonly led by their councillors, the king himself being young, they contrived Somerled's death in another manner'.[57]

By some means they suborned Somerled's nephew and page, called Maurice Macneil, who crossed the river in a small boat to the Gaels' camp which was at the confluence of the River Paisley and the Clyde. He was welcomed and invited to Somerled's tent, where sometime during the night, he stabbed Somerled and his son Gilliecolum to death and escaped in the darkness. Somerled's body was discovered in the morning, and the Gaels, on learning of their leader's murder, became confused – as was their weakness – and deserted the camp to return to their galleys at Greenock, leaving the corpse where it lay.

Malcolm and his men came later in the day to view the body, and one of the escort kicked it. Upon this, the murderer Macneil, conscience-stricken at what he had accomplished and the contempt thus displayed, stabbed that man as well, and escaped by swimming across the river. Malcolm subsequently pardoned him.

The king himself confessed to a certain remorse – and had Somerled's body carried to Iona for burial. Later tradition, perhaps mistaken, holds that he was interred at Saddell Abbey which he is said to have founded. But Iona was the burial place of the Dalriadic kings, and Malcolm's gesture may have been posthumous acknowledgement of his claim to the Isles.

A sepulchre on Iona was Somerled's final right. The Gaelic revival was his achievement. The quarrel with Scotland would be his legacy.

CHAPTER 12

The Sons of Somerled

Thy fair fresh cheek thou hast bathed;
In thine eye is blue beam soft as summer showers;
Over the locks of thy hair, O descendant of Fergus
The wind of paradise has breathed.
O man of the white steed,
O man of the black swan,
The fierce band and the gentle mood,
The sharp blade and the lasting flame.

Descendant of Conn, and descendant of Cormac;
Thou with the speckled ship of ships;
Pursue thy raids on a worthy steed,
For a foolish steed carries one away.
'Eamhain of the Apples': on Ranald mac Somerled, trans. W. F. Skene

According to the custom which then prevailed in the Isles, Somerled's lands were 'gavelled' equally among his surviving sons. By Ragnhilda he had four sons with title to the Isles: Ranald, Dugall, Angus, and Olaf (who may have died young since his life is not otherwise recorded), and a daughter, Beathag – or Beatrice. However, he also had children by at least one other previous marriage, notably Somerled (the Younger) and Gilliecolum, and two natural sons – Gillies, got by a woman of the Bissets from the Glens of Antrim, and Gall ('the Foreigner') MacSgillin by a Lowland woman. These early unions may have been 'handfast' marriages – a common practice in medieval Scotland, whereby the couple clasped hands through a monolith and declared themselves married in front of witnesses. Such marriages were valid for one year, although if the woman became pregnant they were usually confirmed by a proper ceremony and the children regarded as legitimate. Nevertheless, the practice often resulted in quarrels or confusion later, and genealogists have disagreed over the seniority (and even the parentage) of Somerled's several heirs.

In the apportionment of lands, only Somerled's children by Ragn-hilda, through their mother (a daughter of the King of Man), had claim to the possessions in the Isles. Ranald, as the ancestor of Clan Donald, is generally taken to be the senior, although a similar claim has been of Dugall by the MacDougall genealogists. There was no great amity among the brothers. A quarrel over the possession of Mull would persist for generations, and this family division was to have significant consequences later. Somerled's descendants by his earlier handfast marriages were restricted to a mainland inheritance, and their careers shortlived but occasionally troublesome. Gilliecolum was probably assassinated with Somerled at Renfrew in 1164. The bastard son Gillies inherited some land in Kintyre and lapsed into insignificance until a generation later his daughter married Donald son of Ranald son of Somerled.

Somerled the Younger aspired to the title of Thane of Argyll and claimed lands in Morvern and possibly Glassary – in opposition to the sons of Ragnhilda whose mainland portion he also coveted, and with whom his relations were seldom cordial. Unwisely, he began reiving into the debatable lands of Cowal and the Lennox on the flimsy excuse that the people of these regions were harassing Argyll. When they com-plained to the King of Scots, an army under the Earl of March was sent to subdue the young Somerled, who was forced to treat. According to the Sleat account, he told March 'at a private conference, that since he lost his affection for his brethren, by seizing on those lands which his father left them, he could not stand out against both the King of Scots and them' – and therefore preferred to seek the king's pardon, which he duly obtained. He died shortly after, leaving a boy, John (or Ewen) who was taken into tutelage by his uncle, Ranald mac Somerled.

Ranald was at that time in dispute with his brother Dugall over the possession of Mull, and this young John took it upon himself to exacerbate the feud by murdering Dugall's supporter Muchdanach, Chief of Ardnamurchan and Moidart, by whose daughter Dugall 'had most of his children'. Ranald, by contrast a peaceable man, became 'very wrath' at this, and even contemplated executing him, but 'John said that he would ask no more of his father's but the lands of Ardnamurchan and Glassary in Argyll, and twenty pounds land in Islay, which Ranald granted.'[58] John then disappears from the history and his descendants possibly merged with the later MacIains of Ardnamurchan. Somerled the Younger also left a second son called Maolmory who went to seek his fortune in Ireland, and caused no trouble in the Isles.

The surviving sons of Ragnhilda – Ranald, Dugall, and Angus – divided the bulk of Somerled's possessions between themselves. Angus, the youngest, received a scattered patrimony comprising the 'rough bounds' of Garmoran – Moidart, Morar, Knoydart, and Arisaig, to the north of Ardnamurchan, and also the islands of Arran and Bute. In 1192 he quarrelled with Ranald and defeated him in a battle, but in 1210 he was himself killed together with his three sons by the Norsemen of Skye who had invaded Moidart. His possessions were seized by Ranald's descendants, although his eldest son James had left an heiress, Jane, who married Alexander, son of Walter Fitz-Alan the Steward. Through her the Stewarts prosecuted a claim to Arran and Bute – which they eventually obtained after some resistance. Walter, son of Jane and Alexander, was sixth High Steward and married Marjory, daughter of the Bruce, and their son in turn became Robert II, the first of the Stewart Kings of Scotland.

Dugall inherited Lorne (from the head of Loch Leven to Asknish on Loch Fyne) with the strongholds of Dunollie and Dunstaffnage, the islands of Jura, Coll, and Tiree, and a disputed claim to Mull. The descendants of Dugall styled themselves 'de Ergadia' (of Argyll) with the title of 'king' after the Norse fashion (so that in this period there were several 'Kings of the Isles'). Of his three sons, Duncan de Lorn, Dugall Scrag, and Ospak Hakon, the last two were killed or dispossessed during the Norwegian raids in 1230. Duncan de Ergalite (Argyll) was among the nobles who signed a letter and oath to the Pope on the Treaty of Ponteland in 1244, but the family later contracted an alliance with the Comyns and suffered forfeiture under the Bruce. Dugall's descendants are later referred to as the MacDougalls of Lorne.

Ranald (or Reginald as he is sometimes called) inherited Kintyre and Islay (which were the principal centres of the Kingdom of the Isles), and all the other islands to the south of Ardnamurchan, but not the Isle of Man which reverted to a Norse king also called Ragnvald, who continued to claim overlordship of the northern islands of Lewis, Skye, and the Uists.

In strong contrast to the character and policy of his father, Ranald was a pacific and deeply religious man, and descriptions of his popularity in Scotland and Ireland may owe something to the religious bias of their authors. His principal achievements were the monastic foundations associated with his name – and in further contrast to Somerled's Gaelic preference, his piety was of the Roman sort.

During Malcolm Canmore's reign, the queen, St Margaret, had restored the abbey at Iona, but despite her contempt for the Celtic Church, she did not attempt its Romanisation at that time. Following the suppression of the culdees of Columban tradition by the later Scottish kings, it was nevertheless inevitable that pressure would be brought to bear on the Iona clergy to conform with the Roman usage, and in order to prevent this, during the last year of his life in 1164, Somerled had tried unsuccessfully to secure the appointment of a culdee abbot.

By the middle of the twelfth century, the buildings on Iona were again falling into ruin, and in addition to restoring the abbey church itself, Ranald founded a Benedictine community of Black Monks on the site of the early monastery. He also established a Benedictine convent and made his sister Beatrice the first Prioress – a foundation strangely inconsistent with the tradition of St Columba, who had expressly forbidden women to set foot on Iona:

Where there is a cow there is a woman,
And where there is a woman there is mischief

The deed of confirmation of the Benedictine monastery is dated December 1203, but there seems to have been some opposition to the introduction of the Roman Order, since in 1204 the *Annals of Ulster* record that Cellach (Celestine, the new Abbot of Iona)

built a monastery in the middle of the island, without any right and in dishonour of the community, thereby inflicting great damage on the place. When North Ireland heard of this, a party of Derry men came over, led by the Bishops of Tyrone and Tyrconnel and the Abbots of Armagh and Derry, and pulled down Cellach's building. Then the Abbot of Derry who was a lineal descendant of St Columba's brother Ewan was elected Abbot of Iona.[59]

Gaelic protest was thus shortlived.

The principal religious foundation associated with Ranald – although sometimes ascribed to Somerled – was the Cistercian Abbey of Saddell in Kintyre. Ranald is said to have made a pilgrimage to Rome and returned with consecrated dust which was scattered on the foundations, and to have lived there for three years during its building 'without coming under a roof'. He further endowed the monastery with the patronage of a number of parishes in Kintyre and Arran, and this example was followed by his son Donald and grandson Angus Mor who were also generous benefactors. Donald in particular was not a religious man, but having killed his uncle, brother-in-law, and an envoy of the king, probably had an especial need to atone:

He went to Rome, bringing seven priests in his company, to be reconciled to the Pope and Church. These priests declaring his remorse of conscience for the evil deeds of his former life, the Pope asked if he was willing to endure any torment that the Church was pleased to inflict upon him? Donald replied that he was willing should they please to boil him in a cauldron of lead. The Church seeing him so penitent dispensed with him.[60]

Saddell is a ruin, and the old cruciform church a confusion of tumbled stones. It ages slowly by the shore of Loch Fyne, and close to the castle of the same name. In what was once the choir, a recess contains a warrior's tomb – a sculpted figure in conical helmet and a skirted war-coat, clasping a great, two-handed sword. Some would say that this is the sepulchre of Somerled but the church was not completed until 1256, nearly a hundred years after his death. More likely it is another, unknown Gaelic warrior, who is sleeping there.

Rather more unusual was the connection of Ranald and his successors with the monastery of Paisley, since this lay outside the territory of the Isles. It was a Cluniac foundation, the offshoot of Wenlock Abbey, established in the North by Walter Fitz-Alan in commemoration of his Shropshire origin and dedicated to St Milburga of Wenlock, St James, and St Merrin of Ireland. Sometime before 1200, Ranald became a brother of the order and 'granted to the monastery eight cows and two pennies for one year, and one penny in perpetuity for every house on his territory from which smoke issued, and his peace and protection whithersoever the monks should go'. His wife, Fiona, also became a sister of the convent and granted to the monks a tithe on all her goods 'whether in her own possession or sent for sale by land or sea'. These endowments were confirmed by Ranald's successors.[61]

Ranald married Fiona, daughter of the Earl of Moray, by whom he had three sons – Donald, who gave his name to the clan; Ruairi, who founded the collateral clan of that name; and Angus, whose life is not a matter of authentic record. Ranald styled himself '*Reginaldus Rex*

Insularum Dominus de Argile', and his great seal on the charter of Paisley Abbey is described as having on the one side the Galley of the Isles, and on the obverse the figure of an armed man on horseback with a drawn sword in his hand. His successors struck similar seals to transact their business, and as heraldry and the devices of coat armour were adopted in the Highlands, the Clan Donald took the Black Galley of the Norse Kings of Man and the Isles as the emblem of their house. The Lords of the Isles bore the Galley alone and later added to it the Eagle of the Earls of Ross, while branches of the Clan Donald and other western clans who claimed descent from the Norse kings of Man bore it quartered on their arms.

A reflection on the sons of Somerled was that during this first generation they were rarely united – a situation which would have worked greatly to their disadvantage had Malcolm IV pressed the claims which he had made at Renfrew. But Malcolm the Maiden died in 1165 at the age of twenty-five, his death foretold by storms and comets, and the crown passed to William I called 'The Lion' after the device embroidered on his battle-standard. A man of warlike ambition but indifferent ability, he regained the northern regions of Scotland from the Earldom of Orkney (1196) and sold a large portion of Caithness to Ranald, but the chief preoccupation of his early years was to conquer the provinces of Cumbria and Northumberland, promised but never ceded by the English king. He invaded Northumbria, where the atrocities committed by his army earned for Scottish soldiery a sinister reputation and dubious renown, but after an unsuccessful attack on Carlisle he was captured outside Alnwick and carried prisoner to England – a useful windfall for Henry II who had recently murdered Becket and was smarting from the penance. The Plantagenet leopard caged the Scottish lion in France while English armies seized the strongholds of Berwick, Jedburgh, Roxburgh, and Edinburgh, and wasted through the Lowlands. The price of freedom was homage, and in 1174 William the Lion swore to hold Scotland as Henry's vassal – a servitude which he endured for fifteen years. Only the Scottish Church resisted, and by the Papal Bull of 1192, retained its independence.

With twenty Scottish barons hostage in England, and faced with rebellions in Moray and Galloway, William had neither the means nor inclination to undertake any military adventures in Argyll and the Isles. He did, however, pursue a policy begun – or at least attempted – by his predecessors of designating sheriffdoms, and granting rights and jurisdiction over lands in the west. The Earl of Atholl and the Abbot of Glendochart were made responsible for administering the law in Argyll, while the Earl of Menteith had jurisdiction in Kintyre (which actually belonged to Norway) and Cowal. Such measures were largely ineffective, but foreshadowed a later confusion.

After Henry II's death and Richard I's disinterest, William conducted a prolonged and tortuous negotiation with King John, which resulted in a large payment and a doubtful conclusion. He died in 1214, bequeathing a troubled kingdom to his son Alexander II, and the Lion Rampant to posterity. His successors were of sterner disposition, and in the reigns of Alexander II and Alexander III, the lands of Argyll and the islands came under increasing pressure as the Scottish kings fought to obtain the submission of Ranald's successors and challenged the sovereignty of the kings of Norway – who had now also decided to reassert their authority in the Hebrides.

CHAPTER 13

Donald of Islay and Angus Mor

These runes the man wrote
Who is the most rune-skilled west-over-sea,
With that axe that Gauk owned –
Trandil's son from the South country.

Ranald died in 1207 and was buried at Iona. His eldest son, Donald, inherited Islay, southern Kintyre, and the South Isles, while after the death of Angus mac Somerled in 1210, the lands of Garmoran – from Ardnamurchan to Glenelg – were taken by the second son, Ruairi, who also acquired a disputed claim to Arran and Bute. In addition, Ruairi possessed some estates in northern Kintyre and Ugadale.

The name Donald was Gaelic *Dhomhuill* (world-ruler), and the later Lords of the Isles, descended from this eldest son of Ranald mac Somerled, bore the Gaelic style of *Mac Dhomhuill* – 'the son of Donald' as the use of patronymics distinguished between the different western clans. However, Macdonald as a common surname did not come into use until the sixteenth century, although from an early period a member of the family might be referred to as one of the *Dhomhnullach* – of the Clan Donald. Donald and his immediate descendants called themselves *de insulis*, that is 'of the Isles'.

In contrast to their father Ranald, who had the reputation of being a man of peace, Donald and Ruairi inherited the warlike and predatory attributes of Somerled and their Norse ancestors, and in 1211, in alliance with Thomas of Galloway, they raided Ireland with a great fleet of seventy-six galleys to plunder the town of Derry and the peninsula of Innisowen. The following year Ruairi and Thomas of Galloway made a second raid and pillaged the churches of the province – for which, after a wild and turbulent career, Ruairi subsequently made retribution.

Donald married the daughter of Gillies mac Somerled, but some years later he quarrelled with his father-in-law, killing Gillies' son

Callum Alin, and inciting the MacNeils of Lennox to expel him from Kintyre. Gillies escaped to Ireland 'where some of his offspring remain until this day'. Some accounts state that Donald made a second marriage to a daughter of Walter the Steward, although this may be doubtful in view of his brother Ruairi's feud with the Stewarts over Arran. Donald had two sons, Angus and Alasdair, and possibly a natural son called Murchad.

Together with his uncle Dugall mac Somerled, Donald took the precaution of visiting the court of Norway (which at that time was one kingdom with Denmark) 'whereby his own rights and the peculiar rights he had for the Isles by Olaf the Red's daughter were confirmed by King Magnus', and he returned with 'many of the ancient Danes of the Isles, namely the Macduffies . . . ' whom he settled in Colonsay and Oronsay as his vassals in those islands. The Macduffies (whose name meant 'son of the black peace') established themselves in the stronghold of Dun Evan – the old fortress of Earl Gilli – and later became the hereditary Keepers of the Records in the Lordship of the Isles. 'After this, Donald and Dugall became enemies,' states the old history, 'so that at last Donald was forced to kill Dugall.'[62] The quarrel was probably over the continuing dispute in Mull.

The need to confirm his Norwegian title to the islands may have been in response to growing pressure from the Scottish crown. In 1214, William the Lion was succeeded by Alexander II whose accession to the throne triggered fresh rebellions by the MacEth and MacWilliam claimants. These were crushed mercilessly by Ferchar Macantagart of Ross, but the support afforded the rebels by Donald and Ruairi (who may have given the Mackays refuge in Ugadale) prompted Alexander to reconsider the question of Norwegian sovereignty in Kintyre and the Isles. He sent as his envoy Sir William Rollock to demand that Donald should repudiate the king of Norway and acknowledge the sovereignty of the Scottish crown. Donald's reply, as recorded by the Sleat historian, was reminiscent of that given by Somerled to Malcolm IV:

. . . that his predecessors had their right to the Isles from the Crown of Norway, which was renewed by the present king thereof and that he held the Isles of his Majesty of Norway before he renounced his claim to his Majesty of Scotland.[63]

Sir William Rollock argued that the King of Scotland could (and would) grant the superiority of the Isles to whomever he pleased;

whereupon Donald retorted that, when it came to the point, Olaf the Red, from whom he had the Isles, had taken them by conquest, and therefore technically he owed allegiance to neither the King of Norway nor the King of Scotland (a claim which reflected more accurately his true opinion). No accommodation seemed possible, and 'being advised by wicked councillors', at dawn the next day Donald surprised and killed Sir William and most of his men.

Advised of this, and concerned for his frontier in Strathclyde, Alexander II decided to invade Argyll. In 1220 a seaborne expedition failed due to bad weather, but in the following year he mounted an extensive land campaign, expelling Ruairi from Arran and Bute, and driving another Somerled, son of Gilliecolum, out of Kintyre. A number of western chieftains apparently submitted (at least temporarily – as was their custom), and Alexander used the opportunity to confirm land titles on certain of his own nominees – among them Dufgallus son of Syfyn (possibly in the region of Castle Sween where the MacNeils had recently displaced Gillies), and more notably, a certain knight of Strathclyde descent called Colin Wry-mouth or 'Cam-beul', who married the heiress of Duncan mac Duibhne the Irish chieftain of Lochow, and built his castle of Innis Chonnel on an island in Loch Awe.

The peace of the Hebrides was thereafter disturbed by a civil war in the Isle of Man, which on Somerled's death had been repossessed by the sons of Godred the Black. Ragnvald Godredson, King of Man, had given the Isle of Lewis to his brother Olaf – who lived there 'a sorry life', unable to support his followers, and eventually rebelled. Possibly through the agency of Ranald mac Somerled (who favoured Ragnvald), Olaf was captured and handed for safe-keeping to William the Lion who imprisoned him for seven years. Following his campaign in the west, Alexander II released Olaf, and after a pilgrimage to the shrine of St James of Compostela he became reconciled with Ragnvald, marrying his sister-in-law, Lavon, 'daughter of a certain noble in Kintyre', – and once more settled peaceably in Lewis. No sooner had this truce been effected, however, than the Bishop of the Isles (who was Olaf's nephew) visited Lewis and pronounced the marriage null and void on the grounds of consanguinity (since Olaf had previously been married to Lavon's cousin). Olaf repudiated Lavon and married instead Christina, daughter of the redoubtable Ferchar Macantagart of Ross.

This insult to her sister so offended the wife of Ragnvald that she sent a message in her husband's name to their son Godfrey in Skye, ordering him to seize the Isle of Lewis and put Olaf to death. Godfrey invaded the island and caused great devastation, but Olaf, together with the Sheriff of Lewis called Paul Balkison, escaped to the mainland territory of Macantagart where they gathered a band of followers and planned revenge. Sailing to Skye, they hid 'in the remote places' of the island until they heard that Godfrey was staying with only a small escort at the lake settlement of St Columba. Paul and Olaf then dragged their galleys overland to the lake and attacked the island, killing many of the defenders and capturing Godfrey, who, against Olaf's wishes, was blinded and mutilated by Paul the Sheriff. Having taken hostages from the people of Skye, Olaf gathered a fleet of thirty-two ships and sailed to Man, where he forced Ragnvald to come to terms. The brothers agreed to divide the northern Hebrides – although Ragnvald was to retain the title of King. This second truce was broken by Ragnvald who sought help from Allan of Galloway to repossess Olaf's share, but the Manxmen supported Olaf, and Ragnvald was deposed and killed in the fighting which followed.

These events had caused 'a great dispeace in the Hebrides', and having received a large number of complaints from the chieftains of the region, King Hakon of Norway decided to reassert his authority over the Western Isles. Hearing also that 'the Kings of the Hebrides who were of Somerled's race were very unfaithful to him' (possibly on account of their dealings with Alexander II), he fitted out an expedition of twelve ships under the nominal command of Ospak Hakon, whom he intended to make 'Overlord' of Somerled's old territories in the Isles. This Ospak Hakon was the son of Dugall who had earlier gone to seek his fortune at the Norwegian court. He had since earned the reputation of a pirate, having mildly plundered Iona in 1209 – for which he had been severely admonished by the Norwegian bishops.

An advance force under Paul Balkison sailed to Skye where they fought the ancestors of the MacLeods. In a sea battle at Loch Dunvegan the Norse killed Thorkell Thormodson and two of his sons, but the third son Thormod escaped by jumping into a barrel which drifted to Scotland. Thorkell and Thormod are generally held to have been the descendants of Leod, a younger son of Olaf the Black from whom the MacLeods of Skye take their name.

Ospak Hakon sailed to the Sound of Islay where he was met by his brothers, Duncan of Lorne and Dugall Scrag, together with a cousin named Somerled (Gilliecolum's son), and 'a great company'. The islanders invited the Norsemen to a feast with plenty of strong wine, but the Norse suspected treachery and 'each side gathered their company together, for neither side trusted the other'. Duncan of Lorne slept aboard Ospak's galley – which was a fortunate precaution, since during the night the Norse suddenly attacked the Islesmen, slaying Somerled. and taking Dugall Scrag prisoner:

King Ospak was not at this, and when he became aware of it, he hastily got his brother Duncan away, but his brother Dugall he took under his own protection. Now they gathered a company over the islands, and got together eighty ships, and sailed south by the Mull of Kintyre and so east to Bute.[64]

This diversion was possibly instigated by Ruairi in pursuance of his dispute with the Stewarts who were at that time in possession of the island: 'The Scots sat there in a castle and a certain Steward was over the Scots. The Norwegians attacked the castle, but the Scots defended it, pouring down boiling pitch. The Norwegians hewed the wall with axes because it was soft . . .'[65] (presumably the fortifications were built of wood), and took it after three days' fighting. The fleet then raided Kintyre, but Ospak, who had been badly wounded during the siege, died there, and the Norse sailed on to Man where they reinstated Olaf. Apart from this, King Hakon achieved little by this expedition. On the death of Duncan mac Dugall he appointed King Ewen of Lorne, Duncan's son, as overlord of the Norwegian territories in the Hebrides.

Meanwhile, Alexander II 'was very covetous of dominion in the Hebrides and constantly sent men to Norway to demand purchase of the lands'. In 1249 he decided to seize the Isles by force, and gathering a large army, declared 'that he would not desist until he had set his standard on the cliffs of Thurso, and had reduced under himself all the provinces which the Norwegian monarch possessed to the westward of the Solunder sea'. In the summer he sailed to Kintyre and invited Ewen of Lorne to meet him under truce. Alexander demanded that Ewen should repudiate his allegiance to Hakon of Norway and surrender Cairnburgh Castle in the Treshnish Islands together with three other fortresses in return for 'a much larger dominion in Scotland', and the king's friendship. Ewen, however, declined to break his oaths to the King of Norway and fled to Lewis, while Alexander proceeded to the island of Kerrera off Oban, where according to the saga of Hakon, he had an ominous premonition:

When King Alexander lay in Kerrera Sound he dreamt a dream. He thought three men came to him. One seemed to him to be dressed in royal robes. That man was very unfriendly and ruddy of face and rather thick-set, and a man of middle height. The second seemed to him slim-built and young, of all men the fairest, and nobly dressed. The third was by far the tallest and most unfriendly looking of men; he was very bald on the forehead. He threw words at the King and asked if he meant to make way in the Southern Isles. Alexander thought he answered that of a surety he meant to lay the Isles under him. The dream-man bade him turn back; and said there were not two ways about it. The King tells his dream when he awoke, and most were eager that he should turn back, but he would not ... The South islanders say that those men who appeared to the King in slumber were these: King Olaf the Saint, King of Norway, and Saint Magnus of the Orkneys, and Saint Columba.'[66]

Shortly after arriving at Kerrera, Alexander (who had been in poor health for some time) was taken ill and died at Gylen Castle. His body was taken back to Melrose for burial and the expedition was abandoned. Ewen of Lorne seized this opportunity to invade and occupy the Isle of Man for himself, but at the command of Hakon, Donald and Ruairi (family ties notwithstanding) drove him out and forced him to confine his activities to Lorne. During Ruairi's absence on this foray the Stewarts repossessed themselves of Bute.

At about this time (1249) Donald of Islay either died or retired from active life, leaving his lands to his eldest son Angus Mor. (His second son, Alasdair, founded the Clan MacAlisters of Loup.) Towards the latter part of his life, Donald journeyed to Rome to obtain remission for his numerous sins, although he may have had an additional purpose in seeking support from the Church since the Sleat historian also commented that 'some affirm that he had his rights of the Pope for all the lands he possessed in Argyll, Kintyre, and the rest of the continent'. On his return he was a generous benefactor to the monasteries of Saddell and Iona, and like his father Ranald, he may have joined the brotherhood of Paisley. He died at Skipness and was buried at Iona.

During the long minority which followed the death of Alexander II, the Isles were unmolested by the Scottish crown, but in 1260 the young and vigorous Alexander III revived his father's ambition to secure the overlordship of the Hebrides. He sent fresh envoys to Bergen offering to buy the islands, but with an implicit threat that what he could not purchase with silver he might more readily take by conquest. Hakon of Norway, by now grown old and irritable, referred him to the treaty between Magnus Barelegs and Malcolm Canmore and bluntly refused to sell the Norwegian territories in the Hebrides.

In 1261 Macantagart of Ross made a ferocious raid upon Skye, and the kings in the Hebrides sent Ruairi to Norway with letters of complaint:

And they brought forward much about the dispeace that the Earl of Ross and other Scots had made in the Hebrides, when they went out to Skye, and burned down a town and churches, and slew very many peasant men and women. And they said also that the Scots had taken the little children, and laid them on their spear-points, and shook their spears until they brought the children down to their hands, and so threw them away dead. They said also that the Scottish king intended to lay under himself all the Hebrides.

And when Hakon learned these tidings, they caused him great concern; and he brought the case before his Council. And whatever each said about it, King Hakon had levying rights sent out in the winter, after Yule, throughout all Norway, and called out a levy both of men and stores, the most that he thought the land could provide.'[67]

While Hakon recruited pilots in Shetland, Ruairi sent messages from Norway to his sons Dugall and Allan, who saw in this enterprise an opportunity of recovering the MacRuairi lands in Arran and Bute. In order to pre-empt any Scottish attack on the Isles, they spread the rumour that forty galleys were already on their way to Hebridean waters. In Scotland there was widespread alarm, and the castles of Stirling and Ayr were put in readiness for defence.

The expedition left Norway in July, encountering fair weather, and after pausing at the Orkneys and Shetland, sailed south through the Kyle of Lochalsh and the Sound of Mull to anchor off Kerrera. King Hakon was there joined by King Magnus of Man and Ruairi's two sons, whom he appointed to command divisions of the fleet. But Ewen of Lorne and Angus Mor, whose support Hakon expected, failed to attend the muster and not liking Norwegian expressions of overlordship any more than Scottish ones, chose to prevaricate. Hakon sent a fleet of fifty ships to plunder their lands until they should come to their obedience, and sailed on to the island of Gigha where he established his headquarters.

Ewen of Lorne came to the Norwegian king at Gigha, but repeating the tactics that he had employed against Alexander II, said that he could not support Hakon since he had sworn an oath to the Scottish king, from whom he held the larger dominion, and he 'bade King Hakon dispose of the dominions he had given him'. Hakon left Ewen his lands for the moment, but held him prisoner as a potential go-between with Alexander III. Angus Mor meanwhile was induced by the plundering of his territory to send a message through Dugall MacRuairi that he was ready to submit. 'And the King said that he would not plunder the headland of Kintyre if Angus Mor and his brother Murchad came into his power the following day before mid-day. Otherwise I let my men plunder.' Angus came to Gigha and formally surrendered his lands in Islay. These Hakon restored, under his sovereignty, but laid a tax of a thousand cows upon Kintyre. The skald recorded:

Terror was caused by the leader of mighty deeds of gaping-beaked ships, about the lands that are washed with the drizzling rain of western storms. Outlawed princes bowed their helmeted heads to the unsparing terror of robbers.'[68]

The Clan Ruairi were more forward in their own interests. Dugall MacRuairi acquired the fortress of Dunavertie when it surrendered to the Norwegians, while Ruairi himself took a squadron of galleys and attacked Rothesay Castle on Bute. The garrison of Scots capitulated but Ruairi is said to have pursued and killed nine of them before hearing that a truce was called. He then led a Norse raid on the mainland which plundered deep into the Stewarts' country:

The renowned and unsparing company of the peace-breaker won broad Bute from the God-hated ring-users; the raven mounted his wing's cloven sword over the vulture's feast in the Hebrides; the ruler's enemies fell.

The dwellings of the untrustworthy husbandmen were burnt; Hell's destruction was hot in the sea-pastures. The fighting-men being attacked in the South by the ocean-skis (longships) fell death-doomed before the warriors of the Swan's field.'[69]

Hakon meanwhile had sailed from Gigha to Lamash Bay where Dominican monks were trying to negotiate peace terms between the Norwegian and Scottish kings. Alexander III had assembled his army at New Ayr, and spun out the discussions through the autumn, waiting until the fair weather should turn to foul. Hakon grew frustrated and advanced slowly to the Cumbraes, while sixty ships under Dugall MacRuairi and Angus Mor were sent reiving up Loch Long to obtain supplies. They landed at Arrochar and hauled their galleys overland to

Loch Lomond to plunder the islands in the loch and raid as far as Lennox and the Stirling plain.

On 1 October 1263, as the Norwegian fleet lay off the Cumbraes, 'a great storm came on, with fury, and a merchant ship and (nine) longships were driven ashore. On the Monday the storm became so violent that some ships were dismasted and others dragged their anchors.' Even Hakon's great ship broke its mooring and was in danger of being wrecked. The Scots on shore attacked the stranded Norwegians and started to plunder the vessels which had gone aground, but Hakon disembarked eight or nine hundred of his men in an attempt to salvage the cargo of the beached supply ship. While this operation was in progress Alexander III arrived with the main Scottish army and immediately assaulted the Norwegian position on the shore. For a while Hakon was unable to reinforce his men, who were being driven back into the sea, but eventually sufficient Norsemen landed and their counter-attack forced the Scots to retreat up the escarpment until the Norwegians could wade out to the waiting ships. The next day, the Norse returned to bury their dead and burn the hulks which were beyond salvage, before the whole fleet withdrew to the shelter of Holy Island.

This was the Battle of Largs, later exaggerated by the Scottish chroniclers into a 'dangerous and cruel fight' in which sixteen thousand Norsemen were claimed to have been killed. Yet although no more than a skirmish, the event was decisive in that it caused the Norwegians to abandon the Hebridean campaign. Hakon contemplated an invasion of Ireland to fight the Normans there, but his people refused to follow him and the old king eventually turned his storm-battered ships to the north. At Mull he parted from the Hebridean kings, confirming Dugall MacRuairi in his possession of Dunavertie and granting him the lands of the faithless Ewen of Lorne. Ruairi himself recovered Bute, while Murchad, brother of Angus Mor, who had distinguished himself in the plundering of Loch Long, was granted the Isle of Arran. But these were empty honours and the beneficiaries could not enjoy them long. Old Hakon did not survive the voyage home, and when he died at Orkney the Norwegian era in the Isles expired with him. Alexander sent a force under Alan Durward to subdue Man and the Isles, but the western chiefs hurriedly submitted. A mission to Hakon's successor, Magnus of Norway, purchased the Isles for the sum of four thousand merks of silver and an annual payment of a hundred merks in perpetuity. In 1266 a Treaty signed in the Dominican Priory at Perth formally ceded the old Norwegian territories in the Hebrides to the Scottish crown.

Alexander III granted a general amnesty to the chieftains of the Isles who had supported Hakon – allowing them the choice of departing to Norway or remaining under Scottish sovereignty. Ewen of Lorne was restored to his lands with certain additions, while Angus Mor of Islay was confirmed in his existing possessions. Even the Clan Ruairi were forgiven and allowed to keep their patrimony in Garmoran. The only important change of land ownership in the islands themselves which resulted from the transfer of sovereignty was the grant by Alexander of Skye and Lewis to Macantagart of Ross, who, by joining his hereditary lands in Applecross with the territories of East Ross forfeited by the MacEths, became the most powerful lord in the north. The Clan Ruairi, though dispossessed of Skye and Lewis, acquired instead the northern islands of Uist, Barra, Eigg, and Rhum, which had formerly belonged to the King of Man.

At the same time, Hakon's invasion had demonstrated the strategic importance of Arran and Bute, which were now confirmed to the Stewarts and so passed permanently out with the dominion of the Isles. Arran itself became the defensive bulwark against further incursions from the west. The regions around the Firth of Clyde which gave access to the lowland plain were garrisoned, and royal fortresses established at Kildonan, Brodick, and Loch Ranza. Wooden fortifications gave place to stone, and castles of *enceinte* became a feature in the west. The stone strongholds of Mingary, Tioram, Dunstaffnage, Duntrune, Dunvegan, and Duart probably date from the end of the thirteenth century.

In 1284 Angus Mor, Alexander of Lorne (Ewen's successor), and Allan MacRuairi, represented the western lands at the Parliament which met at Scone to regulate the succession, and their presence reflected their new position within the Scottish realm. Other families, however, were also appearing as substantial landholders in the western mainland – the Cambels in Lochow, Lamonts in Cowal, the Mac-Gregors of Glenorchy, the MacNachtans of Loch Fyne, and the MacSweyns of Knapdale – who were to play a part in the events which followed. More significant for the moment was the growing influence within Kintyre of the Earls of Menteith. Until 1233 this earldom had been in the hands of the Gaelic line of *mormaers,* but when the last incumbent died without male issue, his heiress married Walter Comyn,

Lord of Badenoch and brother of the Earl of Buchan. Comyn was poisoned (possibly by his wife) and succeeded by Walter, third son of the High Steward and husband of Comyn's sister-in-law. The Stewarts already held Arran and Bute, and Comyn's widow tried to regain possession. In 1285 the Earldom of Menteith was therefore divided between her descendants and Walter Stewart. This Walter had jurisdiction over Knapdale, but the considerable Comyn interests in the west would create divisions in the years that followed.

Alexander III appears to have erected a sheriffdom in Argyll incorporating agreements with the principal barons, and in 1292 when John Balliol created the sheriffdoms of Skye, Lorne, and Kintyre, the twelve great landowners whose names are given as falling within the sheriffdom of Lorne or Argyll included Angus Mor of Islay, Alexander de Ergadia, Colin Cambel of Lochow, the Earl of Menteith, and a Magister Randulph of Dundee, with seven other Gaelic chiefs.

It is doubtful whether the early sheriffdom as an administrative unit succeeded in Argyll, since by 1294 the Clan Dugall of Lorne were at feud with the Cambels of Lochow, and the incident was perhaps the first serious battle between the descendants of Somerled and the family who would, centuries after, become their traditional enemies. (The spelling Campbell did not appear until a later date.)

According to the accepted story, the march which divided the lands of the Lord of Lorne from those of Sir Colin Cambel of Lochow ran along the 'String of Lorne' – a watershed between the Atlantic and Loch Awe. Following a series of boundary disputes, the two sides agreed to call a meeting at a remote spot in the hills beside a burn known as the Allt a'Chomhlachaidh (the stream of the conference). On their way to the tryst, the MacDugalls paused at Loch Scammadale to consult a magic crystal as to how the negotiations would transpire. To their great consternation, the crystal slipped from the seer's hands into the loch, and conceiving this to be a bad omen, many of the clan returned home. The rest continued up Glen Scammadale, convinced that they were walking into a trap.

Sir Colin Cambel and his people meanwhile, had gone to the meeting place, but not finding the MacDugalls there, they also suspected treachery, and advancing down the Glen as far as the Allt an Ath'-Dheirig (the stream of the red ford) promptly attacked the men of Lorne who were coming from the opposite direction. A furious fight ensued, and the burn ran red with the blood of the slain (and hence its name).

The MacDugalls were heavily outnumbered and likely to have been annihilated, until an archer, taking cover behind a boulder (still called the *Cairn Chailein* or 'the cairn of Colin') shot and killed Sir Colin Cambel, whereupon the men of Lochow lost heart and withdrew, carrying the body of their dead leader.

From Sir Colin Cambel of Lochow the later Campbell chiefs took their name of *Mac Chailein Mor* (Great son of Colin). At this time, however, the Cambels were not yet a real power in the west and their principal lands appear to have been in Dunbartonshire. Sir Colin was succeeded by his son Sir Neil Cambel whose support for Robert the Bruce would contribute further to that family's growing fortune.

In 1286, Alexander III – 'the righteous, holy, wise, kind, mild, and merciful' – was killed in a fall from his horse. His first wife had died in 1275, and his youngest son shortly after. In 1284 his only daughter, Margaret, Queen of Norway, also died in childbirth, and in the same year the heir, Prince Alexander, perished of a lingering illness that drove him witless and killed him at the age of twenty. Alexander III was old for his time, and the succession became a matter of paramount importance. A Great Council of magnates agreed that in the event of his dying without further issue the crown should pass to the infant granddaughter, Margaret of Norway. In 1285, Alexander took a second wife, Yolande de Dreux, and there was hope that he might yet beget an heir. It was not to be. In March 1286, after feasting at Edinburgh, he insisted on riding through a winter storm to join his young wife at Kinghorn, and his horse stumbled under him in the sleeting wind and darkness. It was an insignificant end to a promising king, and Scotland, which had grown to prosperity under his rule, was soon plunged into thirty years of relentless and unremitting warfare. And in the struggle for the throne which followed, the descendants of Somerled became divided – to the eventual discomfort of the House of Lorne and the great fortune of the Clan Donald of Islay.

CHAPTER 14

Alasdair and Angus Og –
The War of Independence

With these, the valiant of the Isles
Beneath their chieftains ranked their files,
  In many a plaided band.
There in the centre proudly raised
The Bruce's royal standard blazed,
And there Lord Ranald's banner bore
A galley driven by sail and oar.
A wild yet pleasing contrast made
Warriors in mail and plate arrayed,
With the plumed bonnet and the plaid
  By the Hebrideans worn.

One effort more and Scotland's free!
Lord of the Isles my trust in thee
  Is firm as Ailsa's Rock:
Rush on with highland sword and targe,
I, with my Carrick spearmen charge;
  Now forward to the shock!
Sir Walter Scott, 'The Lords of the Isles'

On the death of Alexander III, the Scottish barons were reminded of their agreement that, failing other issue, the crown should pass to his infant grand-daughter Margaret, called the Maid of Norway. The prospect was viewed without enthusiasm by the family of de Brus of Annandale who had a claim under the law of tanistry by a settlement of Alexander II in 1238. Moreover, the Maid was marriageable, and Edward I of England, fresh from the subjugation of the Welsh, proposed a union with his two-year-old son, Edward Prince of Wales – the which offer, adequately gilded, was grudgingly accepted by the Scots baronage at the Treaty of Birgham in July 1290. The Maid was sent for, while a

Council of lords and clergy appointed six Guardians to govern in her name. These were, benorth the Forth: Bishop Fraser of St Andrews, Duncan MacDuff Earl of Fife, Alexander Comyn Earl of Buchan; and in the south – Bishop Wishart of Glasgow, James the High Steward, and John Comyn Lord of Badenoch. The Bruces were excluded.

But the Maid of Norway did not survive the short voyage to Scotland, and in an attempt to avert a civil war, Bishop Fraser the Guardian wrote incautiously to Edward I, inviting him to arbitrate between the rival claimants to the Scottish throne.

This was followed by a similar request from the Seven Earls of Scotland, who opposed the conduct of the Guardians and asserted their right since Pictish times to elect the king – expressing a preference for Robert de Brus of Annandale (the grandfather of the future King Robert the Bruce). There were no less than thirteen 'competitors' for the throne, all of them Normans, but the two men with the strongest claim were John de Balliol and Robert de Brus, both of whom could show descent from David, Earl of Huntingdon, the youngest brother of Malcolm the Maiden and William the Lion:

JOHN DE BALLIOL'S CLAIM TO THE THRONE

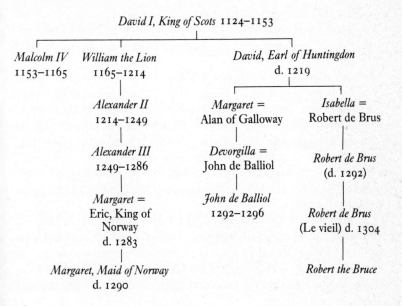

However, it was not established under feudal law whether the succession should devolve on the person second in descent from the elder sister (Balliol), or first in descent from the younger sister (Bruce).

Edward I, the jurist, accepted the invitation, but citing the precedent of William the Lion's submission to Henry II, the price he exacted was that the Scots should acknowledge him as Superior and Lord Paramount – a demand which troubled many, though apparently not the principal contenders. On 13 June 1291 the 'competitors' were summoned to attend the king at Upsettlington and all of them duly appeared, with the temporary exception of John Balliol who mistook the date. Prior to the hearing they set their seals to a formal acknowledgement of Edward's position:

Forasmuch as the King of England has evidently shown to us that the sovereign seignory of Scotland and the right of determining our several pretensions belong to him, we therefore of our own free will and without compulsion, have agreed to receive judgement from him as our Lord Paramount, and we become bound to submit to his award.[70]

After a prolonged debate lasting seventeen months, judgement was given in favour of Balliol, whom possibly Edward considered the most pliable of the principal contenders. The theory of Paramountcy required also that the Scottish king so chosen owed homage, and John Balliol took an oath of fealty to Edward, while the Great Seal of the Guardians was broken and the fragments deposited in the English treasury.

For three years the weak-willed 'Toom Tabard' or 'Empty Coat' as Balliol was contemptuously called, allowed himself to be humiliated by the English king amid a mounting hostility in Scotland. Finally, in 1295, when Edward demanded military and financial support for a war against France, a committee of Scots lords and bishops persuaded their timorous king to renounce his allegiance and conclude a treaty with Philip of France. Enraged by this treason, Edward forfeited the English possessions of all the Scottish lords who supported Balliol, and prepared to invade the north.

In March 1296 Balliol's army under John Comyn, Earl of Buchan, entered Cumberland and besieged Carlisle – which was held for Edward by Robert de Brus ('*le vieil*'). They were repulsed, and set out next on a bloody raid through Tynedale, burning Hexham and Corbridge and massacring the local population. From the outset this war was conducted with particular savagery. On 29 March (Good Friday) the English stormed Berwick and gave no quarter. The sack of the town continued for two days, and the dreadful slaughter of the inhabitants only came to an end when Edward himself saw a woman in the act of childbirth being put to the sword, and turned away shouting '*Laissez, laissez!*' At the end of April Dunbar fell to John de Warenne, Earl of Surrey. James the Steward surrendered Roxburgh and Edinburgh capitulated to Edward. On 7 July, Balliol abdicated and was sent south to captivity in England. Robert de Brus in Carlisle took the opportunity to ask whether Edward might reconsider his own claim to the throne, but Edward is said to have testily replied: 'Have we nothing else to do but win realms for you?'

Scotland was disarmed, and the country looted of its archives and records (including those of Argyll), as well as the Black Rood of St Margaret with its fragment of the True Cross, and the supposed Stone of Destiny itself – carried back to Westminster with the plunder of a nation. At a parliament in Berwick, 2000 Scottish earls, barons, churchmen, burgesses, and freeholders swore fealty to Edward and attached their seals to the document later referred to as the infamous 'Ragman Roll'. English garrisons were installed throughout the country, and the Earl of Surrey made Warden over Scotland.

Beneath this English yoke a national spirit began to smoulder and found expression in the semi-legendary hero Sir William Wallace. Wallace's origins are obscure, but he was possibly a younger son of Malcolm le Waleys of Ellerslie near Paisley, and by his name, 'The Welshman', presumably of Strathclyde British descent. By tradition William Wallace slew the English Sheriff of Clydesdale in revenge for wrongs or atrocities which that official had committed – although from an early reference to a William le Waleys accused of stealing three shillings worth of beer in Perth, it is possible that in the mould of Hereward, his outlawry may first have resulted from youthful lawlessness. In May 1297 Wallace joined a revolt which was being hatched by James the Steward, Bishop Wishart, Sir Andrew de Moray, and Sir William Douglas, and was shortly accepted into their councils. According to the *Lanercost Chronicle* (which set out to denigrate him), Wishart and the Steward 'caused a certain bloody man, William Wallace, who had formerly been a chief of brigands in Scotland to revolt against the king and assemble the people in his support' so that 'the reviving malice of that perfidious race (the Scots) excited their minds to fresh sedition'.

The principal leaders of this rebellion surrendered ignobly to the English at Irvine, but Wallace and de Moray raised an army in the north and declared their intention of restoring King John Balliol. Wallace's revolt had a peculiarly popular aspect since he had little or no support from the great lords of Norman descent whose lands in England led them to equivocate or serve under the banner of de Warenne. His following was made up of small knights, peasants from Galloway and Lothian, Gaels from Badenoch and Moray, outlaws, the landless and the dispossessed, who made up a rude and ragged army, poorly armed and for the most part on foot.

In September 1297 this 'army of the Kingdom of Scotland' descended from the Ochil Hills onto the Stirling plain and camped on the southern slope of Abbey Craig (where the Wallace Memorial now stands). Across the River Forth they were confronted by the forces of de Warenne and the Treasurer, Hugh de Cressingham – whose exactions had made him particularly abominable to the Scots. At this point, close to Stirling, the river could be crossed by a narrow wooden bridge, wide enough for only two or three horsemen to ride abreast, and James the Steward (who had now changed sides) advised de Warenne to make a detour and cross by a ford further downstream. But the English were confident in the weight of their armoured chivalry against the ill-armed rabble whom they saw on the other bank, and de Cressingham led the vanguard across the bridge. Wallace allowed this division to cross and then broke the bridge behind them, so that de Warenne and the main army could only watch helplessly as Cressingham and his force were surrounded by the Scottish spearmen and killed to the last man. De Warenne fled back to Berwick, and Stirling capitulated to the victorious Wallace who then pursued the English over the border and wasted Cumbria. Having no siege engines, the Scots could make no impression against Carlisle which was still held by Robert de Brus, and in November Wallace withdrew again to Stirling and proclaimed himself Guardian of Scotland on behalf of King John Balliol.

In Argyll and the Western Isles, the descendants of Somerled had become divided between the Bruce and Balliol interests. Alexander of Lorne was married to a Comyn of Badenoch and thus attached himself to the fortunes of that family – who were the prominent supporters of Balliol. His son John Baccach, or John the Lame, was particularly active in the Comyn interest and was to become the implacable enemy of Robert the Bruce.

Among the Clan Donald of Islay, loyalties were less clear-cut, since in 1288, Angus Mor and his son Alasdair Og had entered into a bond of association with James the Steward and others to further the claims of the Bruce family. In 1291, with other lords, Angus Mor took an oath of allegiance to Edward I, but he continued to support the elder Bruce, and in 1292 when John Balliol ordered Alexander of Lorne to summon 'Sir Angus, son of Donald and others to do him homage within fifteen days after Easter wherever he may be at the time', he ignored the demand.

Angus Mor was married to a daughter of Sir Colin Cambel of Lochow, by whom he had three sons: Alasdair Og, Angus Og, and John Sprangach (Bold John). (The Clanranald historian also credits him with a fourth son, Duncan, who was the ancestor of the Robertsons of Struan.) When Angus died in about 1300, Alasdair inherited Islay and other mainland territories in Argyll, including Castle Sween in Knapdale, while Angus Og obtained most of Kintyre and Mull – although the latter was still claimed by the House of Lorne. Iain Sprangach was subsequently granted Ardnamurchan.

Some time after 1295, Alasdair of Islay married Juliana MacDugall, sister of Alexander of Lorne – an alliance which also connected him by marriage with the Comyns, whom he then supported against Bruce. In 1296, when the Scottish barons submitted to the English king, Alasdair received a grant of a hundred pounds' worth of land for services rendered to Edward I, and following Balliol's abdication he was appointed Admiral of the Western Isles under the English crown – an office which obliged him to restrain his cousins the Clan Ruairi and caused some conflict with his brother-in-law of Lorne whose son was a hostage in England for a time. The House of Lorne were equivocal in the English interest, their principal affiliation being with the Comyns, with the partial exception of Alexander's younger brother Duncan de Lorn who, together with Sir Neil Cambel of Lochow, fought on at least one occasion with Wallace.

Edward I had appointed as his creature in Argyll an Irishman called Macphadian, who rapidly earned a reputation for cruelty and extortion. In about 1298, this Macphadian, on Edward's commission, attacked Sir Neil Cambel of Lochow and drove him out of his lands on the southern shore of Loch Awe. Cambel and his people retreated towards Cruachan where a small wooden bridge spanned the gorge as the River Awe runs into the Loch. They destroyed this behind them so that Macphadian's larger force was unable to follow, and while Cambel guarded the crossing, Duncan de Lorn rode to Stirling to obtain help from Wallace, who gathered a small force and hurried to Glendochart.

Cambel meanwhile had succeeded in recrossing the Awe, and had taken up a position on Macphadian's flank when he received intelligence that the Irish captain intended to seize the pass at Glenorchy. Cambel hastily joined Wallace and Duncan, and their combined force marched over the hills by Dalmally to reach Glenorchy before Macphadian arrived. They surprised the Irish at the place now called Corrie na Ruaig (the corrie of the fight) and chased them back into the Pass of Brander. Macphadian himself jumped into the River Awe, and supporting himself against a boulder in mid-current, pulled off his armour and swam to the further bank, where he climbed the slope and hid in a cave. Duncan de Lorn followed him across the river, and after a fight in the cave, took his head and placed it on a pinnacle of rock above the battlefield.

Wallace's rule as Guardian of Scotland lasted barely eight months. In 1298 Edward patched up a peace with France, and returning to England, once more turned his baleful eye towards the north. He transferred the seat of government to York, and that summer crossed the Tweed with a massive host of 15,000 men. Wallace's army was caught in the open near Falkirk, and after being decimated under a hail of arrows, the Scottish spearmen were overrun beneath the weight of the English armoured chivalry. Wallace escaped, Guardian no longer, and survived as a fugitive for seven years. He could find none who would support him. The common resistance had been broken at Falkirk, while his own obscure origin offended the fragile honour of a Norman baronage who trembled for their English lands. In 1305 he was betrayed and taken, to be delivered into Edward's mercy. The English paraded him through London garlanded in mockery, and for his treason, sacrilege, homicide, and robbery, prescribed a hideous death. For murder and robbery he was hanged, and cut down still living: for sacrilege, emasculated and his entrails burned before his eyes. As an outlaw he was beheaded, and for treason his head was placed on London Bridge and his quartered body nailed to the gates of Newcastle, Berwick, Perth, and Stirling. Unlike the rest of the Scottish baronage he had never sworn fealty to Edward, and the spectacle of his death was an obscenity even by the standards of that cruel age.

Seven months later, Scotland found a new and greater leader – in an adventurer who suddenly became a king, and who, yet a king, for long years had no kingdom.

Until now the position of Robert the Bruce had been, at the very least, equivocal. During these early wars his father had held Carlisle for the English, and upon the failure of Balliol, the young Bruce had fought with Edward's favour to repossess his lands in Annandale against the Comyn interest. Edward himself seems to have thought well of him, and although associated with the Steward's intrigues, as late as 1298 he had written to offer service to the English king. After Falkirk he provided engines for the siege of Stirling, and in 1304, on being served heir to his father's estates, he swore fealty to Edward for the fourth time. Throughout these years the family of de Brus had looked only to their own interest. Now, the abdication of Balliol and the defeat of Wallace had removed two obstacles from their path, but there remained the powerful family of Comyn upon whom the Balliol claims devolved.

After Falkirk, Edward burned St Andrews and reduced the country to a wasteland of blackened steadings and ruined townships, before he rode south, vowing to return in the spring and put an end to Scottish disobedience and malice. But a new wife distracted him, and amid the desolation, a fresh conspiracy was born. In 1299 Bruce and Comyn met upon some purpose at Selkirk, but the two men quarrelled, and Comyn seized Bruce by the throat. Nevertheless they did agree that the fugitive Wallace should be deprived of the Guardianship, and secretly appointed themselves in his place. Edward's spies reporting the meeting said that Bruce and Comyn had quarrelled over Wallace's property, and Edward apparently suspected nothing more.

Within a year, Bruce and Comyn quarrelled again and the rift grew wider. Bruce began secret negotiations with Philip of France, but he may still have hoped for a promise of the vacant throne. His oaths of fealty were unrewarded, however, and the Guardianship was given to Robert de Soulis. In 1300 and 1301 Edward invaded Scotland again, capturing Caerlaverock but finding no army to fight. In 1304 Comyn led a feeble rebellion and shortly submitted.

In this time, Bruce became prominent in conspiracy with Lamberton and certain other members of the Scottish Church. It is difficult to determine precisely what did happen in 1306. Bruce had just sworn yet another oath of fealty to Edward, on the Lord's Body, the Holy Relics, and the Four Evangelists, and attended the Parliament which approved the execution of Wallace, when it seems likely that he intercepted a messenger from Comyn traducing him to Edward and revealing his French intrigues. He went immediately to Scotland, and sent his brothers to Red Comyn at Dalswinton – probably to contrive his murder, which they failed to accomplish. On 10 February 1306 the rivals met by appointment at the church of the Minorite Friars in Dumfries. In the course of a quarrel, Bruce drew his dagger and stabbed Comyn through the body. Bursting from the church, he told his followers that he thought he had killed Red Comyn, and the Badenoch escort were similarly despatched while Roger de Kirkpatrick went back into the cloister to 'make sure' of the matter.

Edward I, at his hunting lodge near Winchester, was taken by surprise, having only two days previously confirmed the scutage due to Bruce on his English estates. When he learned that Bruce had joined Bishop Wishart at Glasgow and was proclaiming himself King of Scots, he fell into a terrible rage. For the crime of sacrilegious murder, Bruce was excommunicated by the English Church and stood committed beyond the pale of Edward's mercy. 'The liberty of Scotland was now the only cause that might preserve his own.'[71]

The coronation on Palm Sunday 1306 was a sombre affair performed by Isabella, Countess of Buchan, since the Earl of MacDuff whose hereditary right it was to crown the Kings of Scotland was either Edward's man or confined in an English dungeon. Of the traditional Seven Earls of Scotland only Atholl and Lennox were present, with three bishops who were willing to brave the ban of excommunication. The proclamation was made in the time-honoured manner of the ancient Picts and Scots, but the crown itself together with the supposed throne of destiny, upon which all previous Scottish kings were made, had also been removed to England. As Bruce's queen, Elizabeth de Burgh, is said to have remarked, it seemed that 'We are but a summer King and Queen whom children crown in their sport.'[72] They all knew that Edward would exact a terrible and bloody retribution.

Bruce had no strongholds of note nor troops to spare for garrison. His small army consisted mainly of footsoldiers, spearmen, and small knights in his own service. The majority of Scottish lords found excuse –

to shun the excommunicate king or take service with Aymer de Valence, the English Warden in Scotland who was married to Red Comyn's sister. In England, Edward I, although infirm with age, summoned his power and swore he would not rest 'until the Lord has given me victory against the crowned traitor and perjured nation'. It was a doomed endeavour, and Bruce seemed destined to suffer the fate of Wallace. On 26 June, his wretched army was surprised and scattered at Methven Wood near Perth by de Valence and his English knights. The Summer King became a fugitive with no refuge but the Highland hills, and the story of his wanderings has passed into legend.[73]

In the autumn of 1306, Bruce was close to disaster. His queen, daughter, and two sisters were captured at Kildrummie and confined in iron cages. His brother Nigel was taken prisoner with the Earl of Atholl, and hanged and drawn at Berwick. With a few followers, Bruce escaped towards the central Highlands, but near Tyndrum he was ambushed by John the Lame of Lorne who had raised Argyll to avenge the Comyn murder. The MacDugalls 'fawcht with axys sa felounly' that they wounded a number of Bruce's men and killed their horses, so that after a sharp fight, the king only extricated his band with difficulty, himself fighting a rearguard action in the pass. According to the traditional account, John of Lorne was 'rycht angrey in his hart' at the sight of Bruce's escape and called on two brothers, the 'Marthokys', 'the hardiest of the land', to catch and kill him. Together with a third clansman, they sprang upon Bruce in a narrow place between the lochside and the brae, and although Bruce killed all three, one of them tore off the king's plaid together with its brooch, which subsequently became the heirloom of the MacDougalls of Lorne.

Bruce reached Loch Lomond where, fortuitously, he was joined by Lennox, and the fugitives paused to consider where they might find a winter's safety. The whole country was out against them and any refuge could become a trap. The only possible direction was westwards, but there too was danger, since John the Lame pursued the Comyn feud, and Alasdair of Islay, being married to Juliana of Lorne 'would by no means own King Robert's quarrel'. The only potential friend was Angus Og, who held Kintyre with its castles of Saddell and Dunavertie, and had once supported the Elder Bruce against John Balliol.

In 1301 Angus Og had also served the English, and succeeded his brother as Admiral of the Western Isles, but since that time he had not been forward in either cause. At this period his fortunes were depressed while those of Lorne were at their zenith. According to the seannachie MacVurich:

all the garrisons from Dingall in the Ross to the Mull of Kintyre were in the possession of MacDugall during that time while the tribe of Ranald (the Clan Donald and the MacRuairis) were under the yoke of their enemies.[74]

Angus was at feud with John the Lame over the claim to Mull, and Alasdair of Islay was in alliance with Lorne against his younger brother. 'This Angus of the Isles was a little black man, of very amiable and cheerful disposition and more witty than any man could take him to be by his countenance.'

Bruce may not have trusted Angus, but by now he had very little choice. Sir Neil Cambel of Lochow, who had been with the king since Methven Wood, obtained ships and provisions from his people along the Firth of Clyde, and Bruce slipped through the encircling net and sailed to Saddell. Angus Og welcomed him warmly:

> And Angus of Ile at that time was Syr
> And lord and ledar of Kintyr
> The King rycht weill resawyt he
> And undertook his man to be
> And he and his on mony wyes
> He abandowynt to his service
> And for mair sekyrness gaiff him syne
> His Castle of Donaverdyne.[75]

Saddell Castle was strong, but it was exposed and over-close to Alasdair's stronghold at Sween, and Angus transferred the king to his fortress of Dunavertie on the cliff at the southern tip of the peninsula. Even there Bruce was not safe, and it was eventually decided that he should hide out the winter on the island of Rathlin off the coast of Antrim where the storm weather and the MacRuairi galleys would give additional protection. It was wisely done, since shortly afterwards an English force under Sir John de Menteith laid siege to Dunavertie.

At about this time the Macleans made a sudden entry into the history of the Isles. According to the Clan Donald version of events, John the Lame, who was raiding Bruce's lands in Carrick, took into his service one, Gillian son of Gilleusa, and granted him land in the Isle of Sael. This Gillian had three sons: Hector (from whom the Macleans of Lochbuie), Lachlan (from whom the family of Duart), and a third son from whom the others of the name. John of Lorne sent them to prosecute his quarrel with Angus Og over Mull, and while staying at Angus's house in Ardtornish, they were insulted by the steward called MacFinnon.

Angus 'being that same day to cross the Sound of Mull to Aros . . . took a small boat for himself, leaving MacFinnon behind with his great galley and carriage, and the rest of his men. When MacFinnon went to the shore (to witness Angus Og's departure) the sons of Gillian, taking the opportunity for revenge, and calling MacFinnon aside, stabbed him, and straight with his galley and their own men followed the MacDonald across the Sound.' Angus, thinking that it was MacFinnon behind him, was taken unawares and captured.

The Macleans took Angus to Dunstaffnage, and sent a message to John of Lorne (who was at dinner) that they had the Lord of Kintyre prisoner. Lorne was heard to comment that he was pleased enough with the prize, but the Macleans' action had been overbold and 'he would through time bridle their forwardness and insolence'. On learning of this, the Macleans consulted their prisoner who suggested that they would fare better by changing sides, and taking him at his word, they all escaped back to Mull. Angus 'gave fourscore merks of land to Hector MacLean', and made Lachlan the Chamberlain of his house. Lachlan later married the daughter of John, first Lord of the Isles (son of Angus) 'and that by her inclination of yielding' – and through her he acquired lands in Morvern and the keeping of Duart Castle.[76]

In the spring of 1307, Bruce returned to the mainland and resumed the struggle. Christina MacRuairi of Garmoran provided galleys for the crossing, and Angus Og sent a warband of Islesmen to aid in the recapture of Bruce lands in Arran. At the same time, Bruce's brothers, Thomas and Alexander, landed in Loch Ryan with a force from Ireland, but they were captured by Dougal MacDowal of Galloway and hanged at Carlisle. Angus Og is also said to have been present at this defeat but succeeded in escaping from the battlefield.

Bruce's wanderings began anew. Encircled by an English ring of steel, threatened by assassins and hunted with bloodhounds, he gradually gathered an army around him. The country itself was his ally and he skirmished through Glentrool, ambushing the slower-moving English men-at-arms and then withdrawing into the safety of the mountains. On 10 May his small force routed a superior number of

English knights under de Valence at Loudon Hill in present-day Ayrshire – the first real victory – but English reinforcements drove him back into the Galloway hills, too weak to risk a battle against heavy chivalry on open ground.

At Lanercost the old King Edward was dying, but the news of Loudon Hill galled him into leading another army northwards to settle permanently with 'King Hobb' the Bruce. He was now so infirm that he had to be carried in a litter at the head of his soldiers. He died of dysentery at Burgh-on-Sands three miles from the border, leaving instructions that his heart should be sent to the Holy Land, and the flesh boiled from his bones so that his skeleton at least might lead the army to victory over the Scots. His son, who had a weaker stomach, sent the body south intact for burial at Westminster.

The old king's death changed much. Edward II preferred the frivolous capering of the Gascon Gaveston to the dismal Scottish weather and the rigours of a northern campaign. De Valence was replaced by the less competent Ingram de Umfraville, and many English troops were recalled. It was left to the Comyns and their kin to devise Bruce's destruction, and the struggle for independence deteriorated into civil war.

Bruce could take no initiative, having no siege train and every major fortress held against him. But he began to win support – most importantly from the Celtic Earl of Ross, and in the cold and starving Christmas of the year, he defeated the Comyn Earl of Buchan, who, in the extremity of battle, proved coward and incompetent. The lands of Buchan were ravaged from end to end and the devastion left to smoulder. By summer, all the north-eastern castles except for Banff had fallen, and many of the Norman lords submitted. Bruce turned west to settle a score in Lorne.

John of Lorne had 'witteryng' of his coming and laid an ambush in the narrow pass at Brander. The Argyllmen numbered something over two thousand, but John himself (like the later Marquis of Argyll at Inverlochy) watched the battle from his galley in Loch Awe. Bruce, approaching from Dalmally, suspected some such stratagem and sent a force of Highlanders under Douglas to climb the steep slope of Cruachan and so get above the men of Lorne. The MacDugalls made a 'grete and apert defens' but were routed by Douglas's downhill charge and fled back along the pass. Bruce's men pursued them and seized the narrow bridge over the Awe before it could be broken. The army crossed into the lands of Lorne while John the Lame watched helpless from his galley and could only 'thole the ill'.

Bruce's men now plundered the country from Glen Etive as far as Dunstaffnage Castle which he seized and garrisoned. John the Lame escaped by sea, but his father, Alexander of Lorne, submitted to the Scottish king who sentenced him to forfeit his lands but allowed him a safe conduct to England, where he died in poverty soon after.

Meanwhile Edward Bruce was waging a fierce campaign in Galloway, blockading de Umfraville and the English troops in their castles while the Scots reduced the surrounding country. In 1308 he defeated the combined forces of Sir Roland of Galloway and Alasdair of Islay, and in the pursuit Alasdair was captured. He escaped, however, to Castle Sween in Knapdale which was promptly besieged by the king and forced into surrender after a stubborn fight. Bruce imprisoned Alasdair in Dundonald Castle in Ayrshire, where he is presumed to have died. The chieftainship of the Clan Donald passed to Angus Og, and from this time the men of the Isles fought only on the side of Bruce.

In 1309 the Scottish king was strong enough to call a parliament at St Andrews, attended mainly by the Celtic lords, and some months later the clergy also announced their support despite a second papal interdict excommunicating Bruce for 'damnably persevering in iniquity'. Disorder in England and French support for the Scots forced Edward II to negotiate a truce which he promptly broke by leading a half-hearted invasion of the Lowlands that did not penetrate beyond Linlithgow. The English barons grew discontented with trudging after a Scottish army who scorched the earth but would not fight, and became more interested in encompassing the death of the favourite Gaveston.

When Edward withdrew, Bruce struck south across the border into Northumberland and Cumberland, levying a heavy blackmail as the price of truce. During the next three years he concentrated his energies on reducing the English garrisons in Scotland, razing them to the ground or dismantling the fortifications. Forfar fell in 1312. Perth was taken by assault the following January, and Dumfries in February – where Bruce spared MacDowal's life but seized his wealth and lands. In 1313 Linlithgow was captured by a stratagem, and the next year Douglas took the important fortress of Roxburgh.

The campaign now concentrated upon Stirling. Edward Bruce, brother of the king, had closely invested the castle from Lent to Midsummer 1313, when he rashly entered into an agreement with the chatellan Sir Philip Mowbray, that the English garrison would surrender if they were not relieved within twelve months. Such a treaty invited an English invasion.

In June 1314, Edward II mustered a great host at Wark and advanced through Lauderdale to Edinburgh where he obtained fresh supplies carried north by the English fleet. The size of this army has been greatly exaggerated by later (Scottish) chroniclers, and it seems likely that Edward had about four or five thousand mounted knights and about twenty thousand archers and spearmen – but this was perhaps three times larger than any force which the Scots could put into the field.

As Midsummer's Day approached, Bruce assembled his power on the Stirling plain, and camped around the hunting forest of New Park, to the south of the beleaguered castle. His army was largely Celtic in composition – the border fighters of Lothian and Old Strathclyde, *Gallgaels* from Galloway, Picts from Fife, Highlanders from Moray and Ross, and Bruce's own Carrick levies. Allegedly the last to arrive were the Gaels of Argyll and the Isles under Angus Og, who is said to have drawn the relieved greeting from Bruce: 'my hope is constant in thee.'

Bruce expected the English to approach from Falkirk, along the old Roman road which traversed the New Park, crossing the winding Bannock Burn, and continued by an ancient causeway between marshground as far as the castle gates of Stirling. He deployed his army facing roughly south, with his right flank resting on the wooded outcrop of Torwood and his left extending towards the Carse of Bannockburn. The Bannock Stream flowed across the front of this position, but apart from a level stretch between Parkmill in the west and Beaton's Mill in the east (a distance of about a mile) its banks were steep and impassable for heavy cavalry, so that the English would be forced to reduce the width of their line. Between the stream and the Scottish position the causeway carried the road between two extensive bogs. On this ground, and in the firm open meadows along his right flank, Bruce had his men dig a 'honeycomb' of small pits, disguised with a covering of earth and sods and sown with caltrops to disrupt the charge of the heavy English chivalry.

A line of Ettrick archers were posted around the edge of the New Park, while the rest of the army was divided into four 'battles'. On the left, by St Ninian's Church, Bruce placed the division of Sir Thomas Randolph with the men of Ross and Moray. Next to them were the levies of the Steward and Sir James Douglas, and then the division of Edward

Bruce under the great Lion standard. The king himself commanded the right-hand battle, which was composed of his own Carrick spearmen and the men of Argyll and the Isles under Angus Og.

On 23 June, the Scots stood to arms and watched the approach of the English vanguard across the rising ground near Plean – a great armoured column two miles long which seemed to 'cover all the earth'. While Edward with the main body halted at Plean to rest and hold a council of war, the Earl of Gloucester and a party of knights advanced to skirmish along the Scottish front. Crossing the Bannock Burn, one of them – probably Henry de Bohun – recognised Bruce, who was in half-armour and mounted only on a Highland garron some distance ahead of the army. Avid for honour, de Bohun couched his lance and spurred his great destrier at the lonely horseman in front of the Scottish line. Bruce waited until the armoured knight was almost upon him, and then wheeling his little horse away from the lance point, he stood in his stirrups and smote de Bohun as he passed. The blow was such that the battle-axe clove through casque and skull from crest to chin and the haft broke in his hand. The other English, brought up in confusion among the pits and caltrops scattered across the Scottish front, were attacked by the Carrick spearmen and driven back across the stream. The incident took place in full view of the Scottish army, and demonstrated – as perhaps was the king's intention – that on the right ground the lightly armed Scots could overturn the heavy English chivalry.

Gloucester meanwhile, had detached 300 knights under Sir Robert Clifford to circle the Scottish left and relieve Stirling. Randolph's division had been posted to prevent such an attempt, but, possibly diverted by the duel with de Bohun, he almost let the English pass. Bruce saw the move, however, and allegedly rebuked Randolph that he had 'let fall a rose from his chaplet'. Having few mounted men, Randolph led his footsoldiers along the high ground in pursuit, and the English, thinking them an easy prey, halted to fight them in the open. But the Scots formed the bristling spear-ring called the schiltron and the English were beaten off with heavy loss. Gloucester withdrew, badly mauled, and fell back on the main army which now moved slowly into the Carse to leaguer on the narrow land between the Bannock Burn and the River Forth – a fateful choice of ground which may have been prompted by the need for water.

During the night Edward received intelligence (which was probably false) that the enemy intended to retreat to the south, but dawn found the Scots set on battle. Bruce pivoted his divisions upon the left-hand schiltron, and began advancing eastwards towards the English, whose manoeuvre of the previous evening had now placed them in a dangerous position. The River Forth was to their right and rear, and the steep-sided Bannock Burn on their left. The ground was soft and marshy, crossed with bogs and streams, and men and horses began to flounder in the mud. But it was a vast host, confident in weight of numbers, and the advancing Scots army seemed puny by comparison. 'Will they fight?' Edward asked de Umfraville – who assured him that they would.

Some distance into the Carse, the Scots halted and formed their schiltrons, the front ranks kneeling with their spear butts planted in the earth, while those behind advanced their longer pikes to present a barbed and bristling hedge of pointed steel. The English moved towards them in nine solid columns, but the marsh constricted their deployment until they were almost on the Scots defence. In the open ground the pits and caltrops brought the front ranks of mounted men crashing to the ground below the Scottish spears, and the English advance was halted in a confused mêlée.

Gloucester led the vanguard of five hundred knights in a wild and dis-ordered charge against the schiltron of Edward Bruce, and the heavy impact of his armoured cavalry buckled the files around the Scottish standard. But Gloucester was killed in the first few moments, gaffed out of his saddle, and the assault splintered and died against the long Scottish spears. The divisions of Randolph and the Steward now joined the struggle, and the English drew back to seek a respite. Tardily, Edward advanced his archers who began to gall the Scottish flanks, but they were driven off by Bruce's own slender force of cavalry under the Marischal Sir Robert Keith, and played no further part in the desperate hand-to-hand battle which now developed. The Scottish divisions started to advance into the English mass, herding them against the marsh in a choked killing ground where order or deployment became impossible. Now the Selkirk bowmen poured a hail of arrows into the packed concentration of English men at arms who pushed and struggled in the mud – and Bruce unleashed the Highland fighting men of Argyll and the west who hurled themselves into the crush of mounted knights, swinging their axes and great two-handed swords. Somewhere in the press, John Comyn of Badenoch died under the Scottish spears and the fortunes of that family were extinguished with him. Enclosed in a tightening arc of steel the English fought doggedly over the wreck of fallen horses and dead men, until caught at last with their backs against the river, the foot-soldiers began to break and run, and the surviving knights turned to save themselves. On Coxtet Hill the Scottish camp followers heard the exultant shout, 'They fail!', and came pouring down the slope with knives and cleavers to fall upon the fugitives. All order vanished and the English host disintegrated into a fleeing fear-crazed rabble as knights and men at arms tried to escape the battlefield. Some jumped into the river and drowned under the weight of their armour. Many were bogged in the mud and floundered helplessly beneath the Scottish spears. Most ran for Falkirk, and the road became strewn with the litter of a beaten army.

Edward II himself was lucky to escape alive and was nearly taken in the rout. His bodyguard cut a way through to Stirling, but Mowbray was pledged to yield and could grant them no admission. Edward fled through the Torwood and eventually got south to Berwick.

From this day, 'Robert de Brus was commonly called King of Scotland by all men because he had acquired Scotland by force of arms.'[77] His wife and daughter were released from their captivity, along with other prominent Scots who were exchanged for English prisoners. A Parliament at Cambuskenneth close to the battlefield passed sentences of forfeiture on all who had fought for the English at Bannockburn and before, and upon any who did not now declare their allegiance to the King of Scots.

In 1315 Bruce and the Steward sailed again to the Isles to settle affairs in the west. In a gesture deliberately intended to recall the action of Magnus Barelegs, the king landed at Tarbert and had his ships hauled on rollers across the narrow isthmus. It was a time to reward those who had been faithful, and he bestowed on Angus Og the ancient Clan Donald lands of Islay, Mull, Jura, Coll, Tiree, Colonsay, Morvern, Ardnamurchan, and Glencoe, together with part of the old Comyn inheritance of Lochaber. The MacRuairis were granted Lorne (forfeited by the MacDugalls), Garmoran, and the North Isles, and the remaining portion of Lochaber.

Bruce may have been grateful, but he was also king, and he had seen the strategic importance of Kintyre. He was determined that the crown should establish an administrative centre in the region, and he therefore persuaded Angus to relinquish his dominion in Knapdale and the peninsula. These lands passed for a time to the king's grandson Robert, son of the Steward and Marjory Bruce, and in 1325 the stone castle at Tarbert was built as a royal fortress and a Cambel made its keeper. The fidelity of Neil Cambel of Lochow was also recognised, and from this date that family began to expand into the vacuum created by the forfeiture of the MacDugalls, the Lamonts of Cowal, and the other allies of Comyn.

Angus Og remained loyal, and the men of the Isles fought with distinction under Douglas during the great Scottish raid into Yorkshire in 1322. But Bruce never forgot that Angus had been his ally rather than his servant, and he was acutely aware of 'the number, magnitude, and power of the islands' and 'the multitude, ferocity, and hardihood of the inhabitants'.[78] The galleys of the western chiefs amounted to a formidable sea-power, well adapted to the coasts and sea lochs, and were capable in mischievous hands of inflicting great damage on the Scottish mainland. He is said to have left certain counsels to his successors for the guidance of the kingdom, among which was the precept that the Hebrides should never be placed under the dominion of one man, and that royal governors should deal justly in the Isles. Had the later kings of Scotland followed this advice, the history of the Lordship might have been very different.

I *a* Dunadd: the Crowning Stone. Note the footprint and the stoup.
b shows the outline of the boar.

II *a* Pictish stone at Aberlemno. The hole was probably used in handfast marriages.
   b Pictish cross near Aberlemno.

III *a* St Oran's Chapel, Iona.
   b 6th century Christian cave sanctuary at Loch Caolisport.
   c detail of cave wall showing the cross.

IV *a* Aros Castle, Mull.
  b Mingary Castle, Ardnamurchan.

V *a* Castle Sween, Knapdale.
  b Castle of Innis Chonnel in Loch Awe; original stronghold of the Campbells.

VI Kildalton Cross, Islay.

VII MacMillan Cross, Kilmory Knap.

VIII Stone effigies at Kilmory Knap. Note the conical helmet and quilted armour as worn in the western Highlands.

A GENEALOGY OF CLAN DONALD III

The Descendants of Somerled: the Clan Donald and Clan Dougall

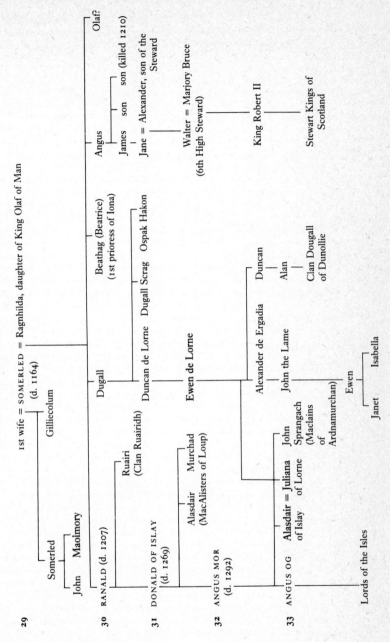

1st wife = SOMERLED = Ragnhilda, daughter of King Olaf of Man
(d. 1164)

29 — Gillieadhamnan/Gilliecolum · Somerled · John · Maolmory

Dugall · Beathag (Beatrice) (1st prioress of Iona) · Angus · Olaf?

30 RANALD (d. 1207) · Ruairi (Clan Ruairidh) · Duncan de Lorne · Dugall Scrag · Ospak Hakon · James · son · son (killed 1210)

31 DONALD OF ISLAY (d. 1269) · Alasdair · Murchad (MacAlisters of Loup) · Ewen de Lorne · Jane = Alexander, son of the Steward

32 ANGUS MOR (d. 1292) · Alexander de Ergadia · Walter = Marjory Bruce (6th High Steward)

33 ANGUS OG · Alasdair = Juliana of Islay of Lorne · John Sprangach (Maclains of Ardnamurchan) · Duncan · John the Lame · Alan · King Robert II

Ewen · Clan Dougall of Dunollie

Janet · Isabella

Lords of the Isles

Stewart Kings of Scotland

A GENEALOGY OF CLAN DONALD IV

The Descendants of Somerled: Clan Donald of the Isles and Clan Ruairidh

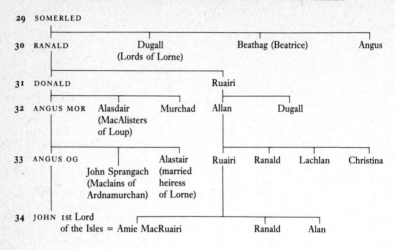

29 SOMERLED

30 RANALD — Dugall (Lords of Lorne) — Beathag (Beatrice) — Angus

31 DONALD — Ruairi

32 ANGUS MOR — Alasdair (MacAlisters of Loup) — Murchad — Allan — Dugall

33 ANGUS OG — John Sprangach (Maclains of Ardnamurchan) — Alastair (married heiress of Lorne) — Ruairi — Ranald — Lachlan — Christina

34 JOHN 1st Lord of the Isles = Amie MacRuairi — Ranald — Alan

PART IV
THE LORDSHIP

34 JOHN OF ISLAY, *1st Lord of the Isles*

Descendants by his two marriages

By his first marriage with Amie MacRuairi of Garmoran:
1 John *died prior to 1369; his son Angus had no issue*
2 Ranald *High Steward of the Isles; ancestor of* Clanranald *and* Glengarry
3 Godfrey *Ancestor of the* Siol Gorrie
4 Mary *married Lachlan Maclean of Duart*

By his second marriage with Margaret Stewart, daughter of Robert II
35 1 DONALD OF ISLAY, *2nd Lord of the Isles*
2 John Mor the Tanister *Ancestor of* Clan Iain Vor *of* Dunyveg and the Glens
3 Alasdair Carrach *Ancestor of the* Macdonalds of Keppoch
4 Hugh *Thane of Glentilt: married the heiress of Mackintosh of Glentilt*
5 Margaret *married Angus Dubh Mackay, Chief of Strathnaver*
6 Agnes *married Sir John Montgomery of Ardrossan*
36 ALEXANDER, *3rd Lord of the Isles, son of Donald, 2nd Lord, d. 1449*
37 JOHN, *Last Lord of the Isles, son of Alexander, 3rd Lord, (in power 1449, deprived of title in 1493, d. 1503)*
38 ANGUS OG, *son of the Last Lord. d. 1490*
39 DONALD DUFF

CHAPTER 15

John of Islay, Lord of the Isles

Great were the marvellous stories told
Of Ossian's heroes,
Giants and witches, and young men bold
Seeking adventures,
Winning King's daughters and guarded gold
Only with valour.

The battle of Bannockburn did not bring an end to the war, for Edward was stubborn and bitter in defeat and would recognise neither Bruce's sovereignty nor Scotland's independence. While England was stricken with famine, and Edward quarrelled with his barons, Scottish armies burned and bled the borders, creating a debatable land against invasion and beginning the reiving tradition which would continue for three hundred years.

In 1318, after an eleven-week siege by Walter the Steward, the great fortress of Berwick finally succumbed to bribery, and Edward II, his army mutinous and unpaid, failed ignominiously to retake it. He concluded a two-year truce but conceded nothing more, and the Pope, who throughout had been his moral ally, issued a further Bull of Excommunication against Robert the Bruce whom he addressed merely as 'Governor of Scotland' with no acknowledgement of his royal title. This provoked from the Scots the eloquent remonstrance called the *Declaration of Arbroath*, which is one of the most significant documents of Scottish history. In this address, the Scottish nation asserted its independence of England – by virtue of its Celtic genesis, its history, and its line of kings. This freedom had been stolen by the English, who had inflicted war and outrage, violence and massacre, and against whom: 'we fight not for glory, nor riches, nor honour, but for that liberty which no true man relinquishes but with his life.' As for Robert the Bruce, 'by the Providence of God, by the right of succession, by those laws and customs which we are resolved to defend . . . and by our just consent, he is our king.' Let the English be told therefore to 'leave us Scots in peace who live in this poor little Scotland . . . and covet nothing but our own . . .' for 'while there exist a hundred of us we will never submit.'[79]

The Declaration reflected the mood of the nation in arms, and although selfish ambitions might later tarnish its finer sentiment, its passion and forcefulness persuaded the Pope that the Scots would not submit to threats, and he advised Edward II to make peace. The English king's response was to attempt another invasion, no more successful than the last. In 1322, while his army mustered at Newcastle, the Scots plundered Lancashire and then withdrew, scorching the country behind them. Edward reached Edinburgh, but his soldiers were dying of famine and the flux, and with his army close to mutiny he retreated south once more, sacking Holyrood in spite, and desecrating the churches of Melrose and Dryburgh. The Scots hung on his heels, crossing Solway to savage the North Riding, and at Rievaulx Abbey in Yorkshire, Edward himself was nearly taken, and lost his treasure chest to Bruce.

In 1323 he agreed to a truce of thirteen years, and Bruce seized the opportunity to send Randolph of Moray as his own envoy to the Pope. John XXII was finding Edward a tedious ally, and on Randolph's suggestion that Bruce could hardly lead a crusade against the infidel while still an excommunicate, he consented in the first instance to recognise Robert I as King of Scots, and eventually to lift the ban. After Avignon, Randolph successfully concluded a treaty of mutual assistance between Scotland and France – to the greater annoyance of the English king. In 1324, after many years of barren marriage, Bruce's queen gave birth to an heir, the Prince David. The omens seemed to brighten, and a strange, uncertain peace settled over the north.

But during this pause the pattern on the chessboard was changing as the kings and queens and knights of the generation of Bannockburn grew old, or were removed, and went to their inevitable hour. Edward II was deposed by his Queen Isabella and her gentle Mortimer, and died mysteriously at Berkeley Castle – murdered it was said by a red hot iron thrust into his rectum which caused his violent end and yet left no mark upon him. In 1327, the boy King Edward III began his reign as the puppet of Mortimer and Isabella.

In 1327 the truce was broken – as much from distrust as any other cause – and once more the beacon fires across the border hills announced the northward progress of an English army. The campaign of Weardale was only memorable in so far as knights wore crests upon their helmets, and primitive cannon were first seen in northern England. The young Edward III had his first experience of war, and wept with shame at his humiliation by the Scots. Again Bruce's army followed the retreating English back across the border, and a parliament in Lincoln sued for peace. The conditions included an acknowledgement of Robert the Bruce as King of Scots and the renunciation of the English claim to sovereignty. The holy relic of St Margaret, the Black Rood, was restored, but strangely not the sandstone Stone of Destiny, which according to some accounts, the citizens of London would not relinquish (although its omission from others might imply that the Scots were not overly concerned about its authenticity). The treaty was to be sealed by the marriage of Prince David of Scotland to Edward's sister Joanna. To the more bellicose among the English barons it was indeed a 'shameful peace', and it cost Mortimer his head.

The marriage of the two children – Prince David aged four, and Princess Joan aged six – was celebrated at Berwick, notwithstanding grim associations, on 12 July 1328. Robert the Bruce, his body rotting from a disease which many said was leprosy, was too ill to attend, and he died at Cardross eleven months later, leaving Scotland to suffer another long minority. His brother Edward Bruce had been killed in Ireland, recklessly pursuing the illusion of an Irish crown. Douglas carried the Bruce's heart to war against the Moors and met a paladin's death in Spain. Randolph, the first regent, also died mysteriously at Musselburgh, and the government passed temporarily to another of Bruce's nephews – the anglicised and less distinguished Donald Earl of Mar. Suddenly almost, the future began to cast long shadows.

Angus Og died at Finlaggan in Islay shortly after Bruce, and was buried at Iona among the former Kings of the Isles. His tombstone bore the inscription: '*Hic jacet corpus Angusii filii Domini Angusi de Ila*', and below was carved a birlinn and four lions above a reticulated pattern of interlacing foliage. Angus had married Agnes O'Cahan, daughter of the great Irish Lord of Limvady who was a descendant of Niall of the Nine Hostages and ruled in Derry. It was a union of consequence, since her dowry had included 140 men out of every surname in the O'Cahan territory – a formidable force of fighting men to augment the Lord of Islay's power. These Irish and their descendants settled in the west, and are numbered now among the Scottish Highland families – the O'Millans from the Roe Water who took the name Munroe, the Roses of Kilravock, Fearns, Beatons, MacLinens, and others, are listed by the historian of Sleat.

By Agnes O'Cahan, Angus had a son, John of Islay, who succeeded him and was the first to be formally styled 'Lord of the Isles'. He also left another son by a handfast marriage with the daughter of Dugall MacEanruig, Chieftain of Glencoe, who was called Iain Fraoch and became the ancestor of the MacIains of Glencoe.

To the end of his life Angus had remained true to his pact with Bruce, but within a short time of succeeding him, John of Islay decided that it was in his better interest to reverse this policy and attach himself instead to the cause of Balliol which was undergoing a brief but somewhat inglorious revival. Old 'Toom Tabard' the Competitor had been dead for twenty years, but his son, Edward, obtained ready sponsorship at the English court and was ambitious to make good his father's claim. In 1332 he landed in Fife with an army consisting mainly of English archers and men at arms, the 'disinherited barons' whom Bruce had banished, and a number of minor English lords and knights to whom he had promised lands in Scotland. The invasion coincided with the death of the regent, Randolph of Moray, and the Scottish forces were led by his successor, Donald of Mar, who had little experience of battle. At Dupplin Moor, the English archers destroyed the helpless schiltrons where they stood, and 'the pile of dead was greater in height from the earth toward the sky than one whole spear length'. The Regent Mar was killed, together with others of greater promise, including Randolph's young heir, a bastard son of Bruce, and many more. Six weeks later, Balliol was crowned king at Scone. Having obtained his desire, he rode south to appease Edward, promising homage to England and offering to marry the Princess Joan if her marriage to the boy David could be dissolved. Behind him the loyal Scots rallied under Randolph's second son and another Douglas, and catching Balliol at Arran, chased him out of the kingdom dressed only in his shirt.

Edward III seized the opportunity of a border incident now to declare openly for Balliol and revoke the Treaty of 1323. Edward Balliol returned to Scotland at the head of a formidable English army and brought the Scots to battle at Halidon Hill, north-west of Berwick. Forgetting the old stratagems of Bruce which had served so well in the early wars, the new regent, Archibald Douglas (another brother of Bruce's great captain), recklessly led his army into a storm of arrows which felled the schiltrons as they advanced – and when the charge was spent and broken, the English chivalry rode down the fugitives 'felling the wretches with iron-shod maces'. Douglas was mortally wounded and taken prisoner, and the Scots lost six earls, seventy barons, five hundred knights and squires, and the flower of their army in one terrible and bloody defeat. Balliol was restored, and duly paid the price which Edward had demanded. Berwick was surrendered to the English and thereafter remained in their possession. The Lothians, together with the counties of Roxburgh, Peebles, Dumfries, and Kirkcudbright, were ceded to the English crown. Balliol acknowledged Edward III as his overlord.

Among the loyal Scots a very few escaped to conjure anarchy and civil war, and challenge Balliol's rule. Significantly, these survivors included Robert Stewart, grandson of the Bruce and Scotland's future king, and John Randolph, Earl of Moray. David II escaped to France and was granted asylum at Château Gaillard, where he enjoyed a comfortable exile and did not return for nine long years.

Apart from a general assumption that a weak or divided monarchy in Scotland ensured greater independence in the Isles, John of Islay's decision to support Balliol appears to have stemmed from a quarrel with the Regent Mar shortly after the death of Angus Og. Alarmed perhaps by the concentration of power in the Hebrides, Mar refused to confirm John in his inheritance, even though Angus Og had been granted the lands by Robert the Bruce. Fear of losing this territory, even if he remained neutral, thus prompted John to side with Balliol, who, anxious to secure so important an adherent, readily granted him not only all the lands possessed by Angus Og, but also Kintyre and Knapdale, then held by the Steward, together with Skye and Lewis belonging to the Earl of Ross, when these last two should be forfeited. On 12 December 1335, John and Edward Balliol entered into a Treaty of Alliance at Perth, the terms of which were subsequently ratified by Edward III at Auckland in the following year:

WE have examined certain letters of indenture drawn up between the magnificent prince Lord Edward King of Scotland, our illustrious and most dear cousin, and John of the Isles, as follows: – In this indenture made at Perth on Tuesday 12 December 1335, between the most excellent prince Lord Edward, by the grace of God the illustrious King of Scots, on the one part, and John of the Isles on the other part, it is certified that the said Lord the King has granted, *in so*

far as in him lay, to the foresaid John for good and praiseworthy service rendered
to himself, and in future to be rendered by him and his heirs,
The Island of Islay
The land of Kintyre
The land of Knapdale
The Island of Gigha
Half the Island of Jura
The Island of Colonsay
The Island of Mull
The Island of Skye
The Island of Lewis
The land of Morvern and Ardnamurchan
– to be held by the same John and his heirs and assignees. The same Lord the
King has also granted to the same John the wardship of Lochaber until the
attainment to man's estate of the son and heir of Lord David of Strathbolgy the
last Earl of Athol. And for these concessions John of the Isles binds himself and
his heirs to be loyal and faithful men to the Lord the King and his heirs for ever,
and he binds himself and his heirs to pursue all his foes and rebels whatsoever,
on what days, in what places and ways he may be able to do so. And in security for
the faithful performance of all these promises the oath shall be given by John on
the holy eucharist, the cup of the altar, and the missal. Likewise, John grants that
if the King should desire to have from him a hostage or hostages for greater
security, that a cousin or cousins of his own under age, very nearly related to
him, may be delivered over the Lord the King when a suitable time has come,
seeing that John has as yet neither son nor heir lawfully begotten of his own
body. Besides, the Lord the King wishes and grants that at whatever time he may
have an heir of his own body legitimately begotten the office of godfather to his
heir may be granted to the foresaid John.
But we accept, ratify, approve, and confirm the whole and each of the contents of
the foresaid letters for ourselves and our heirs so far as in us lies. . . .[80]

A safe-conduct of the same date indicates that John of Islay attended
the king at Auckland to endorse the indenture and the undertakings it
contained. Similar documents relating to the year 1337 also confirm
that, for a time, the relationship between John and Edward III remained
cordial and constant. On 3 December 1337 John was given a further
safe-conduct, informing the sheriffs, baillies, and other faithful subjects
that John and his retinue were under the royal protection, and threatening extreme penalties against any who injured or molested him or his
followers on their way to the king's presence. The Earl of Salisbury,
Edward's legate in Scotland, was instructed to enter into a bond of
association with him, and in the same month, Edward himself wrote an

Epistola blandiloqua addressing him as 'Dearest Friend' and offering guarantees of amity and good faith. These all reflect an assiduous cultivation by the English, although from John's point of view, his support was diplomatic rather than active, since he did not play any strenuous part against Edward's enemies in Scotland, and even when the Steward invaded Lochaber there is no record of his becoming involved.

At the same time, Balliol confirmed Ranald MacRuairi in his lands of Garmoran – which had been forfeited by Bruce when the MacRuairis became engaged in earlier conspiracies against the crown. He also restored some of the old MacDugall lands (but not Lorne itself) to John, grandson of John the Lame – although this may not have pleased the Lord of Islay, who still did not permit the MacDugall to reoccupy his old inheritance.

In 1341 the scene suddenly changed again. Edward III set his ambition on the crown of France, leaving Balliol to work his own salvation in Scotland. The loyal Scots rallied under Robert the Steward, and David II was brought back from France to enter Edinburgh amid scenes of great rejoicing. Balliol fled to England once more.

It was a time again for rewards and punishment, and in 1343 David II, reinstalled as King of Scots, forfeited John of Islay, and gave Islay, Gigha, and Colonsay to his kinsman Angus MacIain (who was descended from a younger son of Angus Mor). John simply ignored the sentence and his authority was not challenged in the Isles themselves. David II had no power to enforce the forfeiture and becoming intent upon an invasion of England, he was obliged to make his peace with the Lord of Islay, whom he confirmed in all the territories held by Angus Og – but not Kintyre, Knapdale, Lewis, and Skye, which remained in the possession of Robert the Steward and the Earl of Ross.

The invasion of England in the autumn of 1346 ended in disaster. At Neville's Cross near Durham, an army of northern barons completely routed the Scottish host. Again the schiltrons were decimated by the concentrated fire of the English bowmen, and when they scattered in confusion under the deadly hail of cloth-yard shafts, the English knights smashed through the ragged line of spears to complete the butchery. The Lion Standard of Scotland fell into the hands of the English, and with the Black Rood, which the Scots had confidently carried to the battle, was laid in triumph on St Cuthbert's shrine at Durham. David II was taken prisoner and led south to captivity in the Tower. He remained eleven years, in some comfort, imbibing English ways and manners, while his people worked to find a crippling ransom. That winter the black pestilence raged through Scotland.

Earlier in the year another violent event had contributed greatly to John of Islay's accumulation of power in the west. Prior to the invasion of England, the Scottish barons were convened at Perth – among them Ranald MacRuairi, who with a tail of followers took lodgings in the monastery at Elcho which was some miles outside the town. Ranald was at that time at feud over the lands of Kintail which he held of the Earl of Ross, who seized this opportunity to settle the matter permanently. During the night he broke into the monastery and killed Ranald and seven of his men, before escaping into the north.

Some years previously, John of Islay had obtained a papal dispensation to marry his third cousin, Amie MacRuairi, who, upon Ranald's death without issue, now became sole heiress to the MacRuairi lands. John therefore claimed the whole of MacRuairi territories of Garmoran, Uist, Barra, Eigg, and Rhum, together with the remaining portion of Lochaber. The Scottish government were reluctant to acknowledge so great a concentration of power reminiscent of the old Norwegian kingdom in the Isles, and so refused to confirm him in this new inheritance. This, together with the defeat at Neville's Cross, may have inclined John to Balliol's cause once more, but Balliol failed to take advantage of the victory – possibly because he received no support from Edward III who was more preoccupied by the expenses of the French war and preferred a king's ransom to an indifferent Pretender. The Steward became Regent of Scotland and John occupied the MacRuairi lands, unconfirmed but also unmolested.

During the years which followed, John of Islay devoted much of his attention to organising his extensive dominions, and it seems possible, in hindsight, that he also began a dynastic negotiation with the Steward. In 1353 he reached a settlement with John of Lorne whom David had restored to some of the old Clan Dugall lands. It was a complicated arrangement whereby Duror, Jura, and Mull were held by John of Lorne as the vassal of John of Islay, together with the fortresses of Cairnburgh and Isleburgh – for which he had to deliver hostages and promise that the Castle of Cairnburgh would never be put into the keeping of the Clan MacKinnon. Apart from certain estates in Tiree, these lands were resigned to John of Lorne with the further condition that as steward only, he could not build any establishment or dwelling without the permission of his superior. He was, however, allowed to retain the island of Coll. (John of Lorne died without male issue, and his heiress married a Stewart. Two generations later, when the male line failed again, the joint heiresses married Campbells.)

In the Agreement, John of Islay styled himself *Dominus Insularum.* Given the old Norse precedents, he may not himself have regarded the address as significantly new, but it is from this document that the title 'Lord of the Isles' derives, and the medieval Lordship may thus be said properly to date from 1353.

In 1354, while negotiations with England continued regarding the payment of David II's ransom, the French offered the Scots 40,000 *moutons d'or* to break the truce and send a force to France. To date, the Scots had not profited greatly from this alliance. A band of French knights had served in Scotland, and even captured Berwick, but English retaliation – called the 'Burnt Candlemas' because Edward's soldiers fired the church of Haddington on the Feast Day of the Purification of the Virgin – deterred any repetition. Nevertheless a contingent of Scots under the Earl of Douglas and John of Islay went to France and served under King John. In September 1356, the Black Prince defeated a numerically superior French army at Poictiers, and John of Islay was among the prisoners taken in the battle. For the next ten months he languished in England, until in December 1357 he was released on parole with four knights and a safe conduct to arrange the collection of his ransom. John's relations with Edward were now considerably less cordial, and although the English later tried to entice him back, he did not renew the former co-operation.

In the same year, David II was released on a guarantee of 100,000 merks to be paid in ten yearly instalments, and the truce which was to run in parallel specifically included 'Monsieur Edward de Balliol and Johan des Isles'. Balliol was now a spent force. In 1356 at Roxburgh, he delivered up the golden circlet and a sod of Scottish soil in token of his renunciation of all claim to the Scottish throne, and Edward pensioned him off with £2,000 per annum – 'unwept, unhonoured, and unsung'.

In Scotland, David II received a muted welcome. The country was pledged to bankruptcy to purchase his release, but he was scarcely more than a stranger, and hardly a creditable king. A self-indulgent young man, he had grown accustomed to English ways and the extravagant pageantry of the southern court. Between him and Robert the Steward grew a mutual hatred and distrust, since by several Acts of Settlement the Steward was the heir presumptive while David had no children. In 1363 the Queen Joan died and David contracted a violent desire for a woman called Margaret Logie – who had been married four times previously albeit without issue – and many barons opposed such a union. David's hatred of the Steward was such that he even offered the Scottish crown to Edward III if the ransom should be lifted, but the Scottish parliament would not ratify so shameful a bargain, and when David married Margaret Logie, the Steward rebelled. It was a feeble rising and short-lived, and Robert Stewart was imprisoned in the Castle of Loch Leven, together with his son, Alexander, Earl of Buchan, called the Wolf of Badenoch.

During the Steward's enforced absence, the office of Seneschal was conferred on John of Islay, who for the period enjoyed the king's trust. In 1360 he was appointed Governor of Edinburgh Castle, and in 1366 he was sent to Flanders to negotiate the wool monopoly with the Flemings. In order to raise the ransom, David II ordered that all wool in Scotland should be 'thirled' to him at a low price for resale to the Fleming textile merchants at a large profit, and the Seneschal, with responsibility for collecting the ransom by this and other means, went to the continent to arrange the export contracts. But the oppressive effect of such exactions, particularly in the Highlands, together with the profligacy and extravagance of David II, drove John also into rebellion, and with other magnates he refused to pay any further taxes or attend the Committee of Estates.

David had no alternative but to release the Steward, whom he charged to bring John of Islay to obedience. This was accomplished with surprising ease, and in 1369 John submitted personally to the king at Inverness, 'coming humbly into the presence of my said Lord' and supplicating for pardon for all his 'late faults' with promises of restitution and amendment. David II accepted him back into the king's friendship, but kept his heir Donald in Dumbarton Castle as a hostage for his good behaviour.

This submission, so easily achieved, would seem uncharacteristic of the Lord of the Isles, were it not apparent in the retrospect that John had a long-standing dynastic agreement with the Steward by which he stood to gain substantially. In about 1358, John divorced Amie MacRuairi of Garmoran and married the Steward's daughter Margaret – 'by the consent of his Council and familiar friends, particularly by the advice of MacInnes of Ardgour, who, being his foster father, advised him to take to wife the (future) king's daughter'.[81] This action possibly met with some opposition in the Isles, since Amie had been 'a good and virtuous gentlewoman', and some settlement had also to be made for the children of this marriage. The eldest son John had died, and the third and youngest, Godfrey, would not be reconciled to an arrangement which denied his mother's rightful claim to Garmoran – or indeed his own as one of the heirs – and he removed to Uist, where he became the ancestor of the *Siol Gorrie*. The second son, Ranald, was more pliant, however, although technically he was the feudal heir, and for his co-operation he was promised all the inheritance of his mother together with the castles of Benbecula and Island Tioram, and the lands of Sunart, Letterlochletter, Ardgour, Hawfaste, and Kilmald and Lochargaig in Lochaber – to be held as a vassal of John, Lord of the Isles, and his heirs. By this arrangement the children of Amie became subordinate to the heirs of John's second marriage to Margaret Stewart.

Amie MacRuairi retired to Island Tioram where she 'lived a solitary life, but was the ruin of the MacInnes'. Presumably in revenge upon the man who had been largely responsible for her repudiation, it is said that she contrived for John to be informed that MacInnes was in the habit of complaining that when he stayed with the Lord of the Isles, he was lodged in a house that 'did not smell well' because it was used as a dog kennel. John of Islay was enraged by this slur upon his hospitality, and commissioned Donald, son of Lachlan MacLean to kill MacInnes – which he did, and 'having also killed his five sons, got himself possessed of Ardgour'. Amie spent the remainder of her life building Castle Borve on Benbecula and completing Island Tioram – which later became the stronghold of the Clanranald. 'She built the parish church of St Columba on Benbecula, and the little oratory at Grimsay – all at the expense of the Lord of the Isles.' In the charter of David II dated 1363, which confirmed John in possession of all the old MacRuairi lands, her name was not mentioned.[82]

Having successfully disposed of Amie, John married Margaret Stewart – who, apart from her other attractions, was heiress to Knapdale and Kintyre. The wedding was celebrated in some splendour, and the story is told that when John sailed up the Clyde with sixty galleys to meet his bride, his councillors advised that since the king would also be present, he 'should behave courteously . . . and uncover himself as others did'. John replied that 'he did not well know how the king should be reverenced, for all men he ever saw should reverence himself; and with that threw away his cap, saying he would wear none.' The tale is probably apocryphal, and rather illustrates the great pride in the Lordship evinced by the later seannachies of the Clan Donald.[83]

In 1371, Robert the Steward succeeded David II as King of Scots, and in a series of charters honoured the agreement which he had made with his 'beloved John of Isla'. The Lord of the Isles was confirmed in all his dominions including the old lands of Knapdale and Kintyre, with the condition that the heir to the superiority of all these estates should be the eldest son by his second marriage to Margaret Stewart.

Between 1372 and 1380 John of Islay did little to record. Like his predecessors he was a benefactor of the Church, making donations to Iona and restoring the roofs on the chapels at Orsay, Finlaggan, and Loch Sween. For this perhaps, he was called 'Good John of Isla' – a paradoxical sobriquet when applied to the rather shadowy figure whose consistent motive was self-interest and the aggrandisement of his house.

In 1380, he was taken ill of a flux while staying at Ardgour 'and was carried yet alive to Ardtornish where he died on the third night thereafter in the fifty-fifth year of his age, and was interred at Icolm-kille'. His heir Donald was still a minor, but Ranald, his son by Amie, remained loyal to their settlement.

Ranald the son of John, was High Steward over the Isles at the time of his father's death, being in advanced age and ruling over them. On the death of his father, he called a meeting of the nobles of the Isles and of his brethren at one place (the island of Eigg), and Donald was nominated Macdonald and Donald of Isle – contrary to the opinion of the men of the Isles.[84]

Ranald became Donald's tutor until he came of age and his leadership was accepted.

It was John of Islay's achievement that his son Donald now inherited a dominion more extensive than ancient Dalriada or the patrimony of great Somerled. The old Celtic lands so long dispersed were reconstituted in a single principality, and the Gaelic revival was consolidated upon the divisions in Scotland and the English war. The Lordship of the Isles which John established consisted of, on the mainland: Lochaber, Garmoran (Moidart, Arisaig, Morar, Knoydart), with Morvern, Knapdale; Kintyre, and Glencoe; and among the islands – Islay, Gigha, Mull,

Colonsay, Jura, Scarba, Tiree, Eigg, Rhum, Lewis, Harris, the Uists,
Benbecula, and Barra.

> Western Albyn thine for croftland
> All her bens and all her cattle,
> All her rowans, all her hazel,
> All her birdland, all her stagland
> Child of Islay shall be thine.
>
> Thine is Jura, thine green Isla
> Far flung isles, from Lewis to Arran,
> Morvern Glens and Moidart waters,
> All the seas from Moyle to Antrim
> Child of Islay shall be thine.

CHAPTER 16

Donald of Harlaw, Lord of the Isles

Victory He giveth, and wealth – at His will,
Wisdom and words – they may win them who can:
As He giveth the boat breeze so he gives the skald skill,
But to each giveth Odin the heart of a man.

Donald of Islay was probably born in about 1362, since he was still a minor at the time of his father's death in 1380. As a child, in 1369, he had been imprisoned in Dumbarton Castle as a hostage for John's good behaviour, but was released in 1371 when his grandfather, Robert II, ascended the throne of Scotland. Shortly after, he was sent to England to be educated at the University of Oxford, returning in 1378 under a safe-conduct granted by Richard II to Donald, '*filio de Johannis de Insulis, clerico*'.

In the years which followed, Donald and his brothers visited the English court on several occasions where they were received with considerable ceremony as independent Celtic princes, and the diplomatic connections established by John of Islay were renewed and strengthened, despite the fact that the family of the Isles were now close blood kin to the Stewart King of Scots. In 1382, Donald's brother Hugh travelled south on a formal embassy to the English king, and in 1388, Donald, with his brother John Mor and his half-brother Godfrey, visited the English court and entered into a league with Richard II. In 1400, after Richard's abdication, they were received by Henry IV and a new defensive alliance, as between sovereign powers, was agreed. Further visits in 1405 and 1408 continued and cemented this relationship.

In the Isles themselves Donald's minority, and the complicated inheritance contrived by John of Islay, proved less divisive than many might have feared. Of John's children by Amie MacRuairi, the eldest son John had been drowned sometime prior to 1369. The second,

Ranald, although by right John's feudal heir, honoured his pledge and governed the Isles as executor and regent until Donald attained his majority. When Ranald died shortly afterwards, his younger brother Godfrey seized his mother's lands of Garmoran – possibly in retaliation for Ranald's having displaced his own people, the *Siol Gorrie,* from South Uist and Canna, or because he was not reconciled to the disinheriting of the MacRuairi branch. Despite his debt to Ranald and his children, Donald did nothing to prevent this, while for his part, Godfrey made no claim to the Lordship as a whole. Godfrey's son was executed by James I in 1460, but it was not until the power of *Siol Gorrie* declined that Ranald's descendants were able to regain their patrimony. John, fourth Lord of the Isles later gave the old MacRuairi lands to his brother Hugh of Sleat, but the Clanranald would not be dislodged and were eventually granted hereditable possession. Ranald had married the daughter of Duncan Stewart of Lennox, and his eldest son Allan became the progenitor of the families of Moidart and Morar, while the second, Donald, was the ancestor of the Macdonalds of Glengarry.

The sons of John's second marriage to Margaret Stewart each received a generous inheritance under the superiority of Donald as Lord of the Isles. The second son, John Mor, called 'the Tanister', obtained a grant of 120 merklands in Kintyre and 60 merklands in Islay including the fortress of Dunyveg. He married Margery Bisset, heiress of MacEoin Bisset, Lord of the Antrim Glens, whose ancestors had been expelled from Scotland for the murder of the Comyn Earl of Atholl, and their descendants, the Clan Iain Mor, styled themselves Macdonalds of Dunyveg and the Glens. By her, John Mor had a son, Donald Balloch, who was fostered by Maclean of Duart (and of whom more hereafter), and he also had an illegitimate son, Ranald Bain, ancestor of the family of Lairgie, whom he got by a daughter of the 'Green Abbot' Finnon. This second handfasting was of perilous conse- quence since the Green Abbot was 'a subtle and wicked counsellor' who together with the chief of the MacFinnons persuaded John Mor that he was entitled to all the islands south of Ardnamurchan, and being 'a subtle, eloquent man brought over to his side the chief of the Macleans and MacLeod of Harris to get the islands for themselves.'[85] When Donald got wind of this rebellion he promptly mustered the fighting men of his dominion – the MacLeods of Lewis, the Mackintoshes, Mackenzies, Camerons, MacNeils of Barra, the Islesmen, and the people of Glenmoriston and Glencoe – and with this formidable force, drove John Mor out of Kintyre. John fled first to Galloway, and when Donald pursued him there, he took refuge with his wife's people in the Glens of Antrim.

When John Mor and his faction saw that both they themselves and their interests were like to be lost unless Macdonald pardoned himself and spared the rest for his sake, they thought it their best course to go to Islay where John resided at Kilcummin. Upon John Mor's coming into his brother's presence, and prostrating himself on the ground, his brother rose and took him up, and embraced him kindly.

The brothers were thus reconciled, but the MacFinnon was hanged and the Green Abbot confined for life on Iona, 'his life being spared because he was a churchman'.[86] The MacFinnons subsequently turned on each other when the sons of the Green Abbot, being 'so wicked and covetous', killed the son of MacFinnon who was the foster-brother of Donald Ferguson. The Fergusons took up the feud and slew the murderers, and the rest of the MacFinnon family made their peace with the Lord of the Isles.

The third son of John of Islay and Margaret Stewart was called Angus, who probably died in childhood since nothing is known of him other than the name. The fourth was Alasdair Carrach, who declined a grant of Trotternish in Skye, and obtained instead a part of Mull, and the forest lands of Lochaber beyond the Lochy in Mamore and Glen Spean. By 1394 the three brothers were on such bad terms with their mother that Robert II ordered the Earl of Fife (her brother, their uncle) to take measures for her protection. Possibly in retaliation, Alasdair Carrach marched into Ross and seized Urquhart Castle on Loch Ness. He was dislodged and captured, and only released a year later when Donald (who probably connived in this escapade) undertook before Parliament to stand surety for his future conduct. Alasdair was a wild spirit, however, and in 1402 he again went raiding into Ross and plundered Elgin. He was once more brought to repentance, and donated a golden torque and a standing cross to the cathedral. Alasdair's descendants were the Clan Macdonald of Keppoch.

The fifth son, Eugenius, or Hugh, who was involved in the negotiations with England, obtained the Thanage of Glentilt, probably through marriage with a Mackintosh (whose name, *Mac-an-Toiseach*, meant 'sons of the Thane').

Apart from these domestic quarrels and the disquiet which his alliance with England may have caused, between 1380 and 1411 Donald did not play an active or significant part in Scottish affairs, and the Hebridean principality was left unmolested. Scotland itself, however, was in a state bordering upon chaos.

The most striking feature of Robert II is said to have been his heavily bloodshot eyes. Having promised fair, the first Stewart king proved to be a timid, hesitant, yet kind-hearted man who 'would rather remain at home than march to the field'. A monarch of little consequence, he was generally incompetent and inactive in every area of government, with the exception of the bedchamber where he sired a prodigious number of children by two wives, and at least eight bastard sons by a variety of other women. Having for so long suffered from the succession of minors and a shortage of heirs, Scotland was now threatened by the very superfluity of them, and the situation was the more irregular in that Robert had already fathered four sons and six daughters by his first wife, Elizabeth Mure, before the Pope was persuaded to agree to their marriage. Despite a Papal Bull legitimising their children, in an age when consanguinity was a serious issue, the spectre of incest, should the barons so choose, might upset the order of succession. On the day after his coronation in 1371, in order to allay such fears, Robert formally named his eldest son John, Earl of Carrick, as his heir. It was hardly a popular choice, since John was a sickly, limping man who was partially crippled from a kick by a horse, but it is unlikely that anyone could have guessed then just how disastrous it would prove. In 1373 a Parliament at Scone confirmed the nomination in order to avoid 'the uncertainty of the succession'.

In Scotland, the authority of the Crown depended upon there being a strong king on the throne, and the royal power once lost, could only be regained by force of arms. Robert II was manifestly weak, and unable to curb the bellicosity of the barons – who 'spent all their time in wars, and when there was no war they fought each other'. 'In those days', says the Chronicle, 'there was no law in Scotland; but the great man oppressed the poor man, and the whole country was one den of thieves. Slaughters, robberies, fire-raising, and other crimes went unpunished, and justice was sent into banishment, beyond the kingdom's bounds.'

The Highlands came under the government of Robert's psychopathic son, Alexander, Earl of Buchan, the Wolf of Badenoch, whose savagery reduced the region to a wasteland. When the Bishop of Moray had the temerity to rebuke him for repudiating his wife, he pillaged Elgin, burning the Cathedral, the churches, and all the religious buildings in the town. The glens became the haunt of reivers, and abandoned homesteads a common sight.

In 1385, while English armies were entrenched in France, the French themselves decided to carry the war to Scotland, and sent their Admiral, de Vienne, to Edinburgh 'with all the flower of chivalry'. If they had thought to benefit from the Auld Alliance they were quickly disillusioned. The Scots did not welcome the intrusion. They received the French coldly, forbade them entry to any castle, charged them for every ounce of grain they ate, and hanged them when they foraged. De Vienne rode south to fight the English, but he found the discomforts of warfare on the border – the sudden raids and burnings, and cattle reiving in the cold bleak landscape of the Teviots – to be not the stuff of chivalry, and the French turned back in disgust. De Vienne himself was held hostage for a time as surety for outstanding 'debts' and he finally left, saying that he had never seen 'such wicked people, nor such ignorant hypocrites and traitors'.[87]

On the border, the families of Douglas and Percy were left to continue what was virtually a personal war, pitilessly devastating the country in raid, and counter raid, and bloody reprisal. In 1388 they fought at Otterburn, the armies grappling through the night, until Douglas fell with lance points through his shoulder, chest, and legs, and Hotspur, not knowing that the hurts were mortal, surrendered to a dead man. The ferocity of their contest inspired one of the finest of the border ballads.

Robert II died in 1390 – 'a tenderer heart might no man have'. As senility overtook him, effective power passed to another of his sons, the Chamberlain, Robert, Duke of Albany – ablest of the brood, but a dissembling man, given to crooked counsels and a devious ambition. Control of Stirling Castle and the Royal Purse made him in all but name the governor of Scotland during the old king's dotage, and although the new monarch initially took his powers from him, his hand was always close upon events. Prince John began his reign by changing his name to Robert III ('John' was thought to be unlucky), but in character he was as inept and weak as the accidental king his father. The anarchy and lawlessness continued without respite.

An incident in 1396 reflected the degree to which the administration of law and justice had been debased, when the Highland clans of

Chattan and Mackay, who were engaged in a dispute the cause of which is long forgotten, were induced to resolve the issue in a 'trial by battle'. Intended no doubt to emulate a chivalrous encounter which had taken place in France some fifty years before, a wooden enclosure was constructed at the North Inch of Perth, and thirty champions from either clan butchered each other in front of a capacity crowd that included Robert III and the ladies of his court. When the last Mackay jumped the palisade and escaped across the Tay, the warriors of Clan Chattan (those who remained) were adjudged the victors and the lawsuit decided in their favour. Tradition avers that the Clan Chattan arrived for the contest with one man short, and a Perth armourer called Hal o' the Wynd volunteered to take his place. He was one of the eleven survivors.

The year 1399 was to be a sad one for kings. In England, Richard II was deposed by Henry Bolingbroke. In Scotland, a General Council forced Robert III to resign his powers on account of the 'sickness of person' which made him unfit for 'restraining trespassers and rebells', and conferred them for three years on his son and heir, David, Duke of Rothesay. Robert's mishandling of affairs had made such a decision desirable and even necessary, but Rothesay was an unhappy choice since his principal talent for dissipation and the dishonouring of nobles' daughters had earned him the deep enmity of the barons. He expired enigmatically in 1402, dying, according to the parliamentary inquiry, 'by Divine Providence' – and with some assistance, said tradition, from the Duke of Albany who starved him to death in Falkland Palace. Albany again became governor of the realm.

The Earl of March defected to the English and once more there was warfare on the border. Albany's son Murdoch with Archibald, fourth Earl of Douglas, were soundly defeated by Percy Hotspur at the Battle of Homildon Hill. Douglas, with five arrows through his body, yielded to Hotspur and then agreed to join him in support of Glendower's Welsh rebellion. It was a doomed adventure which cost Douglas a large ransom and Percy his life.

In 1406 Robert III tried to preserve his surviving heir James from Albany's ambition by sending the boy to France. But by accident or treachery, the ship was intercepted by the English and the young James was carried south into a long captivity which Albany had no inclination to curtail. At Bute, the news caused Robert III to die of grief, in his own words, 'the worst of kings and the most miserable of men'. A General

Council at Perth appointed Albany Governor and Regent in the absence of the rightful heir James I, and having reached a pact with Douglas, his power was undisputed.

In 1411, a major quarrel broke out between Donald Lord of the Isles and the Regent Albany over the Earldom of Ross. This comprised a huge territory, including not only Skye, Ross, and Cromarty, but also part of old Argyll westwards to Loch Broom and the coastlands of Kintail, Lochalsh, Loch Carron, Applecross, and Gairloch. To the south it reached to Urquhart on Loch Ness, and eastwards into the county of Inverness, with the superiority over additional outlying lands in Nairn and Aberdeenshire.

In earliest times this domain had formed one of the seven great *Mormaerships*, of which the last Celtic incumbent had been Macbeth himself. The first to use the title Earl of Ross had been Gillanders, of the Celtic Obeolan family who were descended from the hereditary abbots of Applecross. In the twelfth century it was possessed briefly by the MacEths, and then by Florence Count of Holland, who had married a sister of Malcolm IV and William the Lion. In 1212 it was recovered by Ferchar Macantagart of the Obeolan line, and his descendants held it in turn until, after the death of William, the fifth Earl, without male heirs, it passed to his daughter, Euphemia, Countess of Ross.

Euphemia's first husband, Sir Walter Leslie, died in 1382, and she married Alexander Stewart, Earl of Buchan, upon whom, at her request, the title was conferred to the exclusion of Alexander Leslie, the heir by her first marriage. Alexander recovered the earldom in 1398, and married Isabella Stewart, daughter of the Regent Albany. Alexander's sister, Margaret Leslie, was married to Donald, Lord of the Isles.

In 1402, Alexander Leslie died leaving a sole heiress, Euphemia – a sickly hunchbacked child, who was taken completely into Albany's power. According to the Clan Donald account, 'they persuaded her by flattery and threats to resign her rights to the Earldom of Ross to John, Albany's second son, Earl of Buchan, as it was given out, and *that* much against her will'.[88] Euphemia was to enter a nunnery, and all the territories of Ross would accrue to the Stewart family.

Donald of the Isles, with an eye to his own borders and also to the acquisition of Ross for himself, at once objected, on the grounds that if Euphemia entered a nunnery she was legally dead to the world and so could not lawfully dispose of the earldom – which should therefore pass to his own wife Margaret as the sister and surviving heir of Alexander Leslie. However, he 'could get no hearing from Albany but lofty menacing answers. Neither could he get sight of the rights' which Euphemia was alleged to have made over to John of Buchan. Donald therefore challenged Albany directly that 'he would either lose all he had or gain the Earldom of Ross', and when Albany told him to make good the threat, he called a great hosting in the Isles.

About ten thousand fighting men came to the muster at Ardtornish, out of which number Donald chose six thousand six hundred whom he planned to lead against Inverness and bring the Regent to battle. It was the largest Hebridean army to have come out of the west: Macleans and MacKinnons, MacLeods from Harris and Lewis; the clans of Mull and Morvern; Clan Chattan of Lochaber, and all the scions of Clan Donald and the vassals of the Lordship – a great gathering of Gaelic chieftains, eagle plumes and saffron war-coats, long axes and two-handed broadswords; warriors and red-shanked kerns in yellow shirts and breacons – marshalled for invasion and scenting war beyond the passes.

They sailed by Wester Ross to Stroma, drawing in the clansmen of those parts, and marched to Dingwall where their way was barred by Angus Dubh Mackay and three thousand of his clan. In a fierce assault the Islesmen routed the Mackays, killing many and taking Angus prisoner. Donald seized the Castle of Dingwall and proceeded to Beauly, where he turned aside to savage the lands of the Frasers of Lovat and burned the country along the march to Inverness. The town fell after a short fight.

Donald burns the bridge, the famousest and finest of oak in Britain, burns most of the town because they would not rise and concur with him. John Cumming, a gentleman burgher of the town, putting on his armour and head-piece, and two-handed sword, made such stout resistance at this nearest end of the bridge against the M'donels that . . . if there were ten more like him in Inverness, neither bridge nor burgh had been burnt.[89]

Donald planted his standard in the town and summoned all the northern clans, gathering in the Mackintoshes and bringing his army to something over ten thousand men.

Donald had now gained possession of Ross proper, but he looked for a decisive battle to prove the point. In the south, Albany was slow to muster, and Donald, intending probably to assert his power over the outlying portions of the earldom, and to encourage his men with fresh plunder, started to march through Moray, giving out that he planned to sack the town of Aberdeen.

Words of his advance and the war smoke over the hills caused consternation and alarm, and the gentlemen of Aberdeenshire hastily armed themselves and mustered with their retainers under Alexander Stewart, Earl of Mar. Mar himself was an illegitimate son of the Wolf of Badenoch (and first cousin to Donald), and had inherited many of his father's brigandish tendencies. The heir to Buchan, he had acquired the title of Mar by laying siege to the widowed Countess in her Castle of Kildrummie and marrying her by force – a circumstance to which she apparently became reconciled since she invested the earldom in the ruffian who had ravished her to the exclusion of the lawful heirs.

Mar advanced by Inverury, and the two armies came in sight of each other near the village of Harlaw about fifteen miles from Aberdeen at the junction of the River Ury and the Don. Accounts of the battle were greatly distorted by later Scottish chroniclers and the numbers engaged have been much exaggerated. Donald probably had about ten thousand men, almost all Highlanders on foot, who would have presented a disorganised and outlandish spectacle to the feudal levies of the enemy. The chieftains probably wore the antiquated style of armour then used in the Western Isles – high, conical helmets and quilted war-coats – while the clansmen wore little at all other than saffron shirts knotted between their legs to give them ease of movement, and carried shields of wood and bull-hide, broadswords, long-handled axes, bows, and knives. The Gaels deployed into the traditional crescent-shaped battle front of the Celts, with a centre, two wings, and a reserve.

According to the Sleat historian:

Donald himself commanded the main battle, where he kept most of the islanders, and with the MacLeods, John of Harris and Roderick of Lewis. He ordered the rest to the wings, the right commanded by Hector Roy Maclean, and the left by Callum Beg Mackintosh, who that day received from Macdonald a right to the lands of Glengarry in Lochaber by way of pleasing him for yielding the right wing to Maclean, and to prevent any quarrel between him and Maclean. Mackintosh said he would take the lands and make the left behave as well as the right. John Mor, Donald's brother, was placed with a detachment of the lightest and nimblest men as a reserve, either to assist the wings or the main battle, as occasion required. To him was joined ... Donald Cameron of Lochiel. Alasdair Carrach was young and therefore was, much against his will, set apart, lest the whole of the brothers should be hazarded at once.[90]

In front of the army, the bard Lachlan Mor MacMhuirich declaimed the battle-song to inflame the fighting men of the clans:

Sons of Conn remember
Hardihood in time of strife . . .

– three hundred lines of genealogy, epithet and invocation to conjure the old stories of their greatness and the valour of their chieftains.

By contrast, Mar's force may not have exceeded two thousand men: mounted chivalry, armed in plate and mail, with lances, mace and battle-axe, and all the panoply of feudal war. It was a local levy, composed of the barons and knights of Aberdeenshire, Angus and the Mearns, mustered in defence of their lands – Ogilvies, Lindsays, Carnegies, Lyons, Irvings, Frasers, Arbuthnots, Burnets, and more, with the Lords Marischal and Errol, and Sir James Scrymgeour, Constable of Dundee and Standard-bearer of Scotland. The only notable absentee was Huntly.

Mar divided this army into a main battle commanded by himself, with two small 'fronts': the right under Marischal and Errol, and the left under Sir Alexander Ogilvie, Sheriff of Angus. 'There came several in [Mar's] army to see Macdonald and his Highlanders routed, as they imagined; others came to be rewarded by the Regent.' It seems likely that trusting to the weight of their armour and the shock of mounted chivalry charging home, Mar's levies were confident that they would scatter the lightly armed Gaels.

There are no trustworthy accounts of the fight. The two armies set upon each other and a fierce battle continued until dusk. Mar's charge drove a great wedge into the Gaelic line, but as its momentum failed, the Highlanders closed around the heavily armed knights and chopped them out of their saddles with axes. The attack was brought up short in confusion, and the Islesmen hamstrung the horses, dragging riders down to tear open their armour and stab them on the ground. Unhorsed men fought ponderously on foot, great swords keeping the foe at bay, and the Lowland lords drew together to stand against the wild onslaught of the Gaels. For several hours the fight swung back and forth as the front ranks hewed each other across the battle-wreck, and the wounded, falling underneath the press, bled and suffocated in their heavy mail as the struggle raged fiercely on above them. On Donald's right, Hector Maclean hurled his clansmen at Ogilvie's wing, which was driven backwards against a cattle-pen, and the Gaels swarmed around the shrinking steel ring in a long attrition of sword and axe-work. But Mar's men fought desperately through the day, and the lightly armed Highlanders suffered terrible losses as they recklessly pressed their assault. At dusk the combatants paused exhausted, each surprised by the sheer ferocity of the other.

Donald lost about a thousand men killed, but Mar's losses were proportionately greater and may have amounted to nearly half his force. Mar and Errol escaped to Aberdeen. The dead included Sir Alexander Ogilvie, Sheriff of Angus; Sir James Scrymgeour, the Constable of Dundee, Sir Robert Davidson, Provost of Aberdeen, Maule of Panmure, Abernethy of Saltoun, Sir Thomas Murray, and many more of distinction. Hardly a leading family in Aberdeenshire but lost a laird or son, and the Irvings of Drum were wiped out. The Lord Marischal was captured – 'and died in his confinement of mere grief and despair'. On Donald's side the most notable casualty was Hector Roy Maclean who had led the right wing, and the dead included a number of gentlemen of the Camerons and Munroes, John Macleod and the heir to Macquarie of Ulva.

During the night, Donald withdrew – persuaded according to the Sleat account, by Huntly, who advised him not to sack Aberdeen since 'by his victory in all appearance he gained his own, yet it was ridiculous for him to destroy the town and that citizens would always join with him who had the upper hand'. This gave Lowland historians the opportunity to claim that Donald and his 'weir men' were defeated, and in after centuries it was even alleged that Donald himself was killed. The truth more like was that 'Donald had the victory but the regent had the printer'. Yet the precise reason for Donald's retreat is not known. He had carried his sword through all of Ross and its outlying feus to which he had claim, but he made no attempt to defend his conquest, although the Battle of Harlaw was ever afterwards hailed by the Gaels as the greatest Highland victory over a Lowland army.

The Regent Albany belatedly gathered a large force and recovered Ross without opposition. In 1412 he pursued the campaign into Argyll itself, and Fordoun, in the manner of a propagandist rather than an historian, claimed that Donald was forced to sign a humiliating treaty at Lochgilphead. But there is no other record of such a document, and Donald's rule over the Isles continued undisputed. In 1415 Euphemia did resign the Earldom of Ross to Albany who bestowed it on his son, the

Earl of Buchan. It would pass to the Lord of the Isles in the next generation.

In his declining years, Donald retired to a life of religious seclusion – in the manner of so many of his ancestors. The year of his death is uncertain, but he probably died in 1422 at his castle of Ardtornish in Morvern, and was buried on Iona. Of his children by Margaret Leslie, a number are said to have died in childhood, and he was survived by three sons and a daughter: Alexander who succeeded him; Angus who became Bishop of the Isles; a third son who became a monk; and Marion, who married Alexander Sutherland of Dunbeath.

Wyntoun, the chronicler, tells of a strange incident which occurred in the Isles during the time of Donald's Lordship:

> Quhether he had bene King or nane
> Thare was bot few, that wyst certane.
> Off devotionne nane he wes,
> And seildyn will had till here Mes;
> As he bare hym, like wes he
> Offte halff wod or wyld to be.[91]

In about 1406, a beggarman appeared at the gates of Finlaggan in Islay, starving and witless, whom Donald's sister-in-law, having been in Ireland and at the English court, claimed to recognise as King Richard II. When questioned, the man denied that he had once been king of England, whom men presumed to have been murdered at Pomfret Castle. But he was wild and raving, and the Scots took him into care, first by the Lord of Cumbernauld, and then by the Regent himself. Though well-treated, he never recovered from his madness, but received at the last a respectful burial.

It is a romantic postscript, incapable of proof. Yet strangely, there was a similar legend in the region of the Valle Crucis when Glendower raised the Welsh rebellion – that Richard was abroad in the land, a mendicant touched by God with a holy madness, who cried over the wrongs of an oppressed country. The stones of Pomfret do not give up their mysteries, but it is not impossible that Richard escaped, or was set loose, demented from privation or grief, and found his ways perhaps to Wales and thence to the 'Outleys of Scotland'. There were those who should have recognised him – for Donald and his brothers had often visited the English court – and perhaps also the beggar remembered in

his madness that there was a 'Rune of Hospitality' which the people
recited in the Western Isles.

> I saw a stranger yestreen;
> I put food in the eating place,
> Drink in the drinking place,
> Music in the listening place;
> And, in the sacred name of the Triune,
> He blessed myself and my house,
> My cattle and my dear ones,
> And the lark said in her song,
>   Often, often, often,
> Goes the Christ in the stranger's guise:
>   Often, often, often,
> Goes the Christ in the stranger's guise.

CHAPTER 17

Alexander, Lord of the Isles and Earl of Ross

Pibroch of Donuil Dhu,
Pibroch of Donuil,
Wake thy wild voice anew
Summon Clan Conuil;
Come away, come away
Hark to the summons;
Come in your war array,
Gentles and commons.

Come from deep glen, and
From mountains so rocky,
The war-pipe and pennon
Are at Inverlochy.
Come every hill plaid, and
True heart that wears one;
Come every steel-blade, and
Strong hand that bears one.

Leave untended the herd,
The flock without shelter;
Leave the corpse uninterred,
The bride at the altar;
Leave the deer, leave the steer,
Leave nets and barges:
Come with your fighting gear,
Broadswords and targes.

Come as the winds come, when
  Forests are rended;
Come as the waves come
  When birlinns are stranded:
Faster come, faster come,
  Faster and faster;
Chief, vassal, page, and groom,
  Tenant and master.

Fast they come, fast they come,
  See how they gather!
Wide waves the eagle-plume
  Blended with heather,
Cast your plaids, draw your blades,
  Forward each man set!
Pibroch of Donuil Dhu
  Knell for the onset.

Sir Walter Scott, 'The Battle of Inverlochy', 1431

'If God gives me but a dog's life,' swore James I when first he returned to that unhappy country, 'I shall make the key keep the castle and the bracken bush keep the cow through all Scotland.'

The Regent Albany died in 1420, and the General Council were persuaded to appoint his son Murdoch to succeed him as Governor of the country. Lacking his father's authority and guile, Murdoch was unable to restrain the turbulence of the nobles, and the brigandage and lawlessness increased. Even the crown estates and revenues were plundered and robbed, and when his own son defied him, Murdoch is alleged to have exclaimed, 'Since you pay me so little respect, I shall invite him whom both must obey.' Negotiations began with England for the release of James I, who for eighteen years had been held a prisoner in the south, and in 1424 he was freed on payment of 60,000 marks. Murdoch was not to know that he had uncaged a king indeed.

At thirty, James I was a strong, athletic man of considerable ability and determination. His character had many facets, sometimes in contradiction. He was a poet and musician, given to contemplation and the composing of fine and evocative lyric verse; a scientist with a particular fascination for the machinery of warfare; an administrator with a practical bent for law-making and government; and an uncompromising man of action, unswerving from his purpose. But the long frustrated years of his captivity had embittered him, so that, despite the sensitivity and charm, he was utterly ruthless, and his enemies found him vindictive, and implacable in his revenge.

Immediately after his coronation, James declared that peace would be enforced throughout the realm and 'if any man presume to make war against another he shall suffer the full penalties of the law'. He strengthened the machinery of justice and the king's law replaced the anarchy of the barons. The King's Register promulgated that law through all the towns and sheriffdoms of the country, and a court of the three estates was established to investigate abuses. The spate of legislation and law-giving extended over a variety of social and economic activities, and applied to rich and poor alike without distinction, fraud, or favour. Poaching was prohibited, and the taking of salmon out of season. Archery practice was encouraged; football was banned. The law was enforced with fines, imprisonment, and hempen rope, and those who thought to resist were summarily dealt with.

Among the baronage, James's response to opposition was sudden and drastic. For two years after his return he took no action against his cousins of Albany, but in the middle of his second Parliament, he arrested Murdoch and his two sons, tried them before a court of nobles, and ordered their immediate execution. The other lords were shocked into a cowed submission by the violence of this justice, and the Stewarts, whose avarice and rapacity had contributed in large measure to the disorders of the country, were brought to heel by an uncompromising king who acknowledged no obligation to further the fortunes of his relatives. In due course they would kill him for it, but in the thirteen years between 1424 and 1437, the Scottish barons were forced to endure firm government under a monarch who was capable, energetic, determined – and unpredictable and dangerous.

Alexander, who had succeeded his father Donald as Lord of the Isles, was a member of the jury who convicted Murdoch of Albany and his sons in 1426, but the extermination of that family may have so suited his own interests that he possibly failed to recognise the warning which their sudden execution implied. At that time he had expectations of being confirmed in the Earldom of Ross which had again become vacant in 1424 when Albany's protégé, the Earl of Buchan, was killed at the Battle of Verneuil, leading a Scottish contingent in France. James I appears to have recognised in principle the claim of Alexander's mother, Margaret Leslie, to the title, since she was thereafter referred to as Countess of Ross and Dowager Lady of the Isles, while Alexander himself adopted the style of *Magister*, or Master of Ross. The king was reluctant, however, to bestow the title and found excuse – principally in Alexander's behaviour – to retain the revenues of the earldom, as indeed, by forfeiture and reversion, he also kept the revenues of March, Fife, Mar, Buchan, and Lennox. Nor did James intend to contribute in such measure to the extensive dominions of the Lordship at a time when his prime objective was to curb the power of the great magnates. Within lowland Scotland, the Lordship and the state kept by Alexander were constantly remarked on. 'At that time there happened to be a Spanish traveller in Edinburgh, of whom, after he returned to his own country, it was asked what was the greatest wonder he had seen in Scotland? He said it was a grand man called Macdonald, with a great train of men after him, and that he was called neither Duke nor Marquis.'[92] The envy of the new courtiers who had found positions around the king was more malicious.

The courtiers about King James, and especially the offspring of King Robert II, who were defeated by his father Donald at Harlaw, and disappointed in their designs, became his mortal enemies. These being always in the king's ears, made him believe that Macdonald's power was so extensive that he ought to be crushed in time.[93]

Given the king's preoccupation with law and order it was unfortunately coincidental that at this time a feud had broken out in Ardnamurchan between Alexander of the Siol Gorrie (Godfrey's son) and John MacArthur – a Campbell to whose ancestor, Sir Arthur Campbell, Christina MacRuairi had allegedly bestowed lands in Garmoran. This quarrel, and the constant reiving along the northern bounds, gave credence to the argument that the Highlanders were a wild and uncivilised people whom only rough justice would bring to obedience.

In 1412, after Harlaw, the Earl of Mar as Justiciar of the North, had been commissioned to construct a 'fortalice at Inverness for the utility of the kingdom against the said Lord of the Isles'. During 1426, James had the fortress strengthened and repaired, and in 1427, he summoned fifty of the principal Highland chiefs – those who commanded a thousand men or more – to attend a Parliament in the town.

Despite a warning from the Earl of Douglas (with whom he was on close and almost conspiratorial terms), Alexander and his mother travelled to Inverness, as did the other northern chiefs – among them Angus Dubh Mackay and his four sons, Kenneth Mor Mackenzie, John Ross, William Leslie, Angus of Moray, the Macmahon (Matheson), Alexander MacRuairi of the Siol Gorrie, and John MacArthur. After lodging some days in the town, they were summoned individually to the castle, where they were promptly arrested and placed in close confinement. James I showed 'in the presence of his friends, the pleasure that he felt at this occurrence,' and

bent his face somewhat toward the ground and then repeated before them these two verses which he himself had made:
'Let us carry that gang to a fortress strong
For by Christ's own lot, they did deadly wrong.'[94]

A number, including Alexander of the Siol Gorrie and John Mac-Arthur were executed without the formality of a trial. Alexander himself, described as a principal disturber of the public peace, was kept in prison for two months. In recording this incident, the historian John Major (who was relatively objective by the standards of his age) clearly reflected the contempt in which the 'wild Scots' and Highlanders were held by the people of the Lowlands:

I have nothing but praise for this spirited conduct of the king, and the desire that he showed to deal justice upon all. Those men, all low-born as they were, held in utter subjection some seventy or eighty thousand others; and in their particular tracts they were regarded as Princes, and had all at their arbitrary will, evincing not the smallest regard for the dictates of reason.[95]

What the holders of this view did not understand – or more probably would not countenance – was that in contrast to the stricter applications of feudalism to matters of land and title, within the clan system the chieftainship itself (and with it the loyalty of the clansmen) was an hereditable subject. This factor made it difficult to impose any central or disciplinary control, while the pugnacity of the chiefs themselves was a constant and eventually intolerable threat to the maintenance of law and the king's peace.

While Alexander was in prison, a second violent event in Argyll itself caused a great disturbance in the west. A certain James Campbell, with a commission from King James I, sent to John Mor the Tanister (Alexander's uncle):

desiring him to meet him at a point called Ard-du with some prudent gentlemen, and that he had matters of consequence from the king to be imparted to him. John came to the place appointed with a small retinue, but James Campbell with a very great train, and told of the king's intentions of granting him all the lands possessed by Macdonald, on condition that he held the land of him and served him. John said that he did not know wherein his nephew Alexander wronged the king, and that this nephew was as deserving of his rights as he could be, and that he would not accept of those lands, nor serve for them, till his nephew be set at liberty; and that his nephew himself was as nearly related to the king as he could be.[96]

Campbell thereupon declared that John Mor was the king's prisoner, and when John resisted he was overpowered and killed.

His death made a great noise through the kingdom, particularly among the faction in opposition to the king – namely the Hamiltons, Douglasses, and Lindsays. The king at last being much ashamed at what had happened, he pursued James Campbell as the murderer.

Campbell claimed that he had acted upon the king's authority, but James maintained that his instructions had been to arrest John Mor and nothing else.

And because Campbell had no written order from the king to produce in his defence, he was taken and beheaded – which shows the dangerous consequences of undertaking such a service without due circumspection.[97]

Alexander was released after two months, but he was deeply resentful and intent on revenge. With an army of ten thousand Highlanders from Ross and the Isles, he attacked and burned the town of Inverness, and was besieging the castle when the approach of a large army commanded by James in person obliged him to retire into Lochaber. The king gathered the Mackenzies to his standard and marched south in pursuit. Two of the 'wild clans' – Clan Chattan and a portion of the Clan Cameron – were induced to desert the Lord of the Isles (probably to save their lands which lay along the line of pillage), and James routed Alexander's army somewhere in the braes of Lochaber. There is no account of the battle, but it was recorded that shortly afterwards the Clan Chattan and the Camerons turned against each other, and that the Mackintoshes surrounded a church where the Camerons were attending service and massacred the entire congregation by burning them alive.

James I demanded Alexander's unconditional surrender, and his clansmen advised him to retire to the north of Ireland and wait upon events. Had Alexander done so, or indeed had he taken refuge in the remoter Hebrides, it is doubtful whether James could have followed him. For reasons which are unexplained, however, Alexander eventually decided to submit to the king at Holyrood Palace on Easter Sunday 1429, apparently 'fearing no mischance'.

Alexander of the Isles sent various messages to the king to treat for peace; but to this the king would not consent, and he said in anger that within a few days he would humble him still further. But Alexander, when he saw the fixed purpose of the king, went in secret to Edinburgh, and when he was got within the king's palace went upon his knees, and so came to the presence of the king and queen, carrying his sword by the point, and so gave the hilt into the king's hands, as who should say that he placed his head in the king's hands. Whereupon the queen, and those of the nobles standing round urgently besought the king that he would spare the life of Alexander; and the king sent him to the castle of Tantallon, there to be safely guarded until he should determine what should be further done concerning him.[98]

At the same time, Alexander's mother, the Countess of Ross, was charged with encouraging her son in his violent proceedings, and imprisoned on the island of Inchcolm in the Firth of Forth. Apart from the intervention of the queen, what probably saved Alexander's life was his known connection with the Douglas, Hamilton, Lindsay faction, which, while it increased the king's suspicions, would have inclined James to caution – 'these being the greatest pillars and the most dangerous to be offended of any in the nation'.

It seemed to many that Alexander's power was 'altogether gone and ruined', and a number of the barons thought it a 'convenient time to impair Macdonald's estate and diminish his grandeur' by seizing the lands of Lochaber. The Earl of Mar as Justiciar of the North, obtained the king's commission to raise a large army, with Huntly, Allan of Caithness, Fraser of Lovat, and several Lowland lords, and marched into the west. Invading Lochaber, they leaguered at Inverlochy close to the old castle by the shore of Loch Linnhe and under the shadow of Ben Nevis. Here they were joined by a number of western clans, notably the Mackintoshes, Mackays, and Camerons, and many other vassals of the

Lordship who decided that it would be prudent to throw in their lot with the king.

From Tantallon, Alexander sent a despairing message to the Clan Donald, 'desiring all those whom he trusted most to face the enemy, though they never would see sight of him'. In this hour of need the clan found a warleader in the young Donald Balloch, son of John Mor, who was then eighteen years of age and had been fostered by the Clan Maclean. Donald hurriedly called a muster at the island of Carna in Loch Sunart, where he was joined by MacIain of Ardnamurchan, Allan of Moidart, Ranald Bain of Lairgie, and MacDuffie of Colonsay, with a number of other gentlemen and freeholders of the Clan Donald. With a force of six hundred picked men, they sailed their galleys through the Sound of Mull and up Loch Linnhe to land at Invershippinish, about two miles south of Inverlochy. There they disembarked and prepared to attack Mar's camp which sprawled in careless security along the Lochy to the north of the present town of Fort William.

Now Alasdair Carrach . . . Macdonald's younger uncle, who held the lands of Lochaber, east of Lochy . . . took possession of the hill above the enemy, with 220 archers, being unable, by the smallness of his number to face them, but expected that some of his friends would at last come to his relief. Upon seeing his nephew, Donald Balloch, he was much animated.
Now as Donald Balloch drew near, Lord Huntly stepped into the Earl of Mar's tent, where he and Mackintosh were playing cards. Huntly desired them to lay aside their cards, for the enemy were near at hand. They asked if the enemy were numerous. Huntly answered that they were not very numerous, but he understood by them that they were bent on fighting. Well, said Mackintosh, we'll play this game and dispute with these fellows afterwards. So Huntly looked out again, and saw the enemy driving on furiously towards them. He goes a second time into the tent, saying, Gentlemen, fight stoutly or render yourselves to your enemies. Mackintosh replied that they would play that game, and would do with the enemy what they pleased; since he knew very well the doings of the big-bellied carles of the Isles. Whatever they may be, said Huntly, they will fight like men this day. Mackintosh answered that although (Huntly) himself were to join them, their party would defeat them both. Huntly went out in a rage, saying he would fight against nobody on that day, and so drew his men to one side by themselves, and was rather a spectator than of either party . . .
Then joining battle, Donald Balloch made a main battalion and a front of his men. The front (vanguard) was commanded by MacIain of Ardnamurchan and John MacLean of Coll; the main battle by Ranald Bain (son of the murdered John Mor and Donald's half-brother), Allan of Moidart, MacDuffie of Colon-

say, Macquarie of Ulva, and MacGee of the Rinns of Islay. As they faced one another, Alasdair Carrach came down the brae with the 220 archers and shot their arrows so thick on the flank of the Earl's army that they were forced to give ground. Allan Lord Caithness was killed, a son of Lovat, and 990 men. Hugh Mackay of Strathnavern was taken . . . On Donald Balloch's side was lost 27 men.[99]

The Earl of Mar was wounded through the thigh by an arrow, but managed to escape into the hills around Ben Nevis, where he wandered starving for two days. The story of his flight was of the sort much favoured by the seannachies – and endows him with a character that serves to give flesh to what otherwise is just a name:

At last he [Mar] fell in with some women, who were looking after cattle, who happened to have a little barley meal for their own use with which they relieved the Earl and his servant, mixing it with a little water in the heel of the Earl's shoe. . . . The Earl gave his own clothes to the woman, that he might disguise himself, and travelled in the night time till he came to a little house belonging to a poor man, on a spot of land called Beggich, who was an Irishman by name O'Brien (Obirrin). He was one of the Earl of Mar's own people, and that necessity obliged him to disguise himself for fear of being known. The poor man got a cow from the camp, and beginning to slaughter it, desired his 'guest' to hold the beast. The Earl was more willing to obey the instruction than skilful as a butcher. The man, not pleased with such assistance as he gave him, cursed those who took such a blockhead abroad to be a soldier. At last he cut out come collops, and gave them to the Earl to prepare – which the Earl could not do very well, until the man did it for him by roasting them upon the coals. At going to bed he washed the Earl's feet in warm water, cleansed and washed his wound. When the Earl layed himself down, he could not sleep for the cold, being short of bed-clothes. O'Brien got up, took the cow's hide, and warming it by the fire, wrapped it around the Earl, which warmed him so much that he perspired during the whole night.

In the morning, after such refreshment as they had, the Earl said he would go to Badenoch. O'Brien asked if he knew the way, and on the Earl's saying that he did not but would do his best to get there, O'Brien desired him to take some meat in his pocket, and went with him for some three or four miles to show him the way. As they were about to part, the Earl told him that if his case thereafter should be low, he should go to Kildrummie, the Earl of Mar's seat, and ask for Alexander Stewart, and that he would cause the Earl of Mar reward him for his good offices.

It happened in process of time that O'Brien was reduced to a very low condition, went to Kildrummie and knocking at the gate, the porter asked him who he was and what he wanted. O'Brien said that he wished to speak to Alexander Stewart. The porter said he was a fool, as there was no such man there; but O'Brien continued to knock until the Earl of Mar heard him, and calling the porter, asked who was knocking at the gate. The porter replied that it was some fool enquiring for Alexander Stewart. The Earl, musing a little, starts up, and looking steadfastly at the man, presently recognised O'Brien, causing the gate to be opened, and kindly embraced him.

Immediately the Earl sent for a tailor, and ordered a suit of clothes to be made for O'Brien. He desired O'Brien also to bring his wife and son to Kildrummie, but he told the Earl that his wife was old and could not be persuaded to leave her native country. The Earl, having entertained O'Brien at Kildrummie for some time, sent him home with six milch cows, enjoining him to send his son; who came sometime thereafter, and was made a laird of a small estate – which has fallen since to a gentleman of the names of Forbes. . . .

. . . whereby it may be seen, that a good turn to a generous or noble person is not always lost.[100]

After the battle of Inverlochy, Donald Balloch thoroughly ravaged Lochaber, with particular attention to the lands of the Mackintoshes and those branches of the Camerons who had deserted to Mar, and then prudently retired to Ireland with a great store of plunder. News of Mar's defeat enraged James I, who immediately mustered an army to invade the west – introducing a special tax to finance the campaign – 'for the resistance to the king's rebellers in the north', and ordering that upon 'all lands of the realm where the yield of two pennies is raised, there be ten pennies raised'.

He marched first to Dunstaffnage Castle, where the leaders of the insurgency hurriedly submitted, blaming the rebellion on Donald Balloch, whose power they explained, they had been unable to resist. Some accounts allege that James hanged or beheaded some three hundred of the Clan Donald, but the seannachies emphatically deny this, and indeed, there were no sweeping confiscations, apart from Alasdair Carrach's lands in Lochaber which were granted to Mackintosh. James sent to O'Neill of Connaught with whom Donald Balloch had taken refuge, asking him to return Donald dead or alive if he wished to keep the king's friendship. In due course, a head was delivered, and James was suitably appeased. In the meanwhile, Donald Balloch had, in fact, married O'Neill's daughter with whom he lived prosperously thereafter. The name of the unfortunate who donated his head has not been recorded.

In 1431, a few months after Inverlochy, James released Alexander of the Isles – possibly as part of a general amnesty to celebrate the birth of an heir, and possibly also because he had decided to modify his policy of outright suppression – not least on account of the growing opposition in Scotland. Alexander was restored to all his ancestral rights over the Lordship, but, 'it being impossible to satisfy the humour of the king', James still refused to confirm his mother's claim to the Earldom of Ross. The release was probably conditional also on Alexander's agreeing (after some protest) to confirm the Clan Chattan in the lands of Lochaber, since only this would explain his capricious behaviour in failing to restore his uncle Alasdair Carrach to his proper inheritance. Later, in 1443, Mackintosh received a formal grant of territory in Lochaber, but the Macdonalds of Keppoch continued to hold their lands by sword-right and ignored the Clan Chattan's authority. On the other hand, Alexander did revenge himself upon the chief of Clan Cameron and others who had betrayed him, and conferred their lands on the faithful Maclean of Coll.

On 21 February 1437, James I was assassinated, and two regents – Sir William Crichton and Sir Alexander Livingston – were appointed to govern during the minority of the heir, James II, who was then only six years old. The Earl of Mar had died in 1435, and in a strange reversal of fortune, Alexander of the Isles was created Justiciar of the North – an office which he secured through the influence of Douglas who had been made Lieutenant-General of the realm. Ironically, he thus became Keeper of the Castle of Inverness and warden of the town which he had burned and looted only six years before. Nevertheless, he appears to have discharged his duties efficiently, and the citizens were not heard to complain. Alexander was now also confirmed in the Earldom of Ross and this large territory was added to the extensive dominions of the Isles.

Alexander died on 8 May 1449 at his castle of Dingwall in the Chanonry of Ross, but the Cathedral of Fortrose where he is said to have been buried, was destroyed by Oliver Cromwell. The seannachies give no reason why the old tradition was broken and he was not buried with his ancestors on Iona – unless it was to confer some additional authority to his claim to Ross that caused him to be interred within the Earldom.

During his life, relations with the Ionan community had been strained – largely because of the corruption of Finnon the Green Abbot, whose sons were described in papal correspondence as men 'of a dissolute life who squandered the wealth of the monastery'. In contrast to the old Columban tradition, the community attracted well-born young men who entered the order 'not for the sake of devotion but for the properties of the administration'. In 1420 a reforming abbot, Dominic MacKenneth, secured a Papal Mandate declaring that no one of noble blood could enter the monastery, but he was flouted by a grandson of the Green Abbot known as Fingonius Fingonii. This man was a bastard and thus disqualified from holding any benefice, but he studied canon law and obtained a dispensation. Dominic extracted an oath from Fingonius that he would not attempt to enter the Ionan order, but through influence he not only secured a release from his promise, but Dominic's own Superior ordered that he was to be accepted as a monk. Installed on Iona he lived openly with a woman called Mor, daughter of Mariota MacSween, whom he endowed with forty cows and a dowry looted from the monastery's goods, and when censure and excommunication had no effect, the matter was referred to the Pope. Alexander of the Isles was so enraged at this catalogue of iniquity that he threatened to remove the bones of his forefathers from the Reilig Oran, and suspend all benefactions to the monastery.

Nor was Alexander's own life free of religious scandal. A Papal Mandate of 1445 stated that while 'Elizabeth our daughter well beloved in Christ' (Elizabeth Seton, daughter of Alexander Seton, Lord of Gordon and Huntly), had been married for many years to 'our well beloved son Alexander of Islay, Earl of Ross and Lord of the Isles', the said Alexander had been wrongfully lured away by the wiles and machinations of Christina MacIaide ('our daughter presumably well beloved in Christ') so that he had repudiated Elizabeth and installed Christina in her place. Elizabeth wanted Alexander formally summoned and admonished by the Bishop of the Isles, but since Alexander was very powerful, and the Bishop was his brother, she was obliged to appeal to the Pope. The Bishop of St Andrews and the Archdeacons of Ross and Buchan were accordingly instructed to send an admonition to the adulterous couple, or else to post an edict in a public place provided it addressed itself to the sin in general terms and did not mention any names.

It would seem from the Sleat historian's account that Alexander was susceptible to beautiful women:

A man born to much trouble all his life: first he took to him the concubine, daughter of Patrick Obeolan surnamed the Red, who was a very beautiful woman. . . . She was twice brought before the king, as Macdonald could not be induced to part with her on occasion of her great beauty. The king said it was no wonder that such a fair damsel had enticed the Macdonald.

The result has been some confusion over his several marriages, but excluding the liaisons with Patrick's daughter and Christina MacIaide, these are generally held to have been: first, to Elizabeth Seton by whom he had John, who succeeded him as Earl of Ross and Lord of the Isles; second, to a daughter of MacPhee of Lochaber by whom he had Celestine, who was granted the lands of Lochalsh; third, to a daughter of Gilpatrick Roy, grandson of the Green Abbot, by whom he had Hugh, founder of the Macdonalds of Sleat.

Alexander bequeathed to his son John, fourth Lord of the Isles, the largest dominion in the north outwith the crown of Scotland itself. But at times his power had been demonstrably precarious, and cracks in the political fabric of the Lordship were becoming apparent. Alexander may have owed his preservation to his friendship with the house of Douglas, which was now all-powerful in Scotland – and the greatest menace to the crown. If so, their alliance would ultimately reach a bitter conclusion. In 1438, at Bute, Alexander had conferred with the Earls of Douglas and Crawford, and it was said that they agreed upon some purpose. Precisely what passed between them, or whether they plotted the destruction of the child King James II, is not known, but in the light of what happened later, it was a league of perilous consequence.

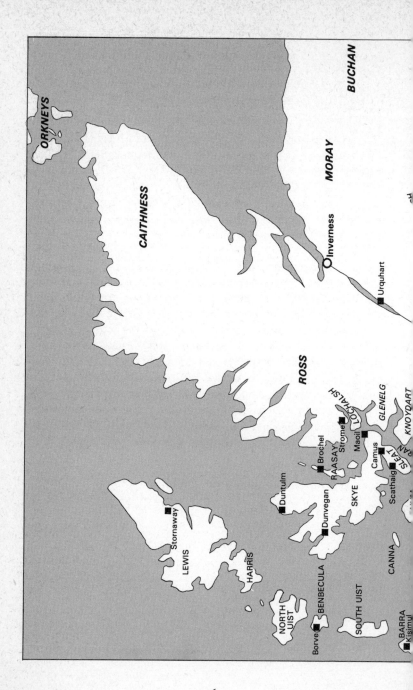

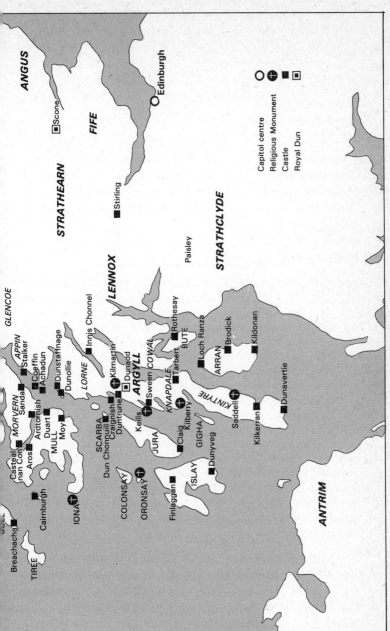

3 The Castles of the Lordship

○ Capitol centre
⊕ Religious Monument
■ Castle
▣ Royal Dun

CHAPTER 18

The Lordship

From the race of Eremon, through Conn of the Hundred Battles and through Coll the Noble, are the Lords of the Isles: to whom pertained a big house and the half of Alba: whose likeness was Cuchullan and he the sun arising; and to whom is the headship of the Gael, as it is but right to proclaim.

K. Macleod, *The Road to the Isles*

In a ceremony reminiscent of the king-making in ancient Dalriada, a Lord of the Isles was proclaimed at the Stone:

At this the Bishop of Argyll, the Bishop of the Isles, and seven priests were sometimes present; but a Bishop was always present, with the chieftains of all the principal families and a *Ruler of the Isles.* There was a square stone, seven or eight feet long, and the tract of a man's foot cut thereon, upon which he stood, denoting that he should walk in the footsteps and uprightness of his predecessors, and that he was installed by right in his possessions. He was clothed in a white habit, to shew his innocence and integrity of heart, that he would be a light to his people, and maintain the true religion. The white apparel did afterwards belong to the poet by right. Then he was to receive a white rod in his hand, intimating that he had the power to rule, not with tyranny and partiality, but with discretion and sincerity. Then he received his forefathers' sword, or some other sword, signifying that his duty was to protect and defend them from incursions of their enemies in peace or war, as the obligations of his predecessors were. The ceremony being over, Mass was said after the blessing of the Bishop and seven priests, the people pouring their prayer for the prosperity and success of their new created Lord. When they were dismissed, the Lord of the Isles feasted them for a week thereafter; and gave liberally to the monks, poets, bards, and musicians.[101]

The description accords with Irish accounts of the inauguration of chieftains after the ancient Gaelic custom. Aside from the rock at Dunadd, several such stones with a footprint cut into them have been found in the Highlands, including one which was discovered in the shallows of Loch Finlaggan in Islay close to the ruins of the manor house which was the administrative centre of the Lordship. It is much smaller, however, than the crowning stone described by the Sleat historian, and may post-date the Lordship itself. While it is generally thought that the ceremony took place in Islay, Donald the second Lord was proclaimed at Eigg, which was geographically more central, and the original stone may have been moved there – or perhaps it was destroyed with so much else.

The constitution of the Isles was thus: Macdonald had his Council at Island Finlaggan in Islay, to the number of sixteen, namely: four Thanes, four Armins, that is to say Lords or sub-Thanes, four Bastards – that is squires, or men of competent estates who could not come up with Armins or Thanes, that is freeholders, or men that had their land in factory, as Macgee of the Rinds of Islay, MacNicoll in Portree in Skye, and MacEachern, Mackay, and MacGillevray in Mull, Macillemhaoel or Macmillan etc. There was a table of stone where the Council sat in the Isle of Finlaggan: the which table, with the stone on which Macdonald sat, were carried away by Argyll with the bells that were at Iona. Moreover there was a judge in every Isle for the discussion of all controversies, who had lands from Macdonald for their trouble, and likewise the eleventh part of every action decided. But there might be still an appeal to the Council of the Isles. MacFinnon was obliged to see weights and measures adjusted; and MacDuffie or MacPhie of Colonsay kept the records of the Isles.[102]

Another account, written by Donald Monro, Dean of the Isles in 1549, states that the Council was composed of four of the greatest nobles, four thanes of lesser estate, and four great men of the royal blood of Clan Donald, presided over by the Macdonald as 'Herdsman of the Isles'. The four great nobles were Maclean of Duart, Maclean of Loch Buie, MacLeod of Harris, and MacLeod of Lewis. The four thanes were MacKinnon, MacNeil of Barra, MacNeil of Gigha, and one other. The four great men of Clan Donald were the Chief of Clanranald, MacIain of Ardnamurchan, Macdonald of Kintyre, and the chief of the Clan, Alasdair Carrach of Lochaber (the Macdonalds of Keppoch). The Council was also attended by the Abbot of Iona and the Bishop of the Isles.

The records of the Isles, maintained by the MacDuffies as the hereditary Keepers, were subsequently lost or destroyed during the troubles which followed the forfeiture of the Lordship, and there is no precise evidence as to the work of the Council itself. It does not appear to have equated in power to the old Norse *Things* and apart from acting as a court of appeal, references to it in the seannachies' accounts would suggest that it was chiefly preoccupied with matters of family policy and custom – the succession, dynastic marriage, tutelage, and occasionally defence. Although feudal theories of primogeniture may have lent additional stability to the succession, the practice of tanistry was still sustained, and during the rule of each Lord, a close relative of full age was appointed Tanister to assume the leadership of the Clan Donald should the situation require it. By such means, and presumably with the assent of the Council, Angus Og had succeeded his brother Alasdair when the latter was forfeited by Bruce, and in more recent times, John Mor had been styled Tanister during the minority of Donald's son Alexander who became the third Lord. Similarly, in the absence of the Lord of the Isles, or on account of some other indisposition, a *Toiseach* (Captain) was appointed as the warleader – and as in the case of Donald Balloch, his authority was accepted by the Islesmen.

The practical administration of the Lordship fell to the brieves or judges – and the posts were usually hereditary in each of the islands. The Morrisons, for example, were the hereditary brieves of Lewis. Few legal tracts have survived, but it seems likely that, in the Hebrides at least, the administration of the law followed older Gaelic custom rather than Lowland feudal practice, and was more concerned with reparation than prevention. The attendance of two prominent churchmen on the Council, apart from their authority in religious matters, indicated the importance of clerics within the administration – particularly in the keeping of records and the drafting of charters and other documents, while the lands of the Lordship were managed by officials called *Tosheadors* who were the equivalent of the medieval *Serjeand of fee*.

The revenues of the Lordship appear to have been considerable. Each 'merkland' paid an annual tax, and a sixteenth-century account of the Isles assessed Islay alone at 'eighteen score merklands' (360), yielding a yearly revenue of 1,420 head of cattle, 5,040 head of sheep, 3,960 bolls of malt and meal, and 720 merks of silver – which is an astonishing indication of one island's productivity at that time. In addition there was payment of a *grassum*, and each merk of land was required to support one gentleman 'who does no labour' – and who was probably a member of the chief's train or household. The old Gaelic dues of *cain* and *conveth* survived – payment of victuals and wine sufficient to support the Lord and his company when they visited the region for one or two nights in the year. Tenants and lesser men who accepted the leadership and protection of one of the more powerful chiefs paid the due of *calp* – the best beast upon the death of a tenant, in addition to other levies at times of special expense – such as the marriage of the chief's daughter, or the building of a house.

Traditional links with Ireland and Norway, together with the maritime experience of the Islesmen, encouraged an extensive sea trade. Under the supervision of the MacFinnons, the Lord of the Isles had his own weights for the *lapidis M'Coull* (standard units of measurement) which were used in most of the islands, since much of the commerce was conducted by barter or commodity exchange. The principal articles of trade were the staple commodities produced in the Hebrides – wool, cloth, flax, linen, fish, and agricultural produce – and since coin was scarce, the tithes and taxes were probably paid in similar currency, while precious metal was usually in the form of torques and rings. In particular, however, the Hebrides were noted for the spinning of wool and flax, and the manufacture of fine cloth. A Lord of the Isles, returning presents, made gifts of mantles and plaids. In the early Norse sagas, elegant heroes wore cloth 'spun in the *Sudreyar*'. Before elaborate tartans became fashionable, the predominant colour was blue.

The administrative centre of the Lordship where the Council met, was Island Finlaggan in Islay. Today it is a disappointing place – a loch set in featureless moorland, with a few pillars of crumbled masonry and outlines in the earth, which convey an atmosphere of dissolution and decay symbolic of the ruin of the Lordship, with no recollection of the period of its splendour. It is an abandoned place, empty of travellers, and a silent testimony to the transience of earthly kingdoms.

The original complex, much of which was probably composed of wooden structures, encompassed a part of the loch side, and two islands close to the shore. Although fortified, it was not a stronghold in the conventional sense, and its position had no defensive purpose. On the shore the approach was guarded by a tower and wall where the *Lucht-taeh*, the personal retainers of the Lord of the Isles, probably were stationed. The larger of the two islands was reached by an artificial causeway. After traversing some marshy ground, this led into a large enclosure which seems to have been surrounded by a dyke, or a not very thick curtain wall, with a number of small towers which may have had some defensive function. The ground within the enclosure is ridged with the foundations of a series of buildings, which probably comprised a Great Hall, the Lords' apartments, guest accommodation for the visiting chiefs, storerooms and servants' quarters. To one side of the main enclosure fragments of the small stone chapel remain – its interior grass-grown, and the old tombstones and grave slabs tumbled in disorder. One such stone has an effigy of a warrior in west Highland armour, with camail habershone and the quilted war coat called the *hektonis*, and bears the inscription '*Hic jacet Donaldus Filius Patrici Celestini*' – belonging therefore to the son of Celestine of Lochalsh who was brother to John, the last Lord of the Isles. A number of the stones are small – about four feet long or less – yet beautifully carved with foliated crosses, and there is a tradition that the children of the Lords who did not survive their infancy were buried in this chapel at Finlaggan. In later centuries the Campbells came, and modern vandals have also done their share of damage. Today the tumbling masonry encloses a derelict museum of nettles and neglect.

A wooden bridge, founded on a narrow stone causeway, once connected the residential Eilean Mor with the second small round island which is said to have been the Council Isle where the sixteen members convened around the great stone table of Macdonald. Only traces of the early foundations in the earth remain, and there is nothing more to recall the last great centre of Gaelic civilisation in Alba.

While Islay was an administrative focal point for the Isles, the Lords are said to have administered Kintyre from their fortress at Kilkerran – the present Campbeltown. A favourite residence seems to have been the castle of Ardtornish in Morvern, built on the rocky headland across from Aros on the Sound of Mull. It lay in beacon-sight of Duart and Lismore and was one of the great chain of strongholds which guarded the sea-ways around Lorne. Some thirty castles, twenty-three of them in the inner isles, are the most evocative relics of the ancient Lordship. Most were built in the three hundred years after 1154 when Somerled introduced the square fortresses of mortared stone after the Norman style which replaced the old earth and rock fortifications of the Dalriadic period. The earliest castles were built with a great wall of *enceinte*, thirty to forty feet high and ten feet thick, but in later period a square keep was sometimes added to provide greater security.

They were strategically sited, many overlooking bays and anchorages to afford protection to the galleys, and at intervals along the coast in line of sight so that the beacon fires could readily be seen, and warning flashed through Lorne and Morvern. Thus, from Dunollie, the flame was seen in Duart, and from there passed to Coeffin in Lismore and by

Sanda northward up Loch Linnhe; or west to Ardtornish in the Sound, by Aros and Casteal nan Con to Mingary in Ardnamurchan and across the hills to Tioram. All but a few are ruined now, picturesque against a landscape of mountain and sea loch, but some, like Dunvegan, Duart, Kisimul (in Barra) and Breachacha in Coll survive, with varying degrees of restoration. Not least they give a sense of scale, for the inner wards seem smaller than their romantic silhouette suggests, and sometimes smaller too than seannachies remembered when the splendour of Clan Donald grew with the telling.

The composition of the Council at Finlaggan reflected the relationship between the Lord of the Isles and the vassal clans which were absorbed into the Lordship. The connections were various. Apart from the clans of direct descent – Clanranald, Sleat, MacIain of Ardnamurchan, Islay, Keppoch, Dunyveg, and other septs or branches of Clan Donald – there were old associations with the families of Islay and Garmoran, tributaries of Somerled, or the vassals of the MacRuairis. Of such were the MacLeods of Harris and Lewis, West Skye, Raasay, Gairloch and Assynt; the Macleans of Mull and Coll, Morvern and Ardgour, Luing, Scarba and the Isles of the Sea; the MacNeils of Barra and the MacNeils of Gigha; the MacKinnons of Skye and Mull, the MacDuffies of Colonsay, the Macquaries of Ulva and Gometra; Mackays, Macmillans, and MacEarchans in Kintyre, MacInnes, MacGillevrays and others. On the mainland there were old connections with the Mackintoshes and the Camerons – frailer perhaps as events had proved – while within the newly acquired Earldom of Ross the Mackenzies and Munroes had been in long possession.

It was the achievement of the Lordship that while it lasted, the authority of the Lords of the Isles was accepted by those clans who were not connected to the family of Islay by ties of kinship, and the latent separatist tendencies which emerged to divide the Lordship after the forfeiture were held in check by a common allegiance. The Macdonald himself had absolute power within the principality to create thanes and sub-thanes at his pleasure, and in the granting of lands to vassals of the Lordship. The enmities aroused in branches of the Clan Donald over the favour shown to certain great vassals, or the seemingly capricious bestowal of lands on more than one family were to lead to bitter divisions and bloodshed after the Lordship was forfeited. The only discernible policy followed by the Lords in this respect was to grant lands in scattered lots, so that no single vassal was able to accumulate a compact block of territory sufficient to encourage thoughts of independence. Nevertheless, notions of landholding were so various that rival claims were inevitable, since some chiefs claimed possession by sword-right, or length of occupation, by verbal grant in front of witnesses, or by a formal charter. The Lords of the Isles appear to have bestowed lands by a variety of means – some by a simple rhyming Gaelic charter recited on the Judgement Mound, or by hereditable grant made in front of witnesses at an appropriate place such as the Black Stones of Iona. Latterly they conferred land largely by formal charter under their Seal, but as the records were destroyed during the later feuds, or when the Clan Campbell occupied Islay, only one such example still survives.

The Clan system, and in particular, comparisons with the feudal system, have been the subject of much elaboration and debate. In reality, the 'Celtic feudalism' or 'Feudo-clanship' which was beginning to emerge, was a hybrid, and its organisation was not uniform through the Highlands. Between the old Gaelic tribal system and feudalism the theories of landholding were manifestly different, but the objectives were often largely the same, and there was much in feudalism which was attractive to the western chiefs. It is therefore an over-simplification to suggest that the two systems were automatically antagonistic, and the points of conflict, notwithstanding that their resolution was often violent and bloody, became more apparent only as the situation evolved.

Under the old tribal system, land was held allodially – of God (that is, without any superior) – and the clan lands were divided between the *cuntrie* and the *duthus*. The latter was territory apportioned to the chief, who granted parts of it at easy rents to members of the *derbfine*. As with successive generations, the relationship became more remote and fresh cadet sons had to be provided for; after three generations such favoured tenants were required to remove and so lost their privileged status. If however, the *derbfine* did not expand and there was no such pressure to displace them, once a family had occupied the land for four generations it became theirs by right.

Under feudalism, only the king held the land by allodial right, but the practice of primogeniture meant that a family which was granted land in perpetuity had security of tenure and would not be displaced after three generations. This contributed to the social stability of the clan, and in this context, the feudal system acted to preserve and give legal effect to clan custom. Both systems gave individual dependants rights to occupy land and guaranteed their protection. Both guaranteed the dependants' loyalty to their chief or lord, by virtue either of kinship or vassalage. Both provided for military service when required and the payment of dues and taxes. There was much in feudalism, therefore, which seemed compatible with custom, while the security of tenure which it offered prompted the rising clans to make good their position through feudal institutions. So long as the chief to whom the clansmen owed their loyalty and the feudal superior of whom they held their land were one and the same, there was no problem, but a point of conflict arose when allegiance was divided. The bonds of loyalty were technically twofold – based on pretence of kin as in the clan or 'family' system, and the place of dwelling as required by feudalism. Rebellion occurred in later times when the king interposed himself, or another, between the clansmen and their hereditary chief, and when many, faced with a choice between the chief and their superior, refused to transfer their allegiance to the latter, they were evicted from their lands and turned into 'broken men'. During the period of the Lordship the problem did not arise, even though the Lords treated the land, not in any tribal sense, but as their own possession as descendants of Somerled. After the forfeiture, however, the variety of conflicting practices made the Highlander an easy prey to unscrupulous superiors and others who saw advantage in fomenting trouble in order to evict the clansmen and seize their land. It was this policy, developed by the Campbells and the House of Huntly, which brought tragedy after the forfeiture and led to the 'danting (subjugation) of the Isles'.

Of the clans not directly related by male descent, the Lords showed special favour towards the Macleans, which inevitably aroused the jealousy of their other vassals. The Sleat historian records an incident which took place at Aros when John, the fourth Lord, returned from the disastrous campaign into Roxburgh during which James II was killed. The account is interesting in that apart from the tensions between the leading families, it also depicts the court of the Isles marshalled after the traditional Irish manner:

When [John] came home to Aros, in Mull, he held a great feast, to which most of the Islanders and many of the Mainland people resorted. On John Macdonald, tutor to Roderick his nephew, Laird of Moydart, and Maclean, and some of the gentlemen conversing, Maclean kept silent for a time; at which John Macdonald asked the reason of his silence. He replied that he had no occasion to speak. The

Tutor said he knew very well Maclean's office (as Chamberlain) was to set the Macdonalds in order tomorrow at dinner, and that he should see all the principal men there placed according to their rank and station; but if Maclean would give him a black hound he had, he would supply his place the next day. Maclean consented to this and gave the hound. At dinner time next day, John stood at the end of Macdonald's table and desired the Laird of Ardnamurchan to sit down. This family indeed might claim to be lords since King David Bruce's time, but the old Scots were careless of their prerogatives. Then he desired MacFinnon and MacQuire to sit, for MacQuire was an ancient Thane. Then he desired Beatton, the principal physician, then MacMurrich the poet, to take their seats. Now saith he, I am the oldest and best of your surnames here present, and will sit down; as for these fellows who have raised up their heads of late, and are upstarts, whose pedigree we know not, nor even they themselves, let them sit as they please. Maclean, MacLeod of Harris, and MacNeil of Barra went out in a rage, and very much discontented. MacLeod of Lewis remained within; the other three were determined, as soon as opportunity offered, to be fully avenged of Macdonald for the affront as they thought he had given. After this, MacLeod of Harris and the family of Moydart were never intimate or on good terms. MacLeod of Harris on his return home, ravaged and plundered the families and Isles belonging to Moydart which was revenged by that family. Thereafter John was made prisoner, and lost his sight during his confinement at Dunvegan, and was thereafter called John Daul, or John the Blind.[103]

The account clearly indicates the rivalries and pressures which were building up during John's rule as Lord of the Isles, and once the focus of authority was removed, the clans would quickly be at each others' throats.

The account also mentions the Beatons (or Bethunes) as being hereditary physicians to the Lord of the Isles. The family had come to the Isles from Ireland in the time of Angus Og, and were famous for their exceptional learning and knowledge of medicine. They followed the teachings of Avicenna the Persian, whose canon was the basis of European practice for over five hundred years. In a period when it was becoming fashionable to think of the Islands as unlettered and barbaric, the Beatons possessed a Gaelic copy of Avicenna's eleventh-century work long before it was translated into English, or faculties of medicine were established in the universities of Scotland and England. Members of the family also became seannachies in Mull and the Outer Hebrides, and their library was known to include the earliest translation into any European language of an account of *The Fall of Troy*.

Other families became associated with particular crafts and skills.

The MacIntyres, descended from MacNeil the shipwright, were known as carpenters. The MacEacherns, originally from Kintyre, became hereditary swordsmiths in Islay and made the famous six-foot blades with the distinctive Islay hilt. Traces of their early forge remain behind the rock face of Creag Uinnsinn, about three-quarters of a mile from Kilchoman Church. In Glenoe, the Fhleistear or MacPheidearin – sometimes simply called Fletchers – were the arrow-makers. The wax for bow strings was furnished by Baill-na-Gail-Bhuin; the arrow shafts came from Esragoin in Lorne, and the bows themselves from the yew trees of Glenmure.

Culturally, the Gaelic revival had meant a conscious return to the Irish heritage of ancient times. Although the Norse influence was reflected in place-names (see p.111) and a variety of loan words, Gaelic again became the language of the Isles, and medieval Celtic art was chiefly indebted to the Irish masters. Islay was the cultural centre of the Lordship, within easy voyage of Loch Foyle on the eastern coast of Ireland, and a sanctuary for the Irish men of skill.

The Lords of the Isles employed Irish stone carvers and masons whose monuments are the great standing crosses, which, together with the tombs and effigies of the chiefs, are the places of pilgrimage for those who wander in the Lordship now. The few that remain are but a fraction of what was once, since most were smashed and destroyed in the centuries which followed the decline of the Gaelic kingdom in the Isles. On Iona it is said that three hundred and sixty crosses were thrown into the sea by the zealots of the Reformation, and today only three remain. Islay, more fortunate, has seventeen, of various sizes and states of preservation, including what is probably the finest example to have survived. The great cross at Kildalton stands a little apart from the Church, nine feet high, and cut from a single block of stone. It has the form of an open circle, resembling St John's Cross at Iona, quartered by four arms which are a fraction out of symmetry. The shaft and arms are finely carved, with close patterns of interlaced work, spirals, and bosses, and with panels of figures and lions' heads in high relief. David fights a charging lion; Abraham offers Isaac to the sacrifice and the Virgin and Child are flanked by guardian angels who spread their wings above them. The cross was probably erected by John, Lord of the Isles, when he founded the Chapel of Cill Daltain in 1360, and the church itself contains two fine effigies of warriors carved in low relief.

On the peninsula of Kintyre, there are crosses at Kilmory Knap and Keills. The Cross of Keills is square and massive, carved down one side only, but lacking the interlaced foliage which was common in the Isles. Strange beasts surround the central boss, and the figure of a cleric gazes from the high shaft, but the general theme of the carving defies a biblical interpretation. In the roofless chapel beyond, a collection of tombstones overgrown with turf and weeds, deteriorates slowly from lack of care. Faint hunting scenes, shears and galleys are just discernible, but they are so worn that preservation comes too late.

At Kilmory Knap stands the tall Macmillan's Cross. In Norse times, the Macmillans inhabited Mull, Tiree, and Iona, and their Gaelic name *Gillamaol* – the tonsured servant – indicates an early connection with the Church. A branch of the clan settled in Tayside, and when they were driven out by David II, removed to Knapdale, where they became vassals of the Lordship, and eventually succeeded to the lands and fortress of the MacNeils of Castle Sween nearby. The Cross is probably of the fifteenth century, and has an interlacing strap design over a hunting scene in which the huntsman wears a curious hood or helmet. In the churchyard, the finest of the tombstones have been moved into the roofless chapel and placed against the wall, where they form one of the most interesting collections to be seen in a single place. In the ground outside, some effigies lie time-worn beyond hope of resurrection, the rain puddles forming in the circles of their eyes, and the faces weathered into anonymity.

More remote, but a place of strong memories, is the Priory at Oronsay where the early MacDuffies are buried. Here too are standing crosses (one sadly damaged), but of greater interest are the mortuary chapel and the tombstones which have been collected in the Prior's House. Within the chapel is the canopied sepulchre of Sir Donald MacDuffie, who was prior in 1549, and it is told that the MacDuffies' rod of office was kept there, even after the last MacDuffie of Colonsay was killed by the MacLeans in 1620, and that until a hundred years ago, it was always replaced whenever it decayed. The Prior's House itself was the scene of the murder of Sir Alexander of Lochalsh, nephew and heir of the last Lord of the Isles. In 1491, as will be told, he had tried unsuccessfully to regain the Earldom of Ross, but by that time the Clan Donald was so divided against itself that MacIain of Ardnamurchan, who had already seized Sir John Macdonald of Islay and his sons, surprised and killed him at Oronsay to obtain, as is said, the favour of the government. One of the effigies, on which is carved a woman buckling on the warrior's spurs, is thought to be his gravestone. The other score of slabs display a variety of designs – dogs and deer, and strange monsters; a few with galleys, and most with the intertwining foliage and floral design which became typical of the art.

There are tombs too at Kilmartin in Lorne, Inchkenneth, Saddell, and Kilberry. At Rodil in South Harris, the effigies of the MacLeods are cut from jet black schist, and the recessed tomb with a sculptured back is probably unique in the islands. There are these, and other places, for the Lordship was wide and its ruins are scattered. So much was lost thereafter, that apart from the Hebridean castles there are few relics that could be called substantial, but time-weathered as they are, the art of the carved stones remains.

The literature of the Lordship was also Irish in its inspiration. Fragments collected by the Dean of Lismore (1512–26) recall a preoccupation with the oral cycles of old Ireland – the ancient myths, the romances of Cuchullain, and the stories of Fionn and his son Ossian. There was a tradition also of religious and secular poetry, panegyrics on the ruling families; and the hereditary bards still took their place at the chieftain's hearth and composed the praise-songs for their patron. Thus the MacMurrichs were the early seannachies and bards of the Lords of the Isles, and the O'Muirgheasains preserved the genealogies of the MacLeods in Harris and Skye. Elsewhere in Scotland their art was less appreciated. In 1612, the 'Regulations for Chiefs' sought to abolish the use of Gaelic, and the bards were proscribed as 'sorners' (beggars) to be punished in the stocks. The Islesmen paid no heed, however, since all knew that bardic memory is the source of knowledge, and the praise of honour, courage, loyalty, and heroic deeds seemed none so sinful to the Gael – although to Lowlands ears it sounded suspiciously like incitement to rebellion.

Above all, the Gaels loved the music of the harp, and the Isles were famous for their harpers. The twelfth-century Welsh historian Giraldus Cambriensis, recalled the Irish harpsong: 'whose music is not slow and solemn as in the instrumental music of Britain, but the sounds are rapid and articulate, yet at the same time sweet and pleasing' – adding, however, that the Scots harpers were more skilful yet 'inasmuch as it is in that country that they now resort as to the genuine source of the art'. The old Irish lyre had been replaced by the Celtic Harp or *Clarsach*, the oldest surviving example of which is the Lamont Harp, dating from 1464, which stood three feet high with thirty-two strings and a sound box hollowed out of a single piece of wood. In 1565, George Buchanan would write of the Gaels:

They are extremely fond of music and employ harps of a peculiar kind; some are strung with brass and some with catgut. In playing they strike the wires with a quill, or with their nails grown long for the purpose; but their strong fancy is to adorn their harps with silver and gems, those who are too poor substituting crystals instead.[104]

The names of some of the great harpers survive: the MacKerral who played for the Lord of the Isles, or Roderick Morrison of Lewis, bard to the MacLeods, and the Galbraiths, of Strathclyde British descent, who were hereditary harpers in Gigha and praised their patron: 'Tomaltach, not mean in his promises, had given me food and wine, a harp as well to reward my song. That hand is the best I have experienced.' They were in the tradition of the ancient *filidh*, and among those who listened to their mystery, who could tell what made a harper?

In one of the Isles, there is a cave known to the lobster fishers and to the otters. In front of it there is a wrecked smack, partly covered in sea-pinks. From its mouth one can see the Coolin Hills.

One day long ago (as the old story is told) three galleys from a different isle anchored in the creek nearby, and the three crews with their harpers met in the cave at the greying of night. Shortly before dawn the harping ceased, and the listening ones asked, softly but eagerly, whence came the desire to make music. Said a harper, 'She was a knee-woman who spent the days among the hills looking for the plants of healing. Now and again, because of her gift, a call would come from the glen below where the children were born and the people died. The boy got the knowing from her, and the wonder of not knowing.' Said the second harper, 'I was herding a widow's one cow in a deserted sheiling. I saw a gnarled oak tree standing alone and a bird's nest in its branches. I climbed up to give the little ones some worms, but the nest was empty and a thought and a sorrow came to me.' Said the third harper, 'It was a boat that came to our creek. There was a woman in her who sang a strange tune, something from another shore. My fingers will always be feeling for that other shore.' 'Which makes you a harper,' said the listening ones. 'Which makes me a little child,' said the harper.[105]

From the early sixteenth century, the bagpipes grew in popularity. The instrument is known to have existed in Mesopotamia and Greece between the eighth and fourth centuries BC, and the early Celts possibly adopted it during the period of their tribal wandering. The Picts had bagpipes in the first century AD, and the Dalriads brought them to the Hebrides from Ireland. They became associated with warfare because they were better than 'buglis blow and hiddeous', and the fierce pibrochs were heard across the marsh at Bannockburn. The Mac-Arthurs were the earliest hereditary pipers in the Lordship, but from 1540 the MacCrimmons of Skye, who were pipers to MacLeod of Dunvegan, were recognised as the finest in the Hebrides. The Scottish court had pipers from 1362.

According to ancient Celtic law, all members of the tribes were equal, but Gaelic society was hierarchical rather than democratic, and the craftsmen, poets, and other men of skill lived on the patronage of their lords and practised their art in the chieftains' halls. But among the people of the Hebrides, a rich tradition of Gaelic folk-lore persisted, expressed in stories, songs, and ballads which outlived the Lordship and imparted a lasting cultural identity to the Isles. Despite the influence of the Church, many of the old faery beliefs continued in a world of Celtic muse and witchery. The sealwomen crooned in the skerries; water sprites and kelpies worked mischief in the tarns; mermaids bathed in the creeks; and the seven great Hags guarded the far-flung Isles of Gaeldom.

They were a sea-people, and from their Norse ancestry came their sea-moods. To the Celt, the Atlantic was infinite and eternal, mysterious in its favours, and terrible in its anger. Their galleys ran the dangerous tide races and the sea reivers dared the currents of Corrievrechan; but sometimes the *birlinns* (a chief's barge) did not return and the songs of sea-sorrow were the chants of Hebridean women. Yet it was thought wrong to grieve for the spirits of the drowned, for they lay with the best heroes of Lochlann beside them, and the best bards in Erin, and the best storytellers in Alba – and which among them indeed had wished for more? *Tir-nan-og*, the Celtic Heaven, the Land-of-the-ever-young, lies somewhere to the west of the Hebrides, where the sun sets:

And the Celtic soul ever waits on the shore of the great sea for the coming of the White Barge which ferries the elect across the waves to the Isles where they would be. But the Barge needs wind nor sail nor rudder to make her speed like a bird over the sea: the wish of the Fate that guides her is her all and her in all. ....

And this was the manner in which a Lord of the Isles would die: Monks and priests being over him, and he having received the Body of Christ, and the Holy Oil having been put upon him, his fair body was brought to Iona or Columcille. And the Abbot and the monks and the vicars came forth to meet him, as it was the custom to meet the body of the King of the Isles, and his service and waking were honourably performed during eight days and eight nights; after which his full noble body was laid in the same grave with his fathers, in the Reilig of Oran.[106]

CHAPTER 19

John, Last Lord of the Isles

True is my praise of Macdonald
A champion with whom I unite;
The hero of every conflict, the lion's heart,
A hand that fails not, pride of the Gael;
The champion of Ulster, the controller of Assemblies,
The eye for causing the stopping of war.
The sun of the Gael, the countenance of O'Colla;
By the banks of the Bann, quick sailing are his ships:
A furious hound that plunders Fodhla,
A modest soul, the tree of Banba,
The country with fire-brands is red after him;
His family ancestor came to Tara,
Putting Meath in commotion, the leopard of Isla;
Root of hospitality, powerful in every land;
He refused no man, nor importunate bard;
The bountiful branch of hospitality, of the land of Oileach,
There did not spring from him but queens and kings,
True are the statements,
True is my praise.

(Book of Clanranald)

When John succeeded his father Alexander as Lord of the Isles in 1449, Scotland was emerging from the throes of a long minority, and the Crown was engaged in a critical struggle for power against the pre-eminent family of Douglas. After James I was assassinated in 1437, the heir James II was still a child of six, and control of the kingdom, manipulated through the Council of Articles, was disputed among the greater nobles. During the early years of the minority, effective government was in the hands of Archibald, fifth Earl of Douglas, as Lieutenant-General of Scotland, but he was an indolent man despite his power, and generally allowed the barons to quarrel or scavenge as they would, while he accumulated the spoils of regency. When he died in 1439, government passed to the two Regents – Sir William Crichton, who had been Master of the Household under James I and Keeper of Edinburgh Castle, and Sir Alexander Livingstone, the Warden of Stirling. These now fought for possession of the boy king, and otherwise the destruction of each other until a common envy of the House of Douglas brought them to uneasy alliance.

On the death of Archibald, the title passed to his sixteen-year-old son William, an impetuous youth who was ingenuously fond of the young king and was in turn admired by James II. In 1440 Crichton and Livingstone profited by this relationship to invite the earl and his younger brother to dine with James at Edinburgh Castle, where they 'banquetted royally with all delicates that could be got' before – according to tradition – the symbolic Black Bull's Head betokening death was set in front of them, and despite the king's entreaties, they were dragged out and beheaded in the castle courtyard:

> Edinburgh Castle, town and toure
> God grant thou sink for sinne!
> And that even for the black dinoir
> Earl Douglas gat therein.

The earldom passed to the murdered boy's great uncle, James the Gross, who reached an accommodation with Livingstone, and when he died three years later, his son William became the eighth Earl and inherited the family's great ambition – which, as many whispered, extended to the throne itself.

James II came of age in 1449, and took over the reins of government determined to rid himself of the factious elements who had tormented the years of his minority. Many who had adhered to the Douglas and Livingstone parties were imprisoned or executed for their various acts of treason, but the king was still not strong enough to proceed so directly against the Black Douglas himself. He therefore did not at once deprive him of his high office as Lieutenant-General, but 'silently withdrew from him his countenance and employment'. Seeing how the wind blew, Douglas found it expedient to leave the country for a while. He travelled to Rome on a visit to the Pope, but he left four brothers in Scotland to oversee his affairs, and through them continued to exercise an influence upon events. He also secretly renewed the old league of mutual assistance, first concluded by Earl Archibald in 1438, with the Earl 'Beardie' Crawford, and the Lord of the Isles.

John of the Isles was aged fifteen and thus also a minor when he succeeded to the Lordship in 1449. Described as a 'meek, modest man, brought up at court in his younger years, and a scholar, more fit to be a churchman than to command so many irregular tribes of people': he was much under the influence of Donald Balloch, now returned from Ireland, as Captain of Clan Donald and President of the Council. At this time, Maclean of Ardgour was Treasurer of his household and Munro of Foulis was Chamberlain of the Isles, while Maclean of Duart, MacNeil of Barra, and Macdonald of Lairgie, were also prominent in ordering the affairs of the Lordship. The Isles were enjoying a period of prosperity, and John kept great state at Dingwall in Ross and at his Castle of Ardtornish.

At the age of sixteen he was partly coerced and partly cajoled by James II into marrying Elizabeth Livingstone, daughter of the Chamberlain of Scotland – whom he appears to have disliked intensely. They had no male issue, but John early had two bastard sons of whom John the younger predeceased him, while the elder, Angus Og, was to become his bane. The marriage to Elizabeth Livingstone was a matter of dynastic convenience conditional upon the grant of certain lands as dowry, and the king's failure to fulfil this promise became the excuse for John's first rebellion in 1451.

In that year, James II of the 'Fiery Face' (on account of a livid birthmark) invaded the Douglas territories, seizing the fortress of Lochmaben and razing Castle Douglas to the ground. This caused the Earl of Douglas to hurry back to Scotland, while his confederates prepared to cause disturbance in other parts of the country. Somewhat imprudently, John of the Isles used the pretext of his wife's unpaid dowry to break into open revolt, and with a large force of Highlanders he captured the royal castles of Inverness, Urquhart, and Ruthven in Badenoch. This last was demolished, but John placed a strong garrison in Inverness and gave Urquhart into the keeping of Sir James Livingstone, his father-in-law, who had escaped from court to join the insurrection. The king was too preoccupied by the Douglas threat in the south to be able to mount an effective campaign against John of the Isles, and so the latter retained possession of his conquests for upwards of two years, collecting rents and revenues as if the lands were his own.

The Earl of Douglas meanwhile had returned to Scotland by way of the English court, and summoned his vassals to his standard for war against the king. James was much enraged, but he still hoped that some accommodation might avert an outright war, and he invited the earl to meet him under safe conduct at Stirling Castle. Douglas went confidently to the meeting, but when the king remonstrated with him over his treasonable conduct and demanded that he renounce his league with Crawford and the Lord of the Isles, he defiantly refused. Whereupon James lost his temper and stabbed him in the neck and body, and as the earl fell wounded, one of the courtiers killed him with a poleaxe. The Scottish Parliament subsequently confirmed that 'the earl was guilty of his own death by resisting the king's gentle persuasion'.

William Douglas was survived by his four brothers – James, the ninth earl who succeeded him, Sir John Douglas of Balveny who had been the principal instigator of the present disturbance, Archibald Earl of Moray, and Hugh Earl of Ormonde – who now declared their open rebellion. In 1452 they entered Stirling with 600 men, and nailing the king's safe-conduct to a board, dragged it through the streets at the tail of a winded horse. They then burned the town and proclaimed their loyalty to the King of England.

In Angus, the Earl of Huntly defeated Crawford near Brechin, and the Douglas faction in the north disbanded. Apart from a half-hearted campaign into Moray, however, Huntly made no serious attempt to dislodge John of the Isles from Urquhart and Inverness, and James continued to concentrate his main forces in the south. In 1453 he reached a hollow truce with Douglas, but when the latter used this interval to intrigue with England, the king descended on the Douglas lands once more, and defeated the rebellious earls at Arkinholme in Annandale in 1455. Douglas himself escaped into England, but the Earl of Moray was killed in the battle, while Ormonde was captured and allowed to recover from his wounds before going to the block. Sir John Balveny, however, fled north into the Highlands and took refuge with John of the Isles.

John immediately fitted out an expedition of 5000 men and a hundred galleys under Donald Balloch to attack the coast of Ayrshire in support of the Douglas faction in the south while the earl himself was soliciting aid from the English Duke of York. The Islesmen landed at Innerkip and wasted the surrounding country, before proceeding to the Cumbraes and the Isle of Arran where they stormed and destroyed the Castle of Brodick. Rothesay on Bute was also razed, and the inhabitants forced to pay a tribute of 100 bolls of meal, 100 cattle, and 100 merks of silver. Finally, Donald Balloch attacked the estates of the Bishop of Argyll who had made himself particularly obnoxious to the Douglas cause by putting his seal to their instrument of forfeiture. Throughout these forays they encountered little opposition since the accounts state that not above twenty persons were killed, but they accumulated a great store of plunder, most of it on the hoof, amounting to 600 horses, 10,000 oxen and kine, and 1000 sheep and goats. Otherwise, however, the campaign achieved very little, and when the Earl of Douglas abandoned his revolt and returned to the English court to await a more favourable opportunity, John of the Isles suddenly found himself dangerously exposed as the only rebel still in arms. He was further embarrassed when in the same year, his wife deserted him and fled to the court, from where she wrote letters to the Pope complaining that John had imprisoned her against her will when she was pregnant, and had attempted to murder her by poison.

John sent a submissive message to the king, asking forgiveness and promising 'as far as it was still left to him, to repair the wrongs which he had inflicted'. At first James refused to listen, but eventually he agreed to put John on 'probation', absolving him from the consequences of his rebellion provided that he demonstrated the sincerity of his repentance by some notable exploit. He also allowed him to retain possession of Urquhart Castle at an annual rent, and in 1457 even appointed him a Warden of the Marches – probably with the intention of weakening his power by forcing him to reside outside the Lordship.

In 1460, James, who was at truce with the Lancastrian Henry VI, took advantage of the Wars of the Roses which had broken out in England, to regain Roxburgh Castle, in English hands since 1362, which was then held by a Yorkist. John of the Isles demonstrated his professed loyalty by joining the king with 3000 fighting men from the Isles – 'all armed in the Highland fashion with habergeons, bows and axes', and he promised James that 'if he pleased to pass any further in the bounds of England, he and his company should pass a large mile afore the rest of the host and take upon them the first press and dint of battle'. He was not required to perform such a service, however, since during the siege of Roxburgh, the king, who had a fascination for artillery, was killed when a great hooped cannon called 'The Lion' exploded close to where he was standing.

The heir James III was only nine years old, and after attending the

Parliament which discussed the administration of Scotland during another long minority, John decided that the new government was not strong enough to compel his obedience, and he reverted to his earlier schemes of independence and his association with Black Douglas. Scotland once more suffered the turmoil of a minority as barons squabbled for the regency or tried to seize the person of the king. In the west, a number of piratical spirits, including John's brothers Hugh of Sleat and Celestine of Lochalsh, together with MacLeod of Harris and 'the young gentlemen of the Isles', set out to attack Orkney, where they killed the earl and a number of his people, and gained a quantity of plunder. Orkney accounts indicate that these raids became a yearly occurrence, but as the islands still belonged to Norway, the Scottish government took no interest.

The intrigue with Douglas at the English court, however, became more sinister. In 1461, after being defeated at Taunton, the Lancastrian Henry VI obtained asylum in Scotland where he plotted to regain his throne, and the Yorkist Edward IV, who had seized the English crown, was ready to support a Douglas diversion in the north.

On 22 June 1461, Edward appointed five commissioners – the Earl of Douglas, Sir John Douglas of Balveny, Sir William Wellis, Dr John Kingscote, and John Stanley – to negotiate with John of the Isles and Donald Balloch, with a view to considering a number of proposals to be discussed in detail at Westminster. On 19 October John, 'by the advice of his principal vassals and kinsmen assembled in Council at Ardtornish', responded by granting a commission in the style of an independent prince to his cousins Ranald of the Isles and Duncan Archdean of the Isles, to confer with the deputies of the English king in London.

During that winter, negotiations continued in England between the representatives of the Isles and the English commissioners, who included the Bishop of Durham, the Earl of Worcester, Lord Wenlock, the Prior of St Johns, and Robert Stillington, Keeper of the Privy Seal. The outcome was an extraordinary Treaty, signed on 13 February 1462, the purport of which was nothing less than the conquest of Scotland by the Earl of Douglas and the Lord of the Isles, with assistance from Edward IV. John of the Isles, Donald Balloch, and John of Dunyveg, Donald's heir, agreed to become forever the sworn vassals of England and to assist Edward in his wars in Ireland and elsewhere. In return for this, John of the Isles was to receive a salary of £200 a year in time of war, and 100 merks in time of peace. Donald Balloch and his son were to receive £40 and £20 a year respectively in time of war and half these sums in time of peace. In the event of their successfully conquering Scotland, the whole of the kingdom north of the Forth was to be divided equally between the Earl of Douglas, John of the Isles, and Donald Balloch, while Douglas would also be restored to all his forfeited lands between the Forth and the English border. When such a division had been implemented, the English salaries would cease.

The Treaty of Ardtornish was a truly perilous engagement, and even without the advantages of hindsight, it is remarkable that the Lord of the Isles, who was already the most powerful noble in Scotland, should have risked his estate and fortune in so wild an enterprise. Moreover, without waiting for the assistance from England to materialise, and under pressure perhaps from the overbold Donald Balloch, John immediately mustered the vassals of the Lordship and Ross, and gathered a great force of Islesmen whom he placed under the command of his natural son, Angus Og, with the veteran Donald to assist him. They seized the town and castle of Inverness, and began to issue proclamations in John's name as Earl of Ross to all the sheriffdoms of the northern counties, ordering the inhabitants to obey Angus Og as his governor under pain of death, to pay to him all the taxes due to the crown, and to refuse obedience to the officers of King James III. These proclamations were generally obeyed, and it is recorded that Angus Og 'succeeded in securing a large part of the burgh dues', besides levying blackmail on Inverness and ravaging the surrounding districts. The eastern counties seemed paralysed by rumours of an English invasion, and the only opposition came from the Frasers, who banded with the Macraes and Forbeses and defeated a Macdonald warband which was raiding in the Aird.

By 1464, however, John again became obliged to make his peace, since Edward IV had signed a truce with Scotland, and the Douglas rebellion had come to nothing. At the same time, John was so powerful and the other barons so intent on their own disputes, that the Regents were reluctant to take any military action against him. John was ordered to appear before Parliament, but when he did not compear, the process against him was suspended, and later in the year he met the young king at Inverness where they apparently were reconciled. For the next ten years, John continued to govern his vast dominions without molestation or interference by the Scottish crown.

In 1474, however, commissioners were invited to England to negotiate a permanent treaty between the two countries, and at some time
during these discussions, details of the Treaty of Ardtornish were either
leaked or became known to the Scottish authorities. The government
immediately summoned John of the Isles to appear before parliament in
December 1475 to answer charges of treason in connection with his
rebellious actions in 1455, 1461, and consequent to the Treaty of
Ardtornish. A commission was given to Colin Campbell, Earl of Argyll,
to prosecute a sentence of forfeiture against him, and when John again
failed to compear, he was condemned to death *in absentia* and the
sentence of forfeiture pronounced. As soon as the weather permitted,
the Earls of Atholl and Crawford were placed in command of a
formidable sea-borne expedition to the Isles in order to enforce the
sentence of parliament, and in the face of this threat, many of John's
councillors advised him to submit. Using Huntly as an intermediary, he
therefore indicated that he wished to sue for pardon, and when the
queen and the States of Parliament were persuaded to intercede on his
behalf, he duly appeared in Edinburgh and 'with much humility and
many expressions of contrition, surrendered himself to the Royal
Mercy'. The king, 'with wonderful moderation', consented to pardon
him.

On 1 July 1476, the Parliament in Edinburgh reversed the sentence of
forfeiture and restored him to his dominions of Ross and the Isles,
whereupon, according to prior agreement, John voluntarily resigned to
the crown the Earldom of Ross (with the exception of Skye), the lands of
Kintyre and Knapdale, and all the castles thereto belonging. In return
for this submission, he was created a Baron Banrent and a Peer of
Parliament, by the title of 'Lord of the Isles'. Thus the Earldom of Ross
was permanently annexed to the crown, and the old claims of the
independent Lordship were exchanged for a feudal title.

By the king's favour, the succession to the title and to the lands of the
Lordship was secured in favour of Angus Og and John, the bastard sons
of John of Islay, and in an attempt to further the cause of reconciliation,
Angus Og was shortly afterwards married to the daughter of the Earl of
Argyll. But 'neither the favour now shown to him by the king nor his
alliance with the Earl of Argyll were sufficient to keep the natural
violence of his temper within bounds, and circumstances soon enabled
Angus Og to establish an ascendancy over his father'. John may have
been lucky to have escaped so lightly, but his submission to the king was

a great blow to his prestige and authority in the Isles, particularly among the chiefs of the Clan Donald, who now held him in contempt, and his efforts to ensure the loyalty of the other vassal clans by further favours and grants of land added to his growing impoverishment and unpopularity. Angus Og, 'observing that his father very much diminished his rents by his prodigality, sought to deprive him of his management and authority',[107] and the allegiance of the Islesmen became divided between the ageing Lord and his rebellious son.

The seannachies, who preferred to recall Angus Og in the heroic mould of his warrior ancestors, described him as a 'bold, forward man, and high-minded',[108] with references to his particular 'sweetness of speech', but there are indications also of a strange streak of madness and instability, and by all accounts he was an exceptionally violent man. Gathering a large number of adherents, he went to Islay where John was then in residence, and turned him out:

forcing him to change seven rooms to lodge in, and at last to take his bed during the whole of the night under an old boat. When John returned to his house in the morning, he found Angus Og sitting with a great crowd about him. MacFinnon rising up, desired Macdonald to sit down; but he answered that he would not sit down till he should execute his intention – which was to curse his son. So leaving Islay with only six men, he went to the mainland and to Inverary, and having waited without till one of Argyll's gentlemen came forth in the morning, and observing Macdonald, immediately told Argyll of the matter, who could scarcely believe him.

Argyll welcomed John, but expressed surprise at his lack of state and the smallness of his retinue.

That is little, said Macdonald, to the revolutions of these times and thou shall be the better of my coming; and so after dinner he bestowed on him the lands of Knapdale from the River Add to the Fox Burn in Kintyre, 400 merk lands, and desired Argyll to convey him to Stirling where the king was at that time, and for his son's disobedience, he would resign all his estates to the king.[109]

It is likely that John's meeting with Argyll and his appearance before the king at Stirling related to a further summons which had been served against him when Angus Og attacked and occupied Castle Sween. John was held responsible for the behaviour of 'his *rebellis* and *traitouris*' and for the 'tresonable stuffing of the said castell with men, vitalis, and armis for weire, and for the tresonable art and part of the holding of the said castell contrare to the Kinge's Majestie', but he strenuously dissociated himself from the actions of Angus Og, and parliament found him innocent.

Angus Og had no intention of relinquishing any part of what he held to be his rightful patrimony, and on the pretext of a feud with the Mackenzies, he invaded the forfeited Earldom of Ross. Kenneth of Kintail, the eldest son of the Mackenzie chief, had married Angus Og's sister, Margaret of the Isles, and on the strength of this intended reconciliation between the Mackenzies and the Macdonalds, Angus Og had taken a house in Balnagown in Easter Ross. It was a marriage of dynastic convenience only, since the lady was considered to be ill-favoured and blind of one eye. At Christmas, Angus gave a great feast to which Kenneth was invited but when he appeared without the Lady Margaret, the Macdonald took offence. Kenneth also considered himself insulted when he and his forty followers were put to lodge in the kiln because the house was full. Angus Og's Chamberlain responsible for these domestic arrangements was a Maclean of Duart, who had quarrelled previously with Kenneth, and so the Mackenzie fetched him a blow on the ear which knocked him to the ground. Angus Og's followers immediately rushed to arms, and the Mackenzies, being outnumbered, hastily retreated and escaped across the river. Finding lodging on the opposite shore, Kenneth felt safe, but humiliated at being obliged to spend Christmas under the roof of a stranger, and so he persuaded his host, 'who had no syrname but a patronimick', to adopt the name of Mackenzie and next day went to Chanonry to obtain feu of the land from the Bishop of Ross to whom it belonged. Kenneth then joined his father at Kinellan, but was further enraged when Angus sent him a message ordering him to leave within twenty-four hours. Kenneth returned a defiant reply, adding that as he no longer wanted peace with the Clan Donald, he did not care to keep one of their name about him, and he sent the Lady Margaret back to Angus Og mounted on a one-eyed horse, attended by a one-eyed servant, and followed by a one-eyed dog.

The Lady, who was pregnant, became greatly distressed, and such an insult required immediate reprisal. In 1480, Angus raised a large force of Islesmen with the Macdonalds of Lochaber, Glengarry and Knoydart, and marched up the Great Glen to Inverness, seizing the town and castle before advancing north to Dingwall, where he stormed the fortress and subsequently defended it for two years. In 1482 the Earl of Atholl raised an army among the Mackenzies,

Frasers, Mackays, Brodies, Rosses, and others who hated the Clan Donald, but was roundly defeated by Angus at the battle of Lagabraad. The government immediately sent another army north under Atholl and Huntly, and Angus was eventually forced to withdraw into Lochaber.

Atholl and Argyll next tried to persuade the clans of the Lordship to reject Angus, 'desiring them to hold of the king . . . who would grant them the same rights that they formerly had of Macdonald'. 'This offer was accepted by several', but 'when the Macdonalds and the heads of their families saw that their Chief and family were to be sunk, they began to look up to Angus Og'.[110] Unfortunately, at about this time, Celestine of Lochalsh died, and John lost the support and counsel of this brother, who was respected in the Isles.

Atholl and Argyll contrived a reconciliation between father and son by arranging a meeting between them, but this achieved nothing and the two factions drew towards war – the vassal clans of Maclean, MacLeod, and MacNeil, adhering to John of the Isles, while the bulk of the Clan Donald itself followed Angus Og.

John gathered his galleys at Tobermory in Mull, while Angus Og's fleet lay storm-bound for five weeks north of Ardnamurchan. When Angus was eventually able to round the point, he came in sight of John's ships lying outside Tobermory, and a desperate sea battle took place in the 'Bloody Bay'. The fight began when Angus, with Donald of Sleat, Alexander of Lochalsh, and Ranald Bain of Moidart attacked the galley of Maclean of Ardgour which was caught in the open waters of the Sound. Maclean, MacLeod of Harris, and MacNeil of Barra steered to Ardgour's relief and the fleets joined battle outside the entrance to the harbour. Ranald Bain ran his galley alongside that of MacLeod of Harris in order to grapple and board her, and one of his men called Edmund O'Brien thrust the blade of his oar below the sternpost of MacLeod's vessel, jamming the rudder and making the ship unmanageable. MacLeod was mortally wounded by two arrows and his galley captured. Angus Og and Ranald of Moidart then attacked Maclean and took him prisoner with great slaughter of his crew. Angus wanted to hang Maclean immediately, but was prevented by the Laird of Moidart who said, whimsically, that he would have no one to quarrel with in future if Maclean was dead. MacNeil of Barra escaped in the direction of Coll with three Macdonald galleys in pursuit, and the rest of John's fleet broke off the engagement and ran for shelter. After this defeat John lost all effective power in the Isles, and withdrew into a temporary retirement, reflecting possibly upon the old Norse proverb:

> Let no man trust an early sown acre,
>   Nor too soon his son.
> Weather makes the acre and wit the son:
>   Each of which is risky.

The Earl of Atholl now thought to bring Angus Og to heel by sailing to Islay and kidnapping his three-year-old son Donald Dubh, or Donald the Black, who was handed for safekeeping to his grandfather Argyll and confined in the Campbell's Castle of Innis Chonnel in Loch Awe 'until his hair got grey'. Angus Og retaliated by leading a ferocious raid over the passes into Atholl. The Earl and Countess took refuge with most of their people in the chapel of St Bride, but Angus violated the sanctuary, taking Atholl and his Countess prisoner and seizing a great store of plunder. During the voyage back to Islay, however, many of his galleys were sunk in a storm, and Angus was so overcome by superstition, believing it to be retribution for his sacrilegious robbery, that after one year he released the earl and returned himself to the chapel where he submitted to a humiliating penance.

From this time onward, in the words of the Sleat historian, 'his father's curse seems to have lighted on the man'. He 'took a journey south where he killed many of the MacAlisters in Arran, and also some of his own name, for seizing and intromitting with some of his lands without his consent'. Returning through Argyll and Lochaber, he occupied Inverness for a fourth time, possibly as a preliminary to another invasion of Ross. But in 1488, his wild career was brought to a sudden and violent end.

In addition to his feud with Mackenzie of Kintail, Angus Og had incurred the hatred of a lady of the MacLeods who was married to his own ally and cousin, Ranald Bain of Moidart. She was the daughter of Rory the Black, Tutor to the young MacLeod of Lewis, who abused his position by trying to dispossess his ward and seize the lands of Lewis for himself. Angus displaced him and restored the young heir to his rightful inheritance, but Rory's daughter was determined to be revenged on him for frustrating her father's scheme, and plotted his death with Mackenzie of Kintail.

The ready instrument of their design was an Irish harper called Art

O'Carby from Managhan, who was often at Angus Og's house, and who had also fallen madly in love with Mackenzie's daughter.

Mackenzie seeing him in that mood, promised him his daughter, provided he would put Angus to death, and made him swear never to reveal the secret. The fellow being afterwards in his cups, and playing on his harp, used to sing a verse composed by himself in the Irish language, saying that the rider of the dappled horse was in danger of his life (for Angus always rode such a one) if there was poison in his long knife, which he called Gallfit.[111]

While the army was at Inverness, Angus shared a lodging with John Cameron, brother of Lochiel, and MacMurrich the poet – but without any other guards. During the night, O'Carby entered the room where he slept and cut his throat. The harper was afterwards torn in pieces by wild horses and never enjoyed Mackenzie's daughter.

On the death of Angus Og, the ageing John of the Isles again resumed possession of the Lordship – although effective government of the Clan Donald passed to his nephew, Alexander of Lochalsh. Some traditions aver, however, that Alexander was not the heir, and acted only as guardian for the captive Donald Dubh.

In the Lowlands, the murder of Angus Og passed virtually unnoticed, since king and barons were once more in contention and the country poised on the brink of civil war. After surviving a troubled childhood during which the several factions had tried to use him as a pawn for power, James III had promised fair, since he was intelligent and gifted and did not seem to lack determination. But he also proved to be morose and unsociable, given principally to solitary and intellectual pursuits and chiefly interested in architecture, astronomy, and the search for the Philosopher's Stone. The barons followed a more robust philosophy and were contemptuous of the 'masons and fiddlers', and other craftsmen who now obtained privileged positions at the court. Both the magnates and the people at large preferred the king's younger brothers, the Earls of Mar and Albany, and their growing popularity encouraged an equivalent ambition. In 1479 James became anxious for his crown, and imprisoned them in Edinburgh Castle. Mar died mysteriously in his bath, bleeding to death from the over-zealous ministrations of the king's leech, but Albany managed to kill his guards and escaped over the castle wall. Taking refuge in London, he proclaimed himself King of Scots, and in 1482 joined an English army which was preparing to invade the borders. James rode south to confront the enemy at Lauder, but the Scottish nobles led by Archibald Earl of Angus, head of the Red Douglases 'whose house had risen on the ruins of the Black', overtook him and in Douglas' phrase, 'belled the cat', by hanging the royal favourites from the bridge at Lauder before escorting James back to Edinburgh. Albany became regent for a short time, but the wheel of fortune turned again and he was eventually driven out of Scotland and died at a tournament in France. The Red Douglas was captured in 1483 when he raided Lochmaben, and James, who could be subtle in revenge, forebore to kill him and forced him instead to become a monk at Lindores Abbey.

In 1488 a fresh rebellion directed against the king's taxation was led by Lord Home with the Hepburns from the border, the Bishop of Glasgow, and Colin Campbell, Earl of Argyll. The conspirators seized the person of the young heir to the throne and proclaimed him King James IV. When negotiation failed, both sides drew to arms at Sauchieburn near Stirling, and in the battle which followed, the king's horse bolted, throwing him from the saddle. Badly injured, he staggered or was carried into the kitchen of Beaton's Mill on the edge of the old battlefield of Bannockburn, where he asked a cottage-wife to fetch him a priest. She returned with a man who claimed to be one (tradition records that it was William Stirling of Keir), and when James asked for absolution the stranger stabbed him to death.

James IV, then aged fifteen, was proclaimed king with Red Douglas as Regent in the interim, and a statement was issued concerning the unfortunate fight at Sauchieburn 'whereat the father of our Sovereign Lord happened to be slain'. The young king evinced some remorse and for the rest of his life wore an iron chain around his body as a penance; but the principal conspirators were richly rewarded. Hepburn was created Earl of Bothwell and Lord High Admiral, while, of more immediate relevance to the Isles, the rapid rise to power of the Campbells of Argyll properly dates from this time.

James IV was the ablest and most attractive of all the Stewart kings – highly intelligent, energetic, charming, confident, lusty, virile, and consequently well beloved. The scholar Erasmus (whom he employed to teach one of his bastard sons) wrote of him: 'He had a wonderful force of interest, an incredible knowledge of all things.' He had as well, a gift for languages, and remarkable for a Lowland king, he spoke Gaelic. The Spanish Ambassador, Pedro de Ayala, reflecting the prejudice of the court, reported to Ferdinand and Isabella: 'He even speaks the language of the savages who live in some parts of Scotland and in the islands.' This ability, and the genuine interest which he showed in the Gaelic regions of his kingdom, explains the exceptional moderation which he displayed, initially at least, in the years following the forfeiture of the Lordship.

In 1491, Alexander of Lochalsh, either on John's advice or in spite of it, attempted another invasion of Ross. Alexander already held lands in Wester Ross, about Lochalsh, Lochcarron, and Lochbroom, and may have had some influence in the region which he believed would support his claim. With a large force of Islesmen he marched through Lochaber and up Glen Spean into Badenoch, where he was joined by the Camerons and the Macdonalds of Keppoch who were also at feud with Mackenzie. The Highlanders sacked Inverness from force of habit and occupied the castle, and then reived north into Cromarty where they plundered extensively along the coastland. The store of *spulzie* (spoil) became so large that Alexander detached a part of his army to carry it back to the Isles, while with the remainder he raided into the Mackenzie country as far as Strathconan. The foray was conducted with customary savagery, and on a Sunday morning the Macdonalds reached the village of Contin and burned down the church which was full of refugees who had taken sanctuary within. Kenneth of Kintail mustered the Mackenzies in revenge, and marched to surprise Alexander at his leaguer in Strathconan. The battle of Blairnepark was fought across a stretch of wild moorland, broken with deep pits and bogs. Kenneth, whose force was much smaller than the Macdonald warband, hid his archers in ambush, and then led his fighting men in a frontal attack against Alexander's camp, intending to draw the Islesmen back into the marsh within range of the bowmen. When Alexander saw Kenneth's small force advancing, he said scornfully that the Mackenzies must be mad to attempt such an assault, but his brother Gillespic, who had more experience of battle, warned him that such extraordinary boldness was probably to a purpose, and he should be wary of such tactics. Alexander scoffed at this advice, calling Gillespic a coward, and 'both parties met with a terrible stour, fighting hansomelie on both sides'.[112] The vanguard, under Maclean of Loch Buie, charged furiously into Kenneth's advancing Mackenzies, and were driving them back when they ran into a withering cross-fire from the hidden archers. Profiting from this confusion, Kenneth wheeled his swordsmen, and the Mackenzies took the main Clan Donald force in the flank and shortly routed them. Alexander himself got safe away, but his brother Gillespic, smarting from the charge of cowardice, was killed in single combat with Kenneth whom he sought out in the battle. The fugitives tried to escape across the River Conan, but there was no ford nearby and many were drowned in the current or killed by the local people as they clung to the bushes along the bank or tried to drag themselves ashore. The exulting Mackenzies raided on into the lands of Kilravock and savaged the estates of the Roses and the Munroes who had supported Alexander. 'So many excesses were committed at this time by the Mackenzies that the Earl of Huntly, Lieutenant of the North, was compelled (notwithstanding their services in repelling the invasion of the Macdonalds) to act against them as rebels and oppressors of the lieges.' Kenneth of Kintail took a thorough revenge.

Alexander's unsuccessful invasion of Ross convinced the Scottish government that John of the Isles was incapable of controlling the western clans, and that the island confederacy had to be broken if order was to be brought to the remoter districts. In the Parliament which met in May 1493, John, fourth and last Lord of the Isles, was forfeited and deprived of his title and estates. (Unfortunately the original document has not been preserved.) In January 1494, he appeared before James IV and went through the form of making a voluntary resignation and surrender of the Lordship. Thereafter he remained some time in the king's household in receipt of a pension, and as he grew older passed long intervals at the Monastery of Paisley.

Immediately after the forfeiture, James IV went to the western Highlands to receive the submission of the vassals of the Lordship. Alexander of Lochalsh, John of Dunyveg (son of Donald Balloch), Maclean of Loch Buie, and Duncan Mackintosh of the Clan Chattan, submitted immediately, and received royal charters for all or most of the lands which they had previously held of the Lord of the Isles, thus becoming independent freeholders under the king. Alexander of Lochalsh was knighted, and by virtue of his having been heir presumptive to the Lordship, was recognised as the leader and spokesman of the islanders. In the hope that a display of leniency might best secure a peaceful settlement, James further promised that he would secure all the free tenants of the Isles in their present holdings.

In 1494, James returned to Kintyre with a strong force sufficient to compel any whom he could not persuade. The castles of Tarbert and Dunavertie were garrisoned, and their defences strengthened by the addition of heavy artillery pieces manned by skilled gunners. The district of Appin was given to the king's cousin, Duncan Stewart, appointed the new Chamberlain of the Isles, who began the construction of Castle Stalker in the Firth of Lorne. A new royal castle was also built at Kilkerran in Kintyre.

Not all the chiefs were ready to submit or carry out the terms of their surrender. John of Dunyveg begrudged the loss of lands in Kintyre which had belonged to Donald Balloch, and when the king dispersed his expedition and was putting to sea with only a retinue, he stormed Dunavertie and hanged the governor in view of the royal fleet. James was unable to act immediately against him, but MacIain of Ardnamurchan, who was anxious to secure the king's favour, later apprehended John and his two sons at Islay and sent them to Edinburgh for summary execution. MacLeod of Lewis also surrendered during the course of the year.

In 1495 James assembled an army at Glasgow and sailed to Mingary in Ardnamurchan. In May, John of Sleat, Donald of Keppoch, Allan of Moidart chief of the Clanranald, Hector Maclean of Duart, Ewen Cameron of Lochiel, and MacNeil of Barra tendered their submissions and received the royal pardon. At the same time, as a precaution against further trouble in the north, Kenneth of Kintail and Farquhar Mackintosh heir to Clan Chattan, were imprisoned at Edinburgh.

These measures were followed by a series of Acts of Council providing, in cases of civil actions against the islanders (of which a large number were in preparation) that each chief was personally liable for the execution of summonses against members of his clan, since the authority of crown officials was likely to be doubtful. The five principal chiefs of rank: Maclean of Duart, MacIain of Ardnamurchan, Allan of the Clanranald, Ewen Cameron of Lochiel, and Donald of Keppoch, appeared before the Lords of Council and bound themselves, 'by the extension of their hands', to the Earl of Argyll on behalf of the king, to abstain from mutual injury or molestation, each under penalty of £100.

In 1497, however, the king's attention was diverted by the pretensions of Perkin Warbeck in England, and during this respite, Alexander of Lochalsh made his final unsuccessful attempt to seize the Earldom of Ross. The Mackenzies and Munroes banded together to rout his army at Drumchatt, and drove him out of Ross for the last time. Alexander failed to obtain any further support in the Isles and withdrew to Oronsay where MacIain of Ardnamurchan, seeing another opportunity to perform an acceptable service to the king, eventually surprised and killed him. At about the same time, Mackenzie and Mackintosh escaped from Edinburgh, but were shortly recaptured at the Torwood by the Laird of Buchanan. Mackenzie died while resisting arrest, and Mackintosh was returned to his dungeon where he remained until after James IV's death at Flodden.

In 1498 the king, impatient to complete the settlement of the Isles, held court at his new castle of Kilkerran, where MacLeod of Harris and MacLeod of Lewis appeared before him and paid homage. Steps were taken to secure the economy of the Isles, and a feud between the Macdonalds of Sleat and the Clanranald of Moydart over the old MacRuairi lands of Garmoran was briefly settled. 'The king soon afterwards returned to the Lowlands, leaving as he imagined, the Isles and West Highlands in a state of tranquillity, not likely soon to be disturbed.'

In January 1503, John, fourth and last Lord of the Isles, died in a small lodging house at Dundee. He seems to have been living in greatly reduced circumstances, since the money due to his landlady, together with the cost of his 'furthbringing and berying, and to louse his gere' were charged to the Scottish treasury. His body was not taken to Iona to rest among his great forebears of Clan Donald, and perhaps there were few in the Isles who mourned him. At his own request he was buried in Paisley by the tomb of his other ancestor Robert II, the first of the Stewart kings, to whose descendant he had submitted.

In this manner fell the Lordship of the Isles, and the great Celtic dynasty of Somerled was divided to its ruin.

CHAPTER 20

The Ruin of the Lordship

It is no joy without Clan Donald:
It is no strength to be without them;
The best race in the round world,
To them belongs every goodly man.

The noblest race of all created,
In whom dwelt prowess and terribleness;
A race to whom tyrants bowed;
In whom dwelt wisdom and piety.

A race the best for service and shelter;
A race the best for valour of hand:
Ill I deem the shortness of her skein
By whom their thread was spun.

For sorrow and for sadness
I have forsaken wisdom and learning:
On their account I have forsaken all things.
It is no joy without Clan Donald.[113]

After the forfeiture of the Lordship,

the islanders and the rest of the Highlanders were let loose, and began to shed one another's blood. Although the Macdonald kept them in obedience when he was Lord over them, yet upon his resignation of his rights – all families, including his own as well as others, gave themselves up to all sorts of cruelties which continued for a long time thereafter.[114]

Had James IV possessed more experience he might have recognised the wisdom of allowing the feudal Lordship to remain, since while the clans accepted its authority and shared a common bond of allegiance, it could have been an effective instrument of government in the Hebrides. By contrast, the central authority in the Lowlands was too remote to enforce order, and the Lieutenants appointed to administer the Highlands and Western Isles were unprincipled, and rapacious, and could command neither loyalty nor respect. By making the Highland chiefs independent tenants of the Crown instead of vassals of the Lordship, James IV had thought to win their co-operation, but in fact he succeeded principally in arousing their cupidity. The effect was to release those latent rivalries which had been held in check by the authority of the Lords of the Isles, and the consequent conflicts between the clans, though often depicted in a romantic light, more truly reflected their decline once the old unity of the Lordship was dissolved. Each tribe strove for aggrandisement at the expense of its neighbours, and since the government's desire was to diminish the Clan Donald, the lesser clans now became the greater, while other families who had never shared any part of the old dominion of the Lordship, profited from the endemic feuding to extend their influence in the western Highlands.

The 'Danting of the Isles' became an abiding preoccupation of the Lowland government, but it was convenient to contract the task of subjugating the Hebrides to certain Highland nobles – in particular the Earls of Argyll and Huntly, and Dougal Stewart of Appin – whose personal ambitions could readily be served by the performance or abuse of such public duty. Moreover, Lowland sentiment towards the Gaels grew more antagonistic as the century progressed, and when coupled with the greed for land and revenue, it was callously accepted that the barbarous inhumanity of the natives was justification enough for depriving them of their hereditary lands, and even for exterminating entire local populations. Thus in 1528, James V could sign an order to the Earl of Moray and others to suppress disorders among the Clan Chattan and 'leave na creature living of that clan, except priests, women, and bairns' (these last to be deported to Shetland). Similarly, in 1607, the North Isles excepting Skye and Lewis were offered to Huntly on condition that he extirpated their whole populations – an atrocity which did not occur only because the feu fee was higher than Huntly wished to pay, while the Presbyterians were not prepared to allow such an increase in property to accrue to a Catholic noble. The same mentality could conceive the massacre at Glencoe and the Clearances of a later century.

In 1499, James IV revoked the charters given at Kilkerran the previous year, and his moderate plans for settlement were replaced by a harsher policy of subjugation. This may have been due to Argyll's persuasion, since he was now given a commission as Lieutenant of the Isles with control over the Castle of Tarbert, and a lease of the entire Lordship except for Islay and Kintyre. Huntly received a similar commission over the northern Highlands:

From this period the great power enjoyed by the Earls of Ross and Lords of the Isles was transferred to Argyll and Huntly; the former having chief rule in the South Isles and adjacent coasts, whilst the influence of the latter prevailed in the northern Highlands.[115]

MacIain of Ardnamurchan was also rewarded for his services to the Crown, and became thereby abhorrent to the other branches of Clan Donald. In the north, Huntly interpreted his commission as a licence to pillage as he pleased, while in the South Isles, through remissions, bonds of manrent, dormant claims, and Lowland law – or more drastically by commissions of fire and sword – the Campbell power crept across the territories of Clan Donald, creating a legacy of bitterness and hatred that would persist for generations. The bellicosity of the western chiefs contributed to their own decline – for their constant feuds provided the excuse, and the rivalries between the clans weakened their ability to resist.

Seeing in the king's measures the likely machinery of their expulsion, the clans rebelled. In 1501, a band of Macdonalds from Glencoe rowed across Loch Awe in dead of night and released Donald Dubh from his island prison of Innis Chonnel. MacLeod of Lewis, Maclean of Lewis, the Clan Donald, with the Camerons, MacKinnons, MacQuaries, MacNeils, and other vassals proclaimed him heir to the Lordship and carried fire and sword into Badenoch and Lochaber. North and south the government forces mobilised but they were unable to bring the Gaels to battle, and a major effort by land and sea failed initially to prevent the spread of insurrection. But the rebellion succumbed to attrition three years later as one by one the chiefs were isolated and brought to submission, and Donald Dubh was sent to a second imprisonment in Edinburgh Castle which was to last for almost forty years.

In 1509, for reasons which are not recorded, Allan MacRuairi of the Clanranald was tried and executed before the king at Blair Atholl, and his successor, Ranald, suffered a similar fate at Perth four years later. Yet during the latter years of his reign the clans accepted James IV's authority since they had a traditional respect for the king, and the administrative reforms, such as the perambulatory courts (the justice ayres), brought a measure of law and order to the Isles. James himself returned to the policy of moderation, and even supported the sons of western chiefs at Lowland universities. A comparative peace returned to the Isles.

It was one of these Highland protégés who next raised the standard of revolt and tried to revive the old confederacy among the island clans. Sir Donald Gallda – the name indicates his Lowland education – was the eldest surviving son of the murdered Alexander of Lochalsh, who had been brought up at court, and was knighted on the field of Flodden. Taking advantage of the minority which followed James IV's death in that battle, in 1513 he proclaimed himself Lord of the Isles on behalf of the true heir Donald Dubh, and led the Macdonalds of Dunyveg and Glengarry down the old war trail into Glen Urquhart, while simultaneously, Maclean of Duart seized Cairnburgh Castle at Mull, and MacLeod of Harris occupied Dunskaith in Skye. The Regent Albany ordered Argyll to deal with the Macleans and use the offices of MacIain to sow division among the vassal clans. Lochiel and Mackintosh were appointed Lieutenants in Lochaber, while the Mackenzies resisted the depredations of Clan Donald in the north. The matter came to treaty and a temporary reconciliation – until English agents incited Donald Gallda to continue the revolt, and he set his mind on the destruction of MacIain of Ardnamurchan in revenge for the murder of his father. But Donald was disliked by many of the island chiefs, and while Argyll worked to suppress the rebellion on the mainland, Maclean of Duart – of the family most favoured by the earlier Lords of the Isles – petitioned James V for the forfeiture of Donald Gallda and the execution of his sons, stressing the need for 'destroying the wicked blood of the Isles, for as long as that blood reigns the king shall never have the Isles in peace'. Donald survived long enough to kill MacIain in battle at Craiganairgid, but he died himself shortly after, and the Hebrides were brought to an uncertain peace. During this time, the new Earl of Argyll (his father had died with James IV at Flodden) began to extend his influence in the old territories of the Lordship.

As clan feuds became endemic, yet on three further occasions a fragile flame of unity gleamed briefly in the Isles and the war-smoke fired the western heather – since so long as Donald Dubh still lived, the nostalgia for the Lordship lingered. In 1531 an insurrection led by Alexander of Dunyveg was suppressed and a temporary truce effected between the king and the island chiefs, but eight years later there was a fresh conspiracy incited by Donald Gorme of Sleat against the Mackenzies of Kintail, and a Macdonald warband once more raided into Ross. Donald Gorme died from an arrow wound beneath the walls of Eilean Donan, and the following year James V, impatient with this perpetual disturbance in the west, undertook a sea-borne expedition to the Isles to pacify the rebel clans. He seized the most influential of the chiefs – Mackay of Strathnaver, MacLeod of Lewis and his vassals, Glengarry, Clanranald, and others of the Clan Colla – and imprisoned them at Dumbarton, taking hostages from others, and leaving garrisons in the principal castles of Argyll and the west. The old Lordship, including north and south Kintyre, was annexed inalienably to the Crown, 'and everything promised an assurance of a more lengthy period of peace than the Isles had hitherto enjoyed'.[116]

That hope disappeared when the untimely death of James V in 1542 exposed the kingdom to the dilapidations of another minority, and an inevitable power struggle between the rival factions who competed for the government. In 1543, Donald Dubh escaped from Edinburgh Castle and once more proclaimed his right to the Lordship and the Earldom of Ross. The Regent Arran imprudently released the chiefs from Dumbarton on condition that they harassed Argyll and Huntly, and with the single exception of James of Dunyveg, the branches of Clan Donald and the vassals of the Lordship united once more under the son of Angus Og. The smoke of war and pillage hung over Argyll as the lands of the Campbells were ravaged and burned, while in the north, the Clanranald of Moidart defeated the Frasers of Lovat at Blar-na-leine, and revenged themselves upon the vassals of Huntly.

The English meanwhile began to stir the pot by assisting the Earl of Lennox and other 'traitorous Scottish Lords' to invade the islands of Arran and Bute, and they now offered a new alliance with the 'Lords of the Isles'. On 23 July 1545, a commission was granted by 'Donald, Lord of the Isles and Earl of Ross . . . with the consent of the barons and Council of the Isles' to the Dean of Morvern and Patrick, brother of Maclean of Duart, to assist Lennox in his negotiations with the English King Henry VIII. The old council included all the traditional vassals of the Lordship. Donald Dubh and the chiefs then removed to Knockfergus in Ireland where they established their headquarters and gathered a fleet of 180 galleys and 4000 fighting men of the western clans. From there they pursued a long correspondence with the English to whom they complained of the many wrongs and injuries which they had suffered at the hands of the Lowland government:

Your Lordships shall consider we have been old enemies to the realm of Scotland, and when they had peace with the King's Highness (Henry VIII) they hanged, beheaded, imprisoned, and destroyed many of our kin, friends, and forebears, as testified by Our Master the Earl of Ross, now the King's Grace subject . . . and many other cruel slaughter, burning, and herschip that has been betwixt us and the said *Scots*, the which were long to write. . . .

Articles of alliance were drawn up, whereby Lennox was to invade the North while Donald Dubh undertook to destroy 'the tane half' of Scotland and compel its submission to the English king. Donald was to receive an annual pension of 2000 crowns for past and future services, and would be confirmed in his dominions, while he himself guaranteed to support Lennox with 8000 fighting men of whom 4000 were currently in Ireland while another 4000 were already confronting Argyll and Huntly in Scotland itself. For his part, Henry VIII would provide money to pay 3000 men, and he undertook not to reach any agreement with Scotland – and in particular with Huntly or Argyll – without the consent of Donald Dubh and the 'barons of the Isles'. These terms were formally agreed on 4 September 1545. Henry VIII wrote to Donald Dubh, urging him to 'proceed like a noble man', and in expectation of Lennox's invasion, the western clans stood poised upon their hour.

This alliance was reminiscent of the former treaties between the Lords of the Isles and the English kings in so far as Donald recognised Henry as his overlord, and yet it echoed also the old claims of Somerled and Donald of the Name to be independent of the Lowland government. Between the 'ancient Scots' and the Scots of the Lowlands there existed an ethnic and cultural divide. The final irony was that the descendants of the ancient *Scotti* who had fought the Romans and founded Dalriada, who gave to Scotland its earlier line of kings and, withal, the name itself, rejected now that name which others had usurped, and reaching further to their past, from this time styled themselves the *Albanach* – the people of Alba. This was the last great Celtic confederacy in the Isles – and the last defiance of a united race.

But Lennox did not invade in time, and the Gaels became disheartened by inaction. Impatient of the delay, and seriously threatened now in Scotland, Donald withdrew into the Isles and tried desperately to hold the clans together. In due course a ship arrived with the promised gold from England, but Maclean of Duart, who undertook its distribution, was accused of misappropriating a portion for himself, and the resulting quarrels between the chiefs finally broke up their confederacy. In November, Lennox's eventual attempt against Dumbarton came to nothing, and Donald Dubh retired to Ireland where he shortly died near Drogheda of a sudden fever. As the only son of Angus Og his inheritance had brought him great misfortune, since he had known only six brief years of freedom in his life. But forty years after the forfeiture, the old bonds of the Lordship still were such that the clansmen had been willing to follow a leader whom they barely knew, because he was a Macdonald, and at the last they buried him as the true Lord of the Isles.

This was the last attempt to restore the Lordship of the Isles, and the vassal clans did not again combine to honour their old allegiance in the Hebrides. The several branches of Clan Donald were never reunited, since Donald Dubh left no successor, and the right to the high Chiefship became so disputed that it served rather to divide them.

The lost Lordship passed into the Gaelic memory, gathering to itself the insubstantial stuff of legend to be preserved by each clan in its pride. And thus to generations who had not known it as it was, the memory of a bygone greatness beckoned still, and the ancient claims brooded in the Celtic mist. The old pride lingered – in genealogy, prose, and praise-song – for such was the manner of the Gael, that after the power and prosperity of the island tribes declined and the chieftains followed each his own ambition, their pretensions still devolved upon the recollection of that former wide dominion. It was left to later seannachies to set tradition down, and in composing their histories of Clan Donald in its might, to lament also the ruin of the Lordship and the passing of its crippled splendour. 'It is no joy without Clan Donald. It is no strength to be without them.'

APPENDICES
LIST OF REFERENCES
SELECT BIBLIOGRAPHY
INDEX

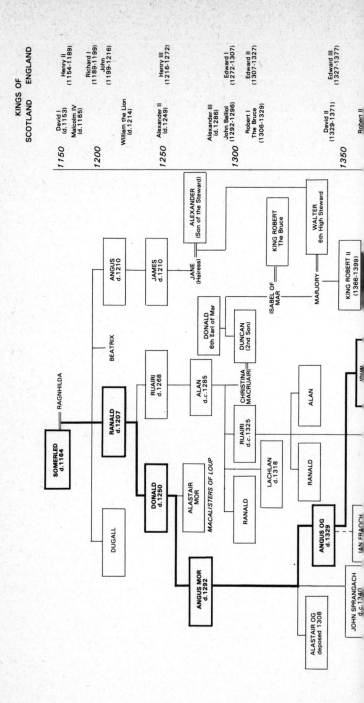

KINGS AND LORDS OF THE ISLES
Origins of the Clan Donald Main Branches
and a Chronology of the Kings of Scotland and England

KINGS OF
SCOTLAND   ENGLAND

1150 David I (d.1153)	Henry II (1154-1189)
Malcolm IV (d.1165)	Richard I (1189-1199)
1200	John (1199-1216)
William the Lion (d.1214)	
1250 Alexander II (d.1249)	Henry III (1216-1272)
Alexander III (d.1286)	Edward I (1272-1307)
1300 John Balliol (1292-1296)	Edward II (1307-1327)
Robert I The Bruce (1306-1329)	
1350 David II (1329-1371)	Edward III (1327-1377)
Robert II	

RAGNHILDA

SOMERLED d.1164

DUGALL

RANALD d.1207

BEATRIX

ANGUS d.1210

JAMES d.1210

ALEXANDER (Son of the Steward)

JANE (Heiress)

DONALD d.1250

RUAIRI d.1268

ALAN d.c.1285

DONALD 6th Earl of Mar

DUNCAN (2nd Son)

CHRISTINA MACRUAIRI

KING ROBERT The Bruce

WALTER 6th High Steward

ISABEL OF MAR

MARJORY

KING ROBERT II (1366-1399)

ALASTAIR MOR

MACALISTERS OF LOUP

RUAIRI d.c.1325

LACHLAN d.1318

RANALD

ALAN

RANALD

ANGUS OG d.1329

JOHN

ANGUS MOR d.1292

ALASTAIR OG deposed 1308

JOHN SPRANGACH d.c.1340

IAN FRAOCH

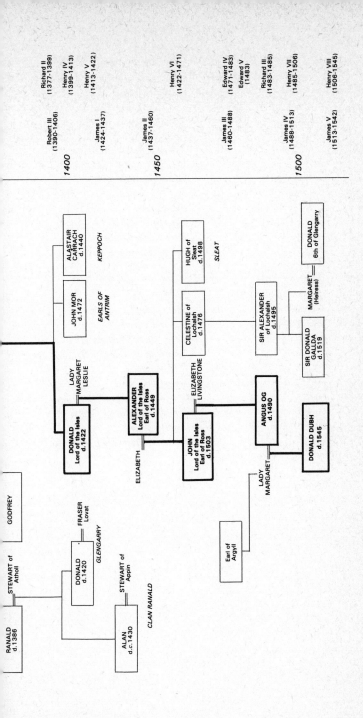

Richard II (1377-1399)
Henry IV (1399-1413)
Henry V (1413-1422)

Robert III (1390-1406)

James I (1424-1437)

1400

Henry VI (1422-1471)

James II (1437-1460)

1450

Edward IV (1471-1483)
Edward V (1483)
Richard III (1483-1485)
Henry VII (1485-1506)

James III (1460-1488)

James IV (1488-1513)

1500

Henry VIII (1506-1545)

James V (1513-1542)

GODFREY

ALASTAIR CARRACH d.1440

JOHN MOR d.1472

KEPPOCH

EARLS OF ANTRIM

HUGH of Sleat d.1498

SLEAT

STEWART of Atholl

LADY MARGARET LESLIE

CELESTINE of Lochalsh d.1476

DONALD 6th of Glengarry

RANALD d.1386

FRASER Lovat

GLENGARRY

DONALD d.1420

DONALD Lord of the Isles d.1422

ALEXANDER Lord of the Isles Earl of Ross d.1449

ELIZABETH LIVINGSTONE

SIR ALEXANDER of Lochalsh d.1495

MARGARET (Heiress)

STEWART of Appin

CLAN RANALD

ALAN d.c.1430

ELIZABETH

JOHN Lord of the Isles Earl of Ross d.1503

ANGUS OG d.1490

SIR DONALD GALLDA d.1519

LADY MARGARET

DONALD DUBH d.1545

Earl of Argyll

THE KINGS OF SCOTLAND I

843–860	KENNETH MAC-ALPIN	*The Hardy: son of Alpin*
860–863	DONALD I	*Brother of Kenneth Mac-Alpin*
863–877	CONSTANTINE I	*Son of Kenneth Mac-Alpin*
877–878	AODH	*Son of Kenneth Mac-Alpin*
878–889	EOCHAIDH	*Great grandson of Alpin*
889–900	DONALD II	*Son of Constantine I*
900–943	CONSTANTINE II	*Son of Aodh*
943–954	MALCOLM I	*Son of Donald II*
954–962	INDULF	*Son of Constantine II*
962–967	DUFF	*Son of Malcolm I*
967–971	COLIN	*Son of Indulf*
971–995	KENNETH II	*Son of Malcolm I*
995–997	CONSTANTINE III	*Son of Colin*
997–1005	KENNETH III	*Son of Duff*
1005–1034	MALCOLM II	*Son of Kenneth II*
1034–1040	DUNCAN I	*Grandson of Malcolm II*
1040–1057	MACBETH	*Grandson of Malcolm II; Mormaer of Moray*
1057–1093	MALCOLM III CANMORE	*Son of Duncan I*
1093–1094	DONALD BANE	*Brother of Malcolm III Canmore*
1094–1094	DUNCAN II	*Son of Malcolm III Canmore*
1094–1097	DONALD BANE	*(Second Reign)*
1097–1107	EDGAR	*Son of Malcolm III Canmore*

THE KINGS OF SCOTLAND II

1107–1124	ALEXANDER I	*Brother of Edgar*
1124–1153	DAVID I	*Brother of Edgar and Alexander I*
1153–1165	MALCOLM IV	*'The Maiden': Grandson of David I*
1165–1214	WILLIAM THE LION	*Brother of Malcolm IV*
1214–1249	ALEXANDER II	*Son of William I The Lion*
1249–1286	ALEXANDER III	*Son of Alexander II*
1292–1296	JOHN BALLIOL	
1306–1329	ROBERT I (The Bruce)	
1329–1371	DAVID II	
1371–1390	ROBERT II	
1390–1406	ROBERT III	
1406–1424	Regency	
1424–1437	JAMES I	
1437–1460	JAMES II	
1460–1488	JAMES III	
1488–1513	JAMES IV	
1513–1542	JAMES V	

Principal references

1 Tacitus, *Agricola*, XXIX–XXXVIII, ed. J. G. C. Anderson
2 Julius Solinus, quoted from W. H. Murray, *The Islands of Western Scotland* (Eyre Methuen, 1973)
3 Ascribed to Cormac MacAirt and quoted from R. B. Hale, *The Magnificent Gael* (Leech, Canada, 1976)
4 *Annals of Ulster*, 576–577. *Annals of Tigernach*, 574
5 Nennius, *Historia Brittonum* (Harley MS 3859, folio 187/A), quoted in Leslie Alcock's *Arthur's Britain* (Penguin Books, 1973)
6 *Annales Cambriae*, 516–518
7 Ibid., 527–528
8 Aneirin, *The Gododdin*, quoted from the translation in I. F. Grant, *The Lordship of the Isles* (Edinburgh, 1935)
9 Gildas, *De Exidio Britanniae*
10 The Venerable Bede, *A History of the English Church and People*, Book III, chapter 3
11 St Adomnan mac Ronan, *Life of St Columba*, ed. W. Reeves (1874)
12 Aneirin, *The Gododdin*, quoted from trans. in I. F. Grant, op. cit.
13 Bede, op. cit., Book I, chapter 34
14 Aneirin, *The Gododdin*, quoted from I. F. Grant, op. cit.
15 A. O. Anderson, *Early Sources of Scottish History, AD 500 to 1286*. 2 vols (1922)
16 *War of the Gaedhil with the Gail*, Rolls Series 48, A. O. Anderson, ibid.
17 Prudentius of Troyes (MGH Scriptores) I, p. 443, A. O. Anderson, ibid.
18 *Heimskringla*, III, chapter iv, trans. S. Laing and Rev. P. Foote (Dent, 1951)
19 *Historiae Norwegiae*, trans. A. O. Anderson, op. cit.
20 *Gretti's Saga*, trans. A. O. Anderson, op. cit.
21 *Laxdaela Saga*, trans. Magnus Magnusson and Hermann Pálsson (Penguin Books, 1969)
22 *Heimskringla*, III, chapter xxii, trans. Laing and Foote
23 *Heimskringla*, III, trans. R. L. Bremner in his *The Norsemen in Alban* (Glasgow, 1924)
24 *Anglo-Saxon Chronicle*, quoted from trans. in Gwyn Jones, *A History of the Vikings* (Oxford University Press, 1973)
25 *Heimskringla*, IV, chapter iv

26 *Olaf Tryggvason's Saga: Flateyjarbók*
27 *Njal's Saga*, trans. G. W. Dasent (Everyman, J. M. Dent, 1957)
28 Ibid.
29 *Njal's Saga*, trans. M. Magnusson & H. Pálsson (Penguin, 1960)
30 *War of the Gaedhil with the Gail*, trans. H. J. Todd (Rolls Series, 1867)
31 Ibid.
32 *Njal's Saga*, trans. Dasent
33 *Wars of the Gaedhil with the Gail*
34 *Orkneyinga Saga*, trans. J. A. Hjaltalin and G. Goudie (1873)
35 Ibid.
36 Ibid.
37 Ibid.
38 Ibid.
39 Ibid.
40 *King Harald's Saga*, trans. M. Magnusson and H. Pálsson (Penguin, 1966)
41 *The Chronicle of the Isle of Man* (Church History Society)
42 Ibid.
43 *Orkneyinga Saga*, from a trans. by A. O. Anderson, *Early Sources of Scottish History*
44 *The Chronicle of the Isle of Man*
45 *Heimskringla*, as quoted in I. F. Grant, op. cit.
46 Ibid.
47 *The Chronicle of the Isle of Man*
48 *Book of Clanranald*, trans. A. Cameron, from *Reliquiae Celticae* (1892)
49 Hugh Macdonald of Sleat, *History of the Macdonalds*. Highland Papers I (1914)
50 Ibid.
51 Ibid.
52 W. H. Murray, *The Islands of Western Scotland*, chapter 6 (Eyre Methuen, 1973); W. C. Mackenzie, *History of the Outer Hebrides* (1903)
53 *The Chronicle of the Isle of Man*
54 Account of William of Newburgh, trans. by R. L. Bremner in his *The Norsemen in Alban* (1924)
55 Hugh Macdonald of Sleat, op. cit.
56 Ibid.
57 Ibid.
58 Ibid.
59 Quoted from I. F. Grant, op. cit.
60 Hugh Macdonald of Sleat, op. cit.
61 A. and A. Macdonald, *The Clan Donald* (Inverness, 1895)
62 Hugh Macdonald of Sleat, op. cit.
63 Ibid.

64 *Hakonar Saga*, quoted from trans. in I. F. Grant, op. cit.
65 Eirspennill; *Hakon Hakonson's Saga*, trans. A. O. Anderson, op. cit.; and see *Hakon Hakonson's Saga*, trans. Dasent (1894)
66 Ibid.
67 Ibid.
68 Ibid.
69 Ibid.
70 J. Bain, *Calendar of Documents relating to Scottish History* (1881)
71 J. Prebble, *The Lion in the North* (Rainbird, 1971)
72 Ibid.
73 J. Barbour, *The Bruce*, trans. A. A. H. Douglas (Glasgow, 1964)
74 *Book of Clanranald*
75 *The Bruce*
76 Hugh Macdonald of Sleat, op. cit.
77 *Chronicle of Lanercost*, trans. Sir H. Maxwell (1913)
78 *State Papers*; Tytler, P. F., *History of Scotland II*; see also G. Buchanan, *Rerum Scoticarum Historia*, trans. W. A. Gatherer
79 *Declaration of Arbroath* (H.M. Stationery Office)
80 Quoted from Donald J. Macdonald of Castleton, *Clan Donald* (1978)
81 Hugh Macdonald of Sleat, op. cit.
82 Ibid.
83 Ibid.
84 *Book of Clanranald*
85 Hugh Macdonald of Sleat, op. cit.
86 Ibid.
87 Froissart's *Chronicles*. J. Prebble, op. cit.
88 Hugh Macdonald of Sleat, op. cit.
89 The Chronicle of the Frazers (*Wardlaw MS*)
90 Hugh Macdonald of Sleat, op. cit.
91 Wyntoun, *Originale Cronykil*
92 Hugh Macdonald of Sleat, op. cit.
93 Ibid.
94 Trans. Sir Walter Scott
95 John Major, *History of Greater Britain*, ed. A. Constable (Scottish History Society, 1892)
96 Hugh Macdonald of Sleat, op. cit.
97 Ibid.
98 Ibid.
99 Ibid.
100 Ibid.
101 Ibid.
102 Ibid.

103 Ibid.
104 G. Buchanan, *Rerum Scoticarum Historia*; W. H. Murray, *The Islands of Western Scotland*
105 K. Macleod, *Road to the Isles* (Edinburgh, 1927)
106 Ibid.
107 Ibid.
108 Ibid.
109 Ibid.
110 Ibid.
111 Ibid.
112 *Family History of the Mackenzies*, (Applecross, Dingwall 1843)
113 as trans. in I. Grimble, *Clans and Chiefs* (Blond & Briggs, 1980)
114 Hugh Macdonald of Sleat, op. cit.
115 Ibid.
116 D. Gregory, *History of the Western Highlands and Isles* (1881)

Select bibliography

Asterisks refer to selected editions of early texts.

Adam, F., *Clans, Septs, and Regiments of the Scottish Highlands* (Macmillan, 1908)

*Adoman, St., *Life of St Columba*, ed. and trans. W. Reeves (Edinburgh, 1874)

Alcock, L., *Arthur's Britain* (Penguin Books, 1971)

Anderson, A. O. and M. O., *Adomnan's Life of St Columba* (Nelson, 1961)

*Anderson, A. O., *Scottish Annals from English Chroniclers AD 500 to 1286* (London, 1908)

* – *Early Sources of Scottish History AD 500 to 1286* 2 vols (Oliver & Boyd, Edinburgh, 1922)

Anderson, J. G. C., see Tacitus

Anderson, M. O., *Kings and Kingship in Early Scotland* (Scottish Academic Press, 1973)

Ashe, G., ed. *The Quest for Arthur's Britain* (Paladin, 1971)

*Bain, J., *Calendar of Documents Relating to Scotland* (1881)

Barber, R. W., *Arthur of Albion* (Barrie & Rockliffe, 1961)

*Barbour, J., *The Bruce*, trans. W. M. Mackenzie (A. and C. Black, London, 1909); and trans. A. A. H. Douglas (Glasgow, 1964)

Barron, E. M., *The Scottish War of Independence* (London, 1914; 2nd edn, 1934)

– *Inverness and the Macdonalds* (Inverness, 1930)

*Bede, The Ven., *History of the English Church and People*; trans. L. Sherley-Price (Penguin, 1955)

*Bellenden, J. *Chroniklis of Scotland*: Boece's *Historia Gentis Scotorum*

Bremner, R. L., *The Norsemen in Alban* (MacLehose, Glasgow, 1924)

Brent, P., *The Viking Saga* (Weidenfeld & Nicolson, 1975)

Bryne, F. J., *Irish Kings and High Kings* (Batsford, 1973)

*Cameron, A., *Reliquiae Celticae* (Inverness, 1892) (see MacVurich, Iain Lom, *Book of Clanranald*)

Chadwick, N., *The Celts* (Penguin Books, 1970)

Chadwick, N. and Dillon, M., *The Celtic Realms* (Weidenfeld & Nicolson, 1967)

*Church History Society, *The Chronicle of the Isle of Man*

*Dasent, G. W., trans.: *Njal's Saga* (Dent, 1957)

– *Hakon Hakonson's Saga* (1894)

258

Select Bibliography

Dillon, M., *The Cycles of the Kings* (Oxford, 1946)

Foote, P. G. and Wilson, D. M., *The Viking Achievement* (Sidgwick & Jackson, 1970)

*Fordoun, J., *Chronica Gentis Scotorum*; trans. W. F. Skene (1871–2)

*Fraser, J., *Chronicles of the Frasers* (The Wardlaw MS) ed. W. Mackay
  – (Scottish History Society, Edinburgh, 1905)

*Garmonsway, G. N., trans., *The Anglo-Saxon Chronicle*
  (Dent, 1953)

Grant, I. F., *The Lordship of the Isles* (Edinburgh, 1935)

Gregory, D., *The History of the Western Highlands and Isles of Scotland*
  (Edinburgh, 1881; reprinted 1975)

Grimble, I., *Clan and Chiefs* (Blond & Briggs, 1980)

*Hailes, Lord, *Annals of Scotland* (1819)

*Hennessey, W. M., trans., *The Annals of Ulster* (Dublin, 1887)

*Hjaltalin, J., and Goudie, G., trans. *Orkneyinga Saga* (1873)

*Jackson, K., *The Gododdin: The Oldest Scottish Poem* (Edinburgh, 1969)

Jones, G., *A History of the Vikings* (Oxford University Press, 1973)

*Jones, G. & T., trans., *The Mabinogion* (Dent, 1949)

Kermack, W. R., *The Scottish Highlands* (Edinburgh and London, Johnston & Bacon, 1957)

Kinvig, R. H., *A History of the Isle of Man* (1950; 3rd edn 1978)

*Laing, S. and Foote, P., trans., *Heimskringla* (Dent, 1951)

*MacCarthy, B., trans., *The Annals of Ulster II–IV* (HMSO Dublin, 1893, 1895, 1901)

Macdonald, A. & A., *Clan Donald* (Inverness, 1896, 1904)

Macdonald, Donald J., *Clan Donald* (Macdonald Publishers, 1978)

*Macdonald (of Sleat), Hugh, *History of the Macdonalds*, Highland Papers
  (Scottish History Society, 1914)

Mackenzie, A., *History of the Macdonalds and Lords of the Isles* (Inverness, 1881)

Mackenzie, W. C., *The Highlands and Isles of Scotland* (Moray, 1937)

Mackie, E. W., *Scotland: An Archaeological Guide* (Faber, 1975)

MacLeod, K., *The Road to the Isles* (Edinburgh, 1927)

*MacVurich, Iain Lom, *The Book of Clanranald*; trans. by A. Cameron in
  Reliquiae Celticae (Inverness, 1892)

*Magnusson, M. and Pálsson, H., trans., *Laxdaela Saga* (Penguin, 1969)

*– *Njal's Saga* (Penguin, 1960)

*– *King Harald's Saga* (Penguin, 1966)

Maxwell, Sir H., *The Making of Scotland* (James MacLehose, Glasgow, 1911)

*– trans., *The Chronicles of Lanercost* (MacLehose, 1913)

Menzies, G., ed., *Who Are the Scots?* (BBC, 1971)

Moncrieffe, Sir Iain of that Ilk, *The Highland Clans* (Barrie, 1967)

*Morris-Jones, J., *Taliesin* (Cymmrodorion Society, 1918)

Murray, W. H., *The Islands of Western Scotland* (Eyre Methuen, 1973)

Nagy, K., *Skocia Pannoniai Királynéja* (Aurora, 1971)

*O'Donovan, J., trans., *Annals of the Kingdom of Scotland by the Four Masters* (Dublin, 1851)

*Palgrave, Sir F., *Documents and Records Illustrating the History of Scotland* (1837)

*Pálsson, H. and Edwards, P., *Orkneyinga Saga* (Penguin Books, 1981)

Prebble, J., *The Lion in the North* (London, 1971)

Skene, W. F., *Celtic Scotland: a history of ancient Alban* (Edinburgh, 3 vols., 2nd edn, 1886–90)

– *History of the Highland Clans* (Highland Society, 1837)

*– trans., *Book of the Dean of Lismore: a selection of ancient Gaelic poetry* (1862)

Smith, G., *The Book of Islay* (1895)

*Stokes, W., trans., *The Annals of Tigernach* (1895)

*Tacitus, *Agricola*, ed. by J. G. C. Anderson (Clarendon Press, Oxford, 2nd edn, 1922)

*Todd, H. J., trans., *The War of the Gaedhil with the Gail* (Rolls Series, 1867)

*Vigfússon, *The Hakon Saga*, trans., (Rolls Series)

*Wade-Evans, A. W., *Nennius's History of the Britons*, with trans. of *Annales Cambriae* (Church History Society, 1938)

Wainwright, F. T., ed., *The Problem of the Picts* (Edinburgh, 1965)

*Williams, H., ed. and trans., *Annales Cambriae* (Clarendon Press, 1912)

*– ed. and trans., *Gildas: Works* (Cymmrodorion Society, 1901)

*Williams, I., *The Gododdin Poems* (Anglesey Antiquarian Society, 1935)

*Wyntoun, A., *Originale Cronykil* (Edinburgh, 1872)

Index

261